Economic Thought and History

Economic Thought and History looks at the relationship between facts and thought in historical economic research, viewing it in the context of periods of economic crisis and providing detailed analyses of methods used in determining the bond between economic history and economic theory.

This interdisciplinary collection brings together international researchers in the history of economic thought and economic history in order to confront varying approaches to the study of economic facts and ideas, rethinking boundaries, methodologies and the object of their disciplines. The chapters explore the relationship between economic thought and economic theory from a variety of perspectives. They highlight the interaction between history and economics and define anew the boundaries of the history of economic thought, in terms of both single authors and schools of thought. The book offers particular insights on the Italian tradition of thought.

The uniquely interdisciplinary and analytical approach presented here bridges the methodological gap between these disciplines, unearthing a fertile common ground of research. This book is intended for postgraduate students conducting further research into the field, or for professors and academics of economic history and the history of economic thought.

Monika Poettinger is a Contract Professor of Economic History and Thought at Bocconi University, Milan, Italy.

Gianfranco Tusset is an Associate Professor of Economics, University of Padova, Padua, Italy.

Modern Heterodox Economics
Edited by Carol M. Connell
Brooklyn College, City University of New York

1 Money as Organisation, Gustavo Del Vecchio's Theory
Gianfranco Tusset

2 Financial Crisis and the Failure of Economic Theory
Angel Rodriguez, Jorge Turmo and Oscar Vara

3 The Invisible Hand of Power
Anton N. Oleinik

4 Economic Thought and History
An Unresolved Relationship
Edited by Monika Poettinger and Gianfranco Tusset

Economic Thought and History
An unresolved relationship

Edited by
Monika Poettinger and
Gianfranco Tusset

LONDON AND NEW YORK

First published 2016
by Routledge
2 Park Square, Milton Park, Abingdon, Oxon OX14 4RN

and by Routledge
711 Third Avenue, New York, NY 10017

First issued in paperback 2017

Routledge is an imprint of the Taylor & Francis Group, an informa business

© 2016 selection and editorial material, Monika Poettinger and Gianfranco Tusset; individual chapters, the contributors

The right of Monika Poettinger and Gianfranco Tusset to be identified as the author of the editorial material, and of the authors for their individual chapters, has been asserted in accordance with sections 77 and 78 of the Copyright, Designs and Patents Act 1988.

All rights reserved. No part of this book may be reprinted or reproduced or utilized in any form or by any electronic, mechanical, or other means, now known or hereafter invented, including photocopying and recording, or in any information storage or retrieval system, without permission in writing from the publishers.

Trademark notice: Product or corporate names may be trademarks or registered trademarks, and are used only for identification and explanation without intent to infringe.

British Library Cataloguing in Publication Data
A catalogue record for this book is available from the British Library

Library of Congress Cataloging in Publication Data
Economic thought and history: an unresolved relationship/edited by Monika Poettinger and Gianfranco Tusset.
pages cm
Includes bibliographical references and index.
1. Economics – History. 2. Economic history. 3. Economics – Study and teaching. I. Poettinger, Monika, editor. II. Tusset, Gianfranco, editor.
HB75.E326 2016330.09–dc232015034092

ISBN 13: 978-1-138-49553-1 (pbk)
ISBN 13: 978-1-138-10139-5 (hbk)

Typeset in Times New Roman
by Swales & Willis Ltd, Exeter, Devon, UK

Contents

List of illustrations   vii
List of contributors   x

Introduction   1
MONIKA POETTINGER AND GIANFRANCO TUSSET

PART I
Economic thought: history and values   15

1 History of economic thought and economic history: who will bring the past to life?   17
BERTRAM SCHEFOLD

2 Economic facts, theoretical beliefs and the 'double movement'   43
CLAUS THOMASBERGER

3 Economic knowledge and value judgments   58
MICHELE CANGIANI

PART II
Theories meet facts   73

4 Between history and theory: Otto Neurath's economics from 1906 to 1917   75
MONIKA POETTINGER

5 The Freiburg scholars and interwar Germany   100
ANITA PELLE

vi *Contents*

6 When a generally accepted theory fails to meet the facts: the case of Real Business Cycles Theory   121
JORGE TURMO ARNAL, ÁNGEL RODRÍGUEZ GARCÍA-BRAZALES AND OSCAR VARA CRESPO

7 The cultural and psychological dimensions of economic development   139
ARTURO HERMANN

PART III
History in the Italian tradition of economic thought   163

8 Economics and history in Italy in the twentieth century   165
PIERO ROGGI

9 Labour as culture: the Lombardo-Veneto School   177
GIANFRANCO TUSSET

10 Sergio Paronetto: an economist in deed, from Alberto Beneduce to Alcide de Gasperi, 1934–1945   192
STEFANO BAIETTI AND GIOVANNI FARESE

Index   202

Illustrations

Figures

I.1	Otto Neurath's taxonomy of historiographic hypotheses	4
I.2	Stage theories and historiographic typologies in Otto Neurath	5
6.1	GDP of the UK, the US, Germany and Japan (1986–2006)	130

Tables

1.1	Approaches to the history of economic thought	21
6.1	TFP in Spain (2003–2007)	134

Contributors

Stefano Baietti is Teaching Assistant of Economic History and of History of Economic Thought at the European University of Rome. He is Adjunct Professor of Public Economics at Link Campus University, Rome. He is a former manager of major state-owned enterprises, namely IRI group, state railways Ferrovie dello Stato, and the national board of state roads ANAS. His latest book, written with Giovanni Farese, is *Sergio Paronetto e il formarsi della costituzione economica italiana* (Rubbettino) about the economist and manager Sergio Paronetto (the closest collaborator of Donato Menichella at IRI, prime minister Alcide De Gasperi, Giovanni Battista Montini, then Pope Paul VI), and the shaping of Italy's economic constitution.

Michele Cangiani is a Contract Professor at Ca' Foscari University of Venice. His main field of research is the history and method of heterodox economic theories. Recent publications include: "Beyond Neoliberalism. An Institutional Approach," *Izmir Review of Social Sciences*, vol. 1, no. 2, January 2014, pp. 37–55; "A Crisis of Freedom," in *Social Costs Today*, ed. by P. Ramazzotti et al., Routledge, 2012; "Karl Polanyi's Institutional Theory," *Journal of Economic Issues*, vol. 45, no. 1, 2011, pp. 177–198.

Giovanni Farese is Assistant Professor of Economic History and of History of Economic Thought at the European University of Rome. He is Adjunct Professor of Economic History at LUISS Guido Carli University, Rome, where he received his PhD. He is Managing Editor of *The Journal of European Economic History* and of *Economia Italiana-Review of Economic Conditions in Italy*. His latest book, written with Paolo Savona, is *Il banchiere del mondo. Eugene Robert Black e l'ascesa della cultura dello sviluppo* (Banker to the world. Eugene Robert Black and the rise of the global culture of development), published in Italian by Rubbettino.

Arturo Hermann is a Senior Research Fellow at the Italian National Institute of Statistics (ISTAT) Rome, Italy. In his main research fields – Institutional and Keynesian Economics, Theories of Social Justice, Political Economy, Sustainable Development, also considered in their relations with psychology and psychoanalysis – he has authored four books and numerous articles in scholarly journals. He is a member of several Associations, in particular, AFIT, AHE, AISPE, EAEPE, ICAPE, Green Economics Institute, PKSG, and regularly participates in their conferences and activities.

Anita Pelle was born in 1975 in Szeged, Hungary. She first worked for a German multinational trading company in Germany and Hungary. She then returned to her alma mater where she is currently Associate Professor and Jean Monnet chair at the University of Szeged, Institute of Finance and International Economic Relations of the Faculty of Economics and Business Administration. She has also been regularly teaching in France. Anita defended her PhD (summa cum laude) in 2010 in the field of European competition regulation. She is the author of 51 scientific publications in English and Hungarian, including four university textbooks.

Monika Poettinger teaches economic history and history of economic thought at Bocconi University, Milan. She has published many articles and book chapters on the industrialization of Lombardy, merchant networks and German entrepreneurial migrations. Recent publications include: *Deutsche Unternehmer im Mailand des neunzehnten Jahrhunderts. Netzwerke, soziales Kapital und Industrialisierung*, Casagrande Editore, Lugano, 2012; *Mercante e società: riflessioni di storia comparata*, Casagrande Editore, Lugano, 2012; (ed.) *German Merchant and Entrepreneurial Migrations*, Casagrande Editore, Lugano, 2012; (ed.) *Firenze e l'Europa liberale. L'Economista (1874–1881)*, Polistampa, Firenze, 2013. Her research interests include: the role of merchants in society from Babylonia to the nineteenth century; European liberal economic thought and its diffusion; and entrepreneurial migrations and the role of merchant networks in industrialization.

Ángel Rodríguez García-Brazales graduated in economics in 1989 and earned his PhD with honors at Universidad Autónoma de Madrid (UAM) in 1997. He has been visiting scholar at George Mason University (VA) and other universities in Spain. Since 1991 he has been involved in undergraduate and graduate courses about Macroeconomics, Microeconomics and Monetary Economics. He has also collaborated in staff training programs with firms such as FNAC, MAPFRE, Deloitte and Accenture. Currently he is Associate Professor at UAM, where he is working and teaching on international monetary issues, focusing on the International Monetary System and its relationship with the Great Recession. During this time, he has published several papers and books on issues such as History of Economic Thought, Evolutionary Economics, Economics of Transition and Monetary Economics. These include: with Oscar Vara and Jorge Turmo Arnal "How the Performance of Firms Leads Economists to Improve their Theories: The Case of Endogenous Growth," in *The Changing Firm. Contributions from the History of Economic Thought*, ed. by Marco Guido and Daniela Parisi, Franco Angeli, 2005; *Rusia: inercias y nuevas perspectivas*, Unión Editorial, 2006 and "La Economía virtual en Rusia," *Cuadernos de Economía*, vol. 29, 2006, about the post-Soviet economies transition; "Austrian Economics as a progressive paradigm," *The Review of Austrian Economics*, 2002, on the methodology and history of economic thought; with Oscar Vara and Jorge Turmo Arnal "The existence of laws in economics and economic theory," in *Y a-t-il des lois en économie?* ed. by A. Berthoud, B. Delmas and Th. Demals, Presses Universitaires du Septentrion, 2007; and "When a Generally Accepted Theory Fails to Meet the Facts: The Case of RBC Theory," a paper in the XII AISPE Conference held in Florence in March of 2013 that will be published as a part of a book. He also served first as Vice-Dean at Management and Economics School and, for the last eight years, as Vice-chancellor of Graduate Programs at UAM. During this time, he has been monitoring the adaptation of UAM's graduate programs to the European Higher Education Area.

Piero Roggi is Full Professor of History of Economic Thought at the University of Florence. His main research interests comprise: Jean Charles Léonard Simonde de Sismondi; economic policies in Italy after WWII; Amintore Fanfani; and methodology of research in economics and history. On these subjects he has published many volumes and essays in Italy and abroad.

Bertram Schefold was born in Basel (Switzerland) in 1943. He studied at Munich, Hamburg and Basel, 1962–1967, and obtained the diploma in mathematics, physics and philosophy. He continued his doctoral studies at Cambridge (GB) and Basel, gaining his PhD in economics in 1971. He then lectured at Basel and was Research Associate at Harvard University, Massachusetts. He became Full Professor (C 4) at the Faculty of Economics of Johann Wolfgang Goethe-University, Frankfurt, in March 1974 and was Dean of the Faculty of Economics at J.W. Goethe-University, 1981/2. He has published more than 40 books and 250 articles on economic theory, history of economic thought, energy policy and general economic policy. He edited the series *Klassiker der Nationalökonomie*.

Honours: Dr. iur. h.c. Tübingen, Dr. rer. pol. h.c. Macerata, Thomas-Guggenheim Prize. A first Festschrift from his pupils is published as: Caspari, Volker (ed.): *Theorie und Geschichte der Wirtschaft: Festschrift für Bertram Schefold*, Metropolis, 2008. A second Festschrift from his colleagues is published as: Caspari, Volker (ed.): *The Evolution of Economic Theory. Essays in Honour of Bertram Schefold*, Routledge, 2011. For further details see: http://www.wiwi.uni-frankfurt.de/fileadmin/user_upload/dateien_abteilungen/abt_ewf/Economic_Theory/admin/curriculum_vitae.pdf

Claus Thomasberger is Professor for Economics and International Policy at the University of Applied Sciences, Berlin, Germany. He gained degrees in sociology and in economics at the Free University Berlin, and his PhD at the University of Bremen. He is a Visiting Professor at Knoxville University, Duke University and the Vienna University of Economics and Business. He has authored and edited numerous books, including: *From Crisis to Growth*,

Metropolis, 2012, and *Das neoliberale Credo*, Metropolis, 2012. Research interests include international monetary relations, European integration, history of economic thought and political philosophy.

Jorge Turmo Arnal was born in Huesca (Spain) in 1958. He has a Bachelor of Arts in Geography and History (University of Zaragoza, 1980), Bachelor of Economics (Central University of Barcelona, 1992) and Doctor in Economics (Autonomous University of Madrid, 2002). He has researched in several fields. In economic growth he published with Ángel Rodríguez García-Brazales and Oscar Vara, "How the Performance of Firms Leads Economists to Improve their Theories: The Case of Endogenous Growth," in *The Changing Firm. Contributions from the History of Economic Thought*, ed. by Marco Guido and Daniela Parisi, Franco Angeli, 2005. He studied the post-communist transition in Russia and published, with Ángel Rodríguez García-Brazales and Oscar Vara, *Rusia: inercias y nuevas perspectivas*, Unión Editorial, 2006, and "La Economía virtual en Rusia," *Cuadernos de Economía*, vol. 29, 2006.

He is also very interested in the methodology of economics and has published, with Oscar Vara and Ángel Rodríguez García-Brazales, "The existence of laws in economics and economic theory," in *Y a-t-il des lois en économie?* ed. by A. Berthoud, B. Delmas and Th. Demals, Presses Universitaires du Septentrion, 2007. He has studied Real Business Cycle Theory and wrote "Las causas de la crisis desde la perspectiva de la Teoría de los Ciclos Reales," in *Crisis global de la economía*, Minerva, 2009. On the same issue he, with Oscar Vara and Ángel Rodríguez García-Brazales, presented a paper in the XII AISPE Conference held in Florence in March of 2013, "When a Generally Accepted Theory Fails to Meet the Facts: The Case of RBC Theory," that will be published as a part of a book.

Gianfranco Tusset is Associate Professor in History of Economic Thought, University of Padua (Italy). His main research interests are economic dynamics in historical perspective and the history of monetary theory. His publications include: "The Italian Contribution to the Early Economic Dynamics," *The European Journal of the History of Economic Thought*, 2009; "Habits and Expectations in the Italian Paretian School" (with M. Pomini), *History of Political Economy*, 2009; "Individual e Market Inertia in Luigi Amoroso's Cycle Model," *History of Economic Ideas*, 2012; "How Heterogeneity Shapes Vilfredo Pareto's Social Equilibrium," *History of Economics Review*, 2013; "The Organizational Properties of Money: Gustavo Del Vecchio's Theory," *Journal of the History of Economic Thought*, 2012; *Money as Organization, Gustavo Del Vecchio's Theory*, Pickering & Chatto, 2014. Since 2004, he has been a member of the board of the Italian Association for the History of Economic Thought (AISPE), and has been its secretary since 2011.

Oscar Vara Crespo was born in Madrid (Spain) in 1967. He has a Bachelor of Economics (Autonomous University of Madrid, 1990) and Doctor in

Economics (Autonomous University of Madrid, 1999). He has been full-time Professor of Economics at the Autonomous University of Madrid since 1992. He has devoted a great part of his research to the history of contemporary Economic Thought. In 2002, in collaboration with Ángel Rodriguez García-Brazales, he published the essay "El Estado y la Teoría Económica" (The State and the Economic Theory), in which they studied how Economic Theory has treated the role of the State in their models. Other publications include: "La fundamental homogeneidad de las teorías monetarias de Georg Simmel y Ludwig von Mises," *Procesos de Mercado, European Review of Economic Policy*, vol. 1, 2004, an analysis of the monetary theories of Georg Simmel and Ludwig von Mises; *Raíces Intelectuales del Pensamiento Económico Moderno* (Intellectual Roots of Contemporary Economic Thought), Union Editorial, 2006, a wider study on the philosophical roots of modern economic thought; with Javier Aranzadi, Jorge Turmo Arnal and Ángel Rodriguez García-Brazales, "The Praxeology of L. von Mises and the Theory of Action of Alfred Schütz," *New Perspectives on Political Economy*, 2010; "Causas de la crisis financiera en el caso español" (Causes for the Financial Crisis: the Spanish case), *Cuadernos de economía: Spanish Journal of Economics and Finance*, 2009, dealing with business cycles. Recently, his research has focused on the complex relation between ethics, economy and society: "Giustizia e Carità dalla Prospettiva della Teoria Economica" (Justice and Charity from the Economic Theory Perspective), in *Alle Fonti dello Sviluppo*, ed. by G. Richi, Marcianum Press, Venice, 2009; "Formazione della Personalità, Pre-concezioni del Mondo e Società Plurale" (Personality Formation, Pre-Comprehension of the World and Plural Society), in *Pensare la Società Plurale*, ed. by G. Richi, Marcianum Press, Venice, 2011.

Introduction

Monika Poettinger and Gianfranco Tusset[1]

It might seem futile to resurrect the long-lasting debate about the relationship between history and economics. The question was born along with the economic science at the end of the eighteenth century and, through the renowned *Methodenstreit*, crossed into the twentieth century, causing harsh debates and a widespread fracture among and inside national traditions of economic thought (Poettinger, 2014). At the eve of the new millennium, the relationship remains unresolved while cultural historians oppose economists over the field of economic history. Even muses have been called into the question and Clio has become the contending point of the opposite sides.[2]

After so long a discussion, every possible angle of the problem must already have been explored, every possible significance and method tried out, every critique voiced and countered. As often happens in such harsh debates, though, when many points are made and traditions of thought are quoted again and again across centuries, theses and concepts lose their original meaning and scientific content. As in family feuds, the youngest generation joins the battle speaking out slogans and formulas of which it does not really know the origin, the evolution or the significance. Mythology, metaphysics or even ideology grow out of the original ideas. In this sense, rethinking the problem of the importance of history in economics and of economics for history might clarify the standing of the opposite sides and even unveil, surprisingly, that despite the ready belligerent attitudes, every generation shared many a philosophical view and across generations certain themes significantly recurred.

It could thus prove useful to briefly overview the evolution of the debate in time, as is done in the first part of this Introduction, in order to correctly define its terms. The second part of the Introduction will then relate the state of the art, highlighting in particular the recrudescence of the question after the economic crisis in 2007, when the current economics orthodoxy was increasingly questioned. The last part of the Introduction will present the rationale of this volume, which collects examples of how mixed methodologies and unorthodox thinking might enrich current economic and historical research.

1 Economics and history: an unresolved relationship

In antiquity, Clio, daughter of Zeus, would not easily meddle in *οἰκονομία*, the management of the house. History was a battlefield for gods and men, the realm of heroic deeds. No merchant ever entered it, nor were markets displayed there. However, acquisition of new and necessary resources abroad was deemed worthy of epics, as were the just and respectful management of the state and the estate. Clio and Calliope chanted the justice of kings as the adventurous search for distant riches (Poettinger, 2012, pp. 31–44). History was, thus, the source of inspiration for present leaders or a religious admonishment. In this sense, it also contained economic prescriptions. As with the biblical jubilee year, such policies were necessary to maintain the equilibrium of society, transforming the earthly reign into a resemblance of the ordered working of Heaven. Abiding by these rules would bring about wealth and growth, ignoring them would end in disaster and chaos. Cycles would only result from injustice and sin.

The attempt of religious elites to gain power over reigning aristocrats is evidently at the base of such epics and histories. Religion prescribed the rules to which kings and princes should abide. External defeats and internal chaos were attributed to the wrath of gods who felt ignored and not properly honoured (Liverani, 2003, 2014). A clear political use of history, made possible by a vision of history that was immutable and circular:

'That which has been is what will be,
That which is done is what will be done,
And there is nothing new under the sun.'
(Eccl. 1, 9)

Thanks to such a premise, situations, people, empires were fully comparable across time and space. Time brought no significant change or progress. History had no end or sense. The actions of men or gods alike would have the same consequences after millennia have passed.

There is a tradition of economic thought that overtly or covertly refers to this kind of historiography. During the difficult years of WWII, Amintore Fanfani named those theories, founded on the existence of an immanent rational economic order, naturalistic (Fanfani, 2011, pp. 71–90). Nineteenth-century liberalism was at the core of this tradition of thought, but also neoclassicism shared its fundaments. Naturalistic doctrines endeavoured to discover natural laws for economics and transform economics into a natural science. Born out of Enlightenment, this tradition of economic thought looked at history as the result of mechanical forces with a limited number of equilibrium points. Economic historiography lost any cognitive value and became a mere collection of examples of the ultimate prevailing of the unbending order of nature (Fanfani, 1960, p. 11).

The simplified vision of history of naturalistic economists, though, was not devoid of value judgements. In their eyes, history represented a sequence of good facts, determined by natural laws, and bad facts, corrupted by man's intervention.

A political use of history could easily follow from such an interpretation. From physiocracy to current economic debates, advocating natural laws and the perfection of an idealistic equilibrium meant for economists to prescribe to politicians their agenda. As ancient kings should have brought to earth the equilibrium of heavenly order, so enlightened rulers and today's politicians should have made perfect markets a reality, to maximise the efficiency of the use of resources and the happiness of men. Much of current economic discourse resembles the antique literary genre of the 'mirror for princes', sharing its conclusions (Kaplan, 2012, pp. 631–636). Chaos and disaster would follow in states that did not abide by the rules dictated by economists, as cycles were caused by impediments in the otherwise frictionless functioning of markets. In this context, history is simply reread to look for the virtuous expanding of market economies and the sinful failures of acquisitive empires or alternative economic orders. Historical research has no other sense than that of exemplifying to current leaders the price of sin and the rewards for virtue.

An alternative to this vision of history was born along with the idea of human progress. If history gains an end, immanent or eschatological, then people or states are no more comparable across time and space. It would make no sense to suggest to today's politicians the same actions that were successful in another epoch. As times change, so should institutions, governments and economies. There is ample space for revolutions, in politics as in economics. Regimes become *ancien* as paradigms in economics change. History goes from normative to narrative: a narrative of transformation, evolution and progress. All stage theories in economics and economic history, from Smith to Rostow, via the German historical school and Marx, adhere to such a vision (Wisman *et al.*, 1988). Whenever economic institutions change in significance, rationale and use, so economies vary in functioning and denomination, obeying different laws and generating new rationalities and theories. No skyward looking for immutable laws of nature is allowed to economics anymore: economic theory and history mix up, given this vision of progressive human nature.

Trespassing from equilibrium to dynamics,[3] though, and leaving laws of nature for laws of history or men, offered economists and historians many alternatives in their relationship to each other.

At the beginning of the twentieth century, Otto Neurath, economist and philosopher, was still caught in the ebbing of the *Methodenstreit* as were most of German and Austrian academia (Poettinger, 2012, pp. 12–29). In 1906 he decided to summarise in his dissertation all possible approaches to the philosophy of history and their consequences as to the comparability of economies in time and space and to the meaningfulness of historical studies in economics.[4] His taxonomy may still be of use in representing all possible interactions between history and theory in the economic discourse (Poettinger, 2012, pp. 12–24).

Neurath distinguished among a historiography of permanence, a historiography of evolutionism and an anarchic historiography (Figure I.1). The first kind of historiography admitted only cyclical or periodical changes of any feature of society in time, while idealistically the same feature remained in time permanent and invariable. A historiography of evolutionism, instead, described the improvement and change of a characteristic of society in time, be it continuous, undulatory or periodical. An anarchic historiography, then, would not admit any permanence or constant improvement in societies. Changes would be continual, undulatory or periodical, but erratic, showing no direction or end.

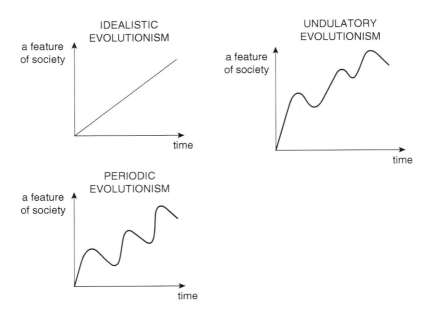

Figure I.1 Otto Neurath's taxonomy of historiographic hypotheses

Adopting one of these three historiographical interpretations would have profound effects on the use of history in economics. The anarchic point of view would render historical studies a futile endeavour and comparative history a nonsense. Neurath proceeded more fruitfully to evaluate the stage theory of Bruno Hildebrand (1848) against a historiography of idealistic evolutionism or periodic permanence (Figure I.2). His choice was not fortuitous. Neurath's analysis had been sparked particularly by the debate between the historian Eduard Meyer (1895) and Karl Bücher (Backhaus, 2000). Bücher (1893) theorised an evolution in stages of economic life that made comparisons between societies difficult if they were not at the same stage of growth. Meyer instead affirmed that the same economic institutions would cyclically return in successive epochs, making appraisals of similar phases of historical development possible and desirable even for the same society (Neurath, 1907, pp. 145–148).

In Neurath's taxonomy, Meyer's stance corresponded to the historiography of periodic permanence, Bücher's position to a historiography of idealistic evolutionism. Considering Hildebrand's stages of a natural, monetary and financial economy (1848), both approaches to history allowed comparisons. Meyer's periodic permanence made comparisons sensible in both time and space, between two societies at the same stage of growth at different times or at the same time, and between similar stages of the same society at different times. Bücher's idealistic

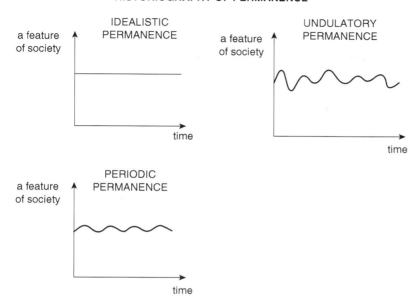

Figure I.2 Stage theories and historiographic typologies in Otto Neurath

evolutionism permitted comparisons only between two different societies at the same stage of growth at different times or at the same time. Idealistic evolutionism could not allow for a particular society to return to an already passed stage of growth.

Whenever comparisons held, both in idealistic evolutionism and in periodic permanence, then an economic theory based in history could maintain and extend its validity; a road chosen by the German historicist tradition of economic thought that would survive up to the 1930s (Heaton *et al.*, 1930) and even further, not only in Marxian tradition (the most notable example is Rostow, 1960).

The Austrian school of thought (Menger, 1883), however, and later, what is collectively termed as neoclassical economic theory, resurrected the positivistic legacy of the classical school, refuting historicism. As Neurath (1907, p. 152) underlined, their methodological attitude was based on Machiavelli's maxim that

> any one comparing the present with the past will soon perceive that in all cities and in all nations there prevail the same desires and passions as always have prevailed; for which reason it should be an easy matter for him who carefully examines past events to foresee those which are about to happen in any republic, and to apply such remedies as the ancient have used in such cases.
>
> (Machiavelli, 2012, p. 98)

Economic actions derived from idealistic permanencies, characteristics that were invariable in respect to time and space. Invariable, the problem of scarcity; invariable, the rationality in the efficient use of resources; invariable, man's self-interest. The economy could thus be studied, in its laws, independently from varying institutions or social norms and uses. Such laws, as seen, were binding to men's will as God's dictates had been in antiquity. Economies worked along mechanical rules, like clocks, determining men and history alike.

Society, in its changing forms and historical nature, became, during the turmoil of the *Methodenstreit*, the realm of sociology. No surprise that among the most important representatives of contemporary historicism,[5] appear many of the founding fathers of sociology, from Max Weber to Karl Mannheim (Rossi, 1991, pp. 57–193). As underlined by Amintore Fanfani, though, sociological researches could end up constraining men via the determination of the historical society in which they lived, while leaving the explanation of facts to historical relativism. The absence of normativity of such studies would deprive them of every possible use, particularly when an economic crisis plagued the entire world and called for policy answers, as in 1929 (Fanfani, 1960, p. 34).

In effect, in the twentieth century, what little space was left for man's *voluntas* was constrained to historicist philosophies with no relationship whatsoever to economics. From Dilthey to Heidegger only philosophy vindicated the historical nature of man. From this contemporary historicism followed many fruitful methodological reflections on the historical approach to the study of society, comprising the French Annales school and American pragmatism (Rossi, 1991, pp. 353–408). In this view, man suffered the constraints of the society she/he was born in, but also shaped society's future by construing cultural symbolisms and institutions. The understanding of men and societies, then, could not happen through the principle of causation, as in the mechanical interpretation of history, but had to rely on the principle of conditioning. Events were unique and researchers had to select, influenced from their worldview and by construing a conceptual framework, some conditions they deemed necessary for a determinate occurrence to take place. To comprehend an event would so mean to understand how it came to happen in relation to other events. Conditions, however, would be necessary but never sufficient to explain an occurrence. Consequently, the principle of conditioning, contrary to that of causation, always implied a grade of probability in its reverse (in time) forecasting capacity.

In such a history, a continuous process of subsequent events conditioning one another, people interacted with their environment. Every moment, they faced an array of events that presented them a set of possible choices among which to choose. Subsequent events, thus, would never be completely determined by past events, man's will being a variable too. Through man's decision and action, ideas – of whatever origin – came to shape history.

These extreme offshoots of historicism in the second half of the twentieth century had more impact on economic history than economics. The influence of contemporary historicism on economics was limited to its very first years and to unorthodox economists such as Thorstein Veblen (Reisman, 2012) and Otto

Neurath. Amintore Fanfani would include among them also American institutionalists, economists he defined as neo-voluntarist (Fanfani, 2011, pp. 105–134), because they implied a measure of human self-determination in contrast to Marxian and positivist determinism. He himself called for a neo-voluntarist economics that studied the economic actions of man as the result of freely chosen ends and rationally systematised means, under the limits posed by natural, social and human restraints (Fanfani, 1960, p. 68). His methodology perfectly resumed the traits of contemporary historicism. As such it called for the simultaneous study of both economic theory and history, the first being the representation of the ends each society chose at a given time, the second being the narrative of the means devised in time to overcome restraints and reach those ends.

A few more words should be said about the effects that postmodernism had on both economic history and theory in the last decades of the twentieth century (Ankersmit, 1990). Starting in the 1980s some classical concepts of economic history writing have increasingly been put under stress by postmodernist criticisms. The whole pantheon of modernisation was accused of being a cultural construction and an imposition of the developed West over the 'Others'. The West had defined itself, starting with Enlightenment, with reference to the irrational, uncivilised, undeveloped, non-Christian rest.

The critique of Eurocentrism to the centuries-old historiography on industrialisation and modernisation brought about a fertile wealth of studies on the economic relations in the world at large, pioneered by Wallerstein's (2005) world-system analysis, and a renewed research interest for areas once condemned to the limiting approach of colonial studies. National economic narratives have also been challenged in a call for a new global history.

What characterises postmodern historical narrative, though, is the accent on power relations as the origin of cultural expressions that are imposed on the weakest part of the relation itself. Historiography is thus usually reread as the result of these power relations and, as such, condemned for its partiality. The construction of a *wertfrei* – or better power-free – new historiographical tradition seems impossible given the postmodernist approach that so loses any cognitive value. In this sense postmodernism becomes part of that branch of contemporary historicist tradition that ended up in historical relativism. If every civilisation creates its own values, symbolisms, language and institutions – a culture that determines men born into it – then no comparison can be made among civilisations or historical moments and no man can understand a civilisation other than her/his. Neurath would have classified this postmodernism as part of anarchic historiography.

Tirthankar Roy (2003) tries to escape from this relativist trap by recovering power relations as a historical permanence, construing around it its own economics and economic history. Both theory and historical research would, thus, have to study the rules set up to control power relations in order to achieve economic efficiency and growth. Power, in this sense, could be not only constraining and submitting, but also liberating. Examples are rules to avoid cheating, polluting and agency problems. Along with the analysis of market failures, game theory would also be a useful part of such a postmodern economics. History, then, would study how a set of rules emerged and which ones were the more conducive to growth. Comparisons, in this historiography, would result from the objective effects of diverse rules on measurable costs: costs of production and costs of governance. By attaching a price label to power relations and the rules emerging from them, Roy attempts to construe a Culture Power Parity that allows comparison of different development paths, without the rhetoric attached to Eurocentric industrialisation historiography. In so doing, he recurs, though, to an idealistic premise like Machiavelli's. Has historiography come back to its beginning?

At the eve of the new millennium, the call of Deirdre McCloskey for a humanistic science of economics,[6] a science that would contemplate ideas as much as quantitative data, remains largely utopian. Historicism and postmodernisms have mined the idea of *Homo oeconomicus*, but the resulting probabilistic and behavioural microeconomics has still little use for history and history has little use for it. Economic history remains the realm of dynamics, while economics has many difficulties yet in abandoning equilibrium. The underlying attitudes towards history are opposite. The history of economics has a clear sense and direction, even if postmodernism reshaped its Eurocentric denomination as industrialisation or modernisation; economic theory lives with a hypothesis of idealistic permanence. Economic theory strives to be value-free, while values are, for historians, the very source of the questions to which they aim to find answers. Norms are as invariable for theory as they are variable for history. Determinism vs. voluntarism is also part of a separation agreement that was consensual as long as historians, economic historians and economists all built the autonomy of their disciplines in order to be granted university positions and funds.

Some attempts at reconciliation resulted from periods of stark economic and political change, as in the middle and at the end of the twentieth century, in the 1930s and 1950s. The same holds for the economic crisis that afflicted the world at large starting in 2007. The current rethinking of the philosophical bases of economic theory and history merits close study as the origin of new fruitful research lines if not of a new paradigm.

2 Economics and history after the crisis of 2007

In 2001, Hodgson wrote that 'History is important, partly because every complex organism, every human being and every society carries the baggage of its past' (Hodgson, 2001, p. 3). The relationship between economics and history remains contradictory: it appears progressively weak when mainstream economics, both micro and macro, are at stake; however, it seems to grow stronger when dealing with evolutionary economics, long-term growth and institutional economics.

Both neoclassical theories of general equilibrium and neo-Keynesian economics avoid or ignore history. At best, one might find an examination of historical series; however, this is not sufficient to analyse or give expression to historical or 'becoming' time. To recognize the relevance of the past or historical time involves stating that each economic thought or reasoning has historical contents expressed in preferences, habits, culture and institutions. What frequently occurs is that economists start from historical data; although they may come back to these data, they follow a mental process that is completely indifferent to history. As a result, the links between mainstream economics and history are definitely weakened, if not broken.

Contrary to this trend in mainstream economics, new connections between the economic and historical disciplines have begun to emerge. The 2007 economic crisis and its subsequent developments made at least two points clear concerning the overlap between economics and history. First, the comparison with past crises could be useful to single out specific policies to deal with the crisis. Given the inadequacy of mainstream economic thought to face long-term economic reversals, historical approaches could reveal useful tools. Second, institutions are called to play a major role to overcome the crisis. Since institutions are deeply rooted in and affected by history, they cannot be treated by means of pure mathematical methods. Therefore, they require new research fields that include both economics and history.

In some way, the aftermath of the 2007 crisis is shaping a new theoretical field where economics, the history of economic theories and economic history can overlap and thus provide new analytical viewpoints and perspectives.

The increasing detachment of economics from a historical perspective has also concerned the history of economic thought, with the consequence that the latter is gradually re-approaching economic history. Intellectual history and factual history are utilised to design new common research areas. What follows are some specific topics in which the two 'histories' seem to accept the challenge of defining a common research field which begins by examining the economic crisis.

An economic crisis should be treated as a phenomenon deeply rooted in the economic development or progress involving periodic reorganisations of the market, often leading to the elimination of non-competitive firms. This implies the necessity of a historical contextualisation in which the theories dealing with economic crisis are read according to facts and their evolution. Economic crisis is often associated with capitalism, where the latter is treated as a historical category more than an economic one. Perhaps this is far from the capitalism depicted as an 'economic style' *à la* Spiethoff (1952) which presents economic crisis as a symptom of this inexorable movement. According to that view, crisis – and not capitalism – was the historical 'fact' requiring theoretical and historical methodologies.

Crisis evokes another more general concept that makes any pure deductive experiment very difficult, i.e. 'economic change', which is really a twisted notion in mainstream economics. The study of how scholars deal with economic change can be useful to sort out the dilemma of an economics studying time as an account of subsequent facts or, on the contrary, an economics explaining deterministic movement, as in mechanics, in which analysing the initial conditions explains all the subsequent developments.

History involves an 'oriented' and 'irreversible' time that, contrary to the mechanical metaphor, is suited to the purpose of representing economic phenomena in their 'becoming'. Just the notion of becoming, frankly so uncommon to both economics and history, represents one of the unresolved points of synthesis between the two areas. According to a historical view, however, economic change is the study of 'economic becoming'.

George L. Shackle, who was one of the greatest interpreters of economic becoming, wrote as follows: 'For the individual human consciousness time is not a mathematician's space nor a historian's panorama but a moment. In this solitary moment all the consequences that the decision-maker seeks or accepts must necessarily be contained' (Shackle, 1967, p. 33). In this excerpt we find the drama of both mainstream economics, which is not able to free itself from mathematical time, and that of economic history, which can depict individual or collective decisions without explaining them. The new fields of research are called upon to overcome these opposite limits by integrating thought and time.

There is another area requiring a historical perspective, from both a theoretical and factual perspective: economic policy. It is unthinkable to detach economic policy from its factual application and its effects; however, it is also unthinkable to separate policy from the thought inspiring it. Here, the history of theories and ideas driving economic policies and the history of their specific historical application demonstrate the widest overlapping. The abstraction implicit in any theoretical analysis must deal with the real economic relationships taken into consideration in policy-making. Theories concerning economic policy and policy-making cannot refer to different semantic and conceptual worlds: a mutual relationship between them must be defined, and this is necessarily a concrete, historical relationship.

The process of beginning from economic thought in order to make and apply economic policies requires a simultaneous analysis of both theoretical and historical features. Then, if we also consider the retroaction from facts to the development of thoughts and theories, what emerges is a circular process rather than a linear one. This is also what emerges when considering the 'history of economic policy', a research area aimed at improving the economic policy outcomes. Thought and concrete political choices are considered together to identify the successes and failures of economic policies which are always historically contextualised. Among the areas in which the history of economic thought and economic history are intertwined, this is certainly the most promising.

Wondering whether economists and historians agree on anything, David B. Ryden wrote that the cultural dimension characterising historical studies does not find room in economics: 'The descriptive models [historians] construct are usually complex, hypertheoretical, particular, and subsequently impossible to empirically measure with quantitative methods' (Ryden, 2011, p. 210). It is true that culture is too complex to be reduced to budget constraints and rational maximisation, but economists have increasingly been engaged with culture in economic growth and economic policy. They have also attempted to include culture into deductive and mathematical models. In the area of economic culture, economic history and the history of economic thought appear to be complementary, which suggests that a promising new common research area can be established. It can be also hypothesised that the same history of economic thought can serve as a proxy to represent the evolution of the economic culture in a specific field.

Economic crisis, economic policy and *economic culture*, to which we can add the study of *monetary regimes* and of *the price of land*,[7] are only some of the research areas in which the history of economic thought and economic history appear complementary in defining new analytical categories grounded on the evolution of ideas besides facts. Intellectual and real histories find a synthesis that appears crucial to understanding the investigated phenomenon. The case of economic policy marked by a retroaction that makes economic theory dependent on policy outcomes is paradigmatic of a circular flow between thought and facts that both economic theory and history are unable to manage on their own.

In conclusion, although still in an embryonic stage, we can suppose that a stronger relationship between the history of economic thought and economic history is possible.

3 An attempt to reshape frontiers

The present volume collects essays of international researchers in the history of economic thought and economic history in order to confront their different approaches to the study of economic facts and ideas, rethinking boundaries, methodology and the objects of their disciplines. The essays face the question from three points of view: the relation between history and economics (Part I); the boundaries defining the history of economic thought in single authors and schools of thought (Part II); the Italian tradition of thought (Part III).

The chapters in Part I of the volume specifically confront the relation of economic theory and history. Bertram Schefold analyses different approaches to economics from antiquity to Islamic, Japanese and Chinese studies, emphasising three main historiographies of economic thought: positivistic, relativistic and political. Claus Thomasberger studies the question with a broad historical perspective, trying to ascertain a dialectical movement between facts and thought. Michele Cangiani, in Chapter 3, stresses the normative boundaries of the Austrian school of economic thought.

The essays in Part II relate the stance of single authors or schools of thought on the problem of history and theory in economics. Monika Poettinger discusses the Austrian philosopher and economist Otto Neurath; Anita Pelle writes about the Freiburg scholars in the interwar period in Germany; Jorge Turmo Arnal, Ángel Rodríguez García-Brazales and Oscar Vara Crespo explain the real business cycle theory; and Arturo Hermann's chapter is about theories comprising economic and psychological variables in order to explain evolution.

Part III hosts chapters assessing the fruitful relationship between economic facts and economics in the Italian tradition of thought. Piero Roggi details the issue for the twentieth century; Gianfranco Tusset analyses the 'paternalistic' approach developed by the Lombardo-Venetian School; Stefano Baietti and Giovanni Farese research in depth the special case of Sergio Paronetto, an economist dedicated, in the interwar period, to the construction of a new economic order.

All contributions are interdisciplinary and cross the usual boundaries of economic history, history of economic thought and economics with the aim of filling the methodological gap between these disciplines and finding a fertile common ground of research.

Notes

1 The second paragraph of this Introduction was written by Gianfranco Tusset, the rest by Monika Poettinger. Thanks must be expressed to the Italian Association for the History of Economic Thought (AISPE), presided over by Prof. Massimo Augello, that organised its XII meeting in Florence (21–23 February 2013) in which the topic of this volume has been widely discussed. Particular thanks to the Organising Committee in the person of its chair Prof. Piero Roggi. The contributions of Cristina Polverosi and Omar Ottonelli were invaluable for the success of the conference and the completion of the volume.
2 On the recent debate over the 'poverty' of Clio, see Boldizzoni (2011) and the reviews by Grantham (2012), McCloskey (2013) and Bodenhorn (2013).
3 On the importance of deriving equilibrium from dynamical laws and not dynamics from equilibrium theory, see Mach (1872).
4 The dissertation was partially published in volume in 1906 (Neurath, 1906a) and then in Schmoller's *Jahrbücher für Nationalökonomie und Statistik* (Neurath, 1906b and 1907).
5 Contemporary historicism is here loosely defined as the tradition of thought born out of the theorizations of Dilthey and Weber at the beginning of the twentieth century and spanning to its last offshoots in the aftermaths of WWII in France and the United States. See Rossi (1991, pp. vii–xxv).
6 For the debate see Whaples (2010), McCloskey (2010) and Mokyr (2010).
7 See the 'substantive economics' theorised by K. Polanyi (Polanyi and Meadow, 1957).

References

Ankersmit, F. R. (1990): Historiography and Postmodernism – Reply. *History and Theory*, vol. 29, no. 3, pp. 275–296.

Backhaus, J. G. (ed.) (2000): *Karl Bücher. Theory – History – Anthropology – Non Market Economies*. Marburg: Metropolis.

Bodenhorn, H. (2013): Review of: *The Poverty of Clio: Resurrecting Economic History* (by F. Boldizzoni; Princeton: Princeton University Press, 2011). *Journal of Interdisciplinary History*, vol. 43, no. 3, pp. 470–471.

Boldizzoni, F. (2011): *The Poverty of Clio: Resurrecting Economic History*. Princeton, NJ: Princeton University Press.

Bücher, K. (1893): *Die Entstehung der Volkswirtschaft: sechs Vorträge*. Tübingen: Verlag der H. Laupp'schen Buchhandlung.

Fanfani, A. (1960): *Introduzione allo studio della storia economica*. Milan: Giuffré.

Fanfani, A. (2011): *Storia delle dottrine economiche: un'antologia*, ed. by O. Ottonelli. Florence: Le Monnier.

Grantham, G. (2012): The Poverty of Clio: Resurrecting Economic History by Francesco Boldizzoni. *The Journal of Economic History*, vol. 72, no. 2, pp. 560–562.

Heaton, H., Gras, N. S. B., Clark V. S., Fay, C. R. and Jenks, L. H. (1930): Stages in Economic History. *The American Economic Review*, vol. 20, no. 1, Supplement, Papers and Proceedings of the Forty-second Annual Meeting of the American Economic Association, pp. 3–9.

Hildebrand, B. (1848): *Die Nationalökonomie der Gegenwart und Zukunft*. Frankfurt am Main: J. Rütten.
Hodgson, G. M. (2001): *How Economics Forgot History*. London and New York: Routledge.
Kaplan, J. (2012): 1 Samuel 8:11–18 as 'A Mirror for Princes'. *Journal of Biblical Literature*, vol. 131, no. 4, pp. 625–642.
Liverani, M. (2003): *Israel's History and the History of Israel by Mario Liverani*. London: Equinox Publishing Ltd.
Liverani, M. (2014): *The Ancient Near East: History, Society and Economy*. London: Routledge.
Mach, E. (1872): *Die Geschichte und die Wurzel des Satzes von der Erhaltung der Arbeit*. Prag: Mercy.
Machiavelli, N. (2012 [1531]): *Discourses on Livy*. Mineola: Courier Corporation.
McCloskey, D. N. (2010): One More Step: An Agreeable Reply to Whaples. *Historically Speaking*, vol. 11, no. 2, pp. 22–23.
McCloskey, D. N. (2013): The Poverty of Boldizzoni: Resurrecting the German Historical School. *Investigaciones de Historia Económica*, vol. 9, no. 1, pp. 2–6.
Menger, C. (1883): *Untersuchungen über die Methode der Socialwissenschaften und der politischen Oekonomie insbesondere*. Leipzig: Duneker und Humblot.
Meyer, E. (1895): *Die Wirtschaftliche Entwicklung des Altertums*. Jena: Fischer.
Mokyr, J. (2010): On the Supposed Decline and Fall of Economic History. *Historically Speaking*, vol. 11, no. 2, pp. 23–25.
Neurath, O. (1906a): *Zur Anschauung der Antike über Handel, Gewerbe und Landwirtschaft. Inaugural-Dissertation zur Erlangung der Doktorwurde genehmigt von der Philosophischen Fakultät der Friedrich-Wilhelms-Universität zu Berlin*. Jena: Fischer.
Neurath, O. (1906b): Zur Anschauung der Antike über Handel, Gewerbe und Landwirtschaft. *Jahrbücher für Nationalökonomie und Statistik*, vol. 32 (87), no. 5, pp. 577–606.
Neurath, O. (1907): Zur Anschauung der Antike über Handel, Gewerbe und Landwirtschaft. *Jahrbücher für Nationalökonomie und Statistik*, vol. 34 (89), no. 2, pp. 145–205.
Poettinger, M. (2012): *Mercante e società: riflessioni di storia comparata*. Lugano: Casagrande Editore.
Poettinger, M. (2014): Besieging the French Liberal Fortress: The Diffusion of Italian and German Economic Thought in the Last Quarter of the 19th Century. *Rivista di Storia Economica*, vol. 30, no. 1, pp. 37–58.
Polanyi, K. and Meadow, P. (1957): The Economy as an Instituted Process. In: K. Polanyi and C. M. Arensburg (eds.), *Trade and Markets in Early Empires*. Glencoe: The Free Press.
Reisman, D. A. (2012): *The Social Economics of Thorstein Veblen*. Cheltenham: Edward Elgar.
Rossi, P. (1991): *Storia e storicismo nella filosofia contemporanea*. Milan: Il Saggiatore.
Rostow, W. W. (1960): *The Stages of Economic Growth: A Non-Communist Manifesto*. Cambridge: Cambridge University Press.
Roy, T. (2003): Economic History and Postmodern Theory. *Economic and Political Weekly*, vol. 38, no. 19, pp. 1874–1878.
Ryden, D. B. (2011): Perhaps We Can Talk: Discussant Comments for Taking Stock and Moving Ahead: The Past, Present, and Future of Economics for History. *Social Science History*, vol. 35, no. 2, pp. 209–212.
Shackle, G. L. S. (1967): *Time in Economics*. Amsterdam: North-Holland.

Spiethoff, A. A. C. (1952): The 'Historical' Character of Economic Theories. *Journal of Economic History*, vol. 12, no. 2, pp. 131–139.

Wallerstein, I. (2005): *World-Systems Analysis, An Introduction*. Durham, NC: Duke University Press.

Whaples, R. (2010): Is Economic History a Neglected Field of Study? Final Thoughts. *Historically Speaking*, vol. 11, no. 2, p. 27.

Wisman, J. D., Willoughby, J. and Sawers, L. (1988): The Search for Grand Theory in Economic History: North's Challenge to Marx. *Social Research*, vol. 55, no. 4, pp. 747–773.

Part I
Economic thought
History and values

1 History of economic thought and economic history

Who will bring the past to life?[1]

Bertram Schefold

1 Introduction

History of economic thought and economic history, as disciplines pertaining both to economics and to history, seem like rivalling brothers. Both claim the birthright, but who was the firstborn? I shall present my view as to how they should relate to each other on the basis of my research and teaching of the matter over forty years (Schefold, 2002b; 2009a) and on the basis of two projects to be mentioned below. I thus hope also to contribute to an ongoing debate about the genesis of modern capitalism which involves both disciplines.

The relationship between the history of economic thought and economic theory once seemed to me to be easy. I still think that this simple view holds truth; it is best illustrated by an analogy: History of economic thought is to economic history as the literary sources about a culture are to the archaeological remains. If we compare excavations of a Polis in Greece of the classical period with excavations of American-Indian cultures in, say, Guatemala, the buildings of the former will be interpreted on the basis of what we know from ancient Greek poetry, history, novels and drama. Indeed, we know fairly well what meaning was attached to religious buildings, administrative buildings and assembly places, because of a tradition, which involves knowledge about ancient Greek philosophy, religion and law. We excavate the Agora in Athens and we imagine Socrates standing there and looking for pupils. In the case of Mesoamerican excavations, the lack of texts, which we could read, often compels us to interpret the architectural structures found exclusively on the basis of additional material remains, such as household equipment, instruments of handicraft and weapons. There may be mythological representations. But the intellectual world once associated with this material culture is difficult to reconstruct; it will explicitly or implicitly depend on what we know from living cultures or texts left by other cultural traditions. Stones will speak differently not only when inscriptions on them can be deciphered, but also – no, principally – if they relate to texts handed down to us by scribes, by monks and humanists. How would you interpret the statue of Laokoon, if you did not know the myth of the destruction of Troy?

The history of economic thought helps to give meaning to the facts uncovered by economic history. Mercantilism may serve as an example. The mercantilists expressed their trust in the market by asserting that exports would pay for imports, preferably with a surplus of precious metals, which could be used to facilitate domestic monetary circulation. It is true that they recommended measures to foster exports. They would protect the domestic industry by means of customs duties and they would help exporting industries by granting privileges and easing the labour supply, but they did not intervene in foreign trade in order to secure specific imports to nourish the population. This, however, had been the concern of many earlier and even contemporary empires (Vidal-Naquet and Austin, 1977). The Athenians in the classical period required exporting ships to show contracts for the import of corn, since the agricultural production of Attica was not sufficient to feed the population. The Ottomans, down to the eighteenth century, wanted internal trade to prosper, but the aim of foreign trade was to secure necessary imports (Ermis, 2013). This attitude has been called provisionism, and it is amply documented in reports by government officials, ambassadors and in the writing of philosophers. An account merely of material facts of economic history might not suffice to establish the difference between mercantilism and provisionism. It was a matter of economic policy, based on a certain vision of how the economy within the state worked. The difference between mercantilism and provisionism, therefore, reflects differences in the history of economic thinking, documented in texts, such as economic historians will use to explain differences in economic development. Provisionism became an obstacle to economic development in the Eastern Mediterranean, when the Western part was carried away by the autonomous dynamics of mercantilism. The cooperation between economic historians and historians of economic thought may be quite easy and peaceful in this case, in that economic historians might explain economic policies and developments using the same sources as historians of economic thoughts, whose aim would be to demonstrate the existence of a coherent body of doctrines. Provisionism would be based on the interpretation of the state as a community with mutual obligations. The sultan would express his paternalism and his concern that the order of a stratified society be maintained. The minister of finance in a Western monarchy in the period of mercantilism had a more dynamic view. Colbert wanted France to be rich in order to be powerful, and he wanted power in order to let it accumulate riches. France should be independent, but everybody else should need France and depend on its supplies (Wolters, 1922).

In other cases, the views of economic historians and historians of economic thought may tend to diverge considerably. This will typically be the case if the economic historians interpret economic history by means of neoclassical theory, which, as a theory, is historically invariant, while historians of economic thought borrow from historical sociology to emphasise the differences of the intellectual worlds of different cultures, often using time-dependent theories, and they interpret economic facts and policies in this light. A famous example is the controversy between primitivists and modernists in the interpretation of ancient history, a debate which began in Germany with the publications of Karl Bücher, a leading figure of the German Historical School, who had a background as a classical scholar, but had become an economist (Schefold, 1988; 2014). He confronted the modernism of colleagues in ancient history, in particular Eduard Meyer. Meyer saw a close parallel between the evolution of the economy in Greece from archaic and classical down to Hellenistic and Roman times with the later development in northern Europe from the early Middle Ages down to mercantilism, in that the stages of economic growth were similar; they went in antiquity from the pre-monetary economy with aristocratic rule to an extended market system spanning the Mediterranean. Bücher objected and tried to identify specific traits of the economy of antiquity. According to him, the Polis economies remained centred around the household, from the royal courts described in Homer down to the family of the Athenian citizen. Where Meyer wrote of export-oriented industries, Bücher saw craftsmanship and personal networks of gift-giving; the goods designated as exports did not result from large-scale enterprise seeking foreign markets but were luxury items produced by migrating artisans. Moses Finley was inclined to justify this primitivism in his well-known book on the ancient economy (Finley, 1973). His influence diminished later, and modernism has gained ground in ancient history in recent years (Schefold, 2013). Bücher and Meyer had in common that they analysed developments in terms of stages. Meyer was interested in material development and the growth of trade and communication. With his primitivist conceptions, Bücher groped towards an integrated view of economy, society and culture, but the analysis of different economic styles and systems came only later.

Max Weber, one generation younger than Bücher, used his ideal types to characterise different economic forms, primarily on the basis of the prevailing rationality. There had always been greed, but profit-seeking merchants are only one capitalist element; they do not constitute capitalism as a system. For Weber, the capitalism of antiquity was largely political (Schefold, 1992a). The institutional and intellectual means for an efficient administration of private firms did not yet exist. Indeed, household and firms had not yet separated. Hence there was a tension between the aim of leading a good life, as the ancients put it, and pursuing material gain. There was not, as in modern life, the separation of roles pursued in one's professional occupation and in the family. Slavery rendered a rational allocation of labour difficult, and the main opportunities to make large profits were associated with the political system. But von Mises, as a leading Austrian economist, would not accept Weber's historical distinctions based on the assumption of changing rationalities. The rationality of action would always be the same, Mises thought, but the means changed. If a seafaring merchant sacrificed a ram in order to cross the Mediterranean and to trade with distant peoples, Weber would see this as evidence of a traditional rationality, while von Mises asserted that the rationality was the same as in modern times: the merchant wanted to make sure that his ship travelled safely, only he was superstitious and therefore wrong in choosing the means (Schefold, 2009c). In this manner, the Austrian form of a historical neoclassical theory was used to criticise Weber's proposal of different forms of rationality underlying economic action.

Historians of economic thought tend to see an evolution of ideas from antiquity and the Middle Ages to mercantilism and beyond, in which economic insights grow and are assembled in more and more coherent representations of the functioning of the economy, until the system of liberalism is born and modern capitalism develops on the basis of a quasi-mechanical understanding of how the economy works. The early ethical rules, which impose cooperation, which demand mutual love, have to be modified and the advantages of letting self-interest dominate at least in the public sphere must be recognised. The main step was taken, once it was recognised by the late scholastics that *lucrum cessans* legitimises the taking of the interest (Lessius, 1999; Schefold, 1999a). Attention is focused on the Occident, special, it was claimed, in its striving for a coherent description of the autonomous functioning of interrelated markets by those mercantilists who prepared the ground for the liberals, such as Serra, who wrote about the advantages of scale and of agglomeration, comparing Naples with Venice (Serra, 2011 [1613]; Schefold, 1994). This representation of the historical process seems to imply that the growth towards a modern world economy is based on unique material and spiritual constellations in the West; modern capitalism then spread to other parts of the globe under the influence of an extension of the European system, by means of colonisation, trade and intellectual influence.

Some economic historians have begun to challenge this view of an exceptional economic development in the West by arguing that high cultures elsewhere reached similar levels of development by the eighteenth century, and that certain provinces in China or Japan and even in other countries attained a level of production such that an industrial revolution could have started; and Britain could be first in the creation of the industrial revolution because of a number of coincidences, such as the availability of coal and iron, an infrastructure provided by navigable rivers and natural ports and by a growth of technical knowledge made possible by an association of theoretical and practical intellectual work in institutions, such as the Royal Society. The California School (Goldstone, 2000; Pomeranz, 2000; Frank, 1998; and, with a similar tendency, Maddison, 2007) hold that capitalism has prevailed most of the time, even if it was contained by feudal and patriarchal rule. The more developed provinces in China and Japan were not so different from, for example, the Netherlands in the seventeenth century or even the Roman Empire. Given the emphasis on material facts and, first of all, the standard of life, and given the reduced importance ascribed to differences of economic systems, the differences in economic thought also lose importance. Max Weber had complemented his theory of the growth of modern capitalism as favoured by the growth of Protestantism by analysing the world religions and showing that the economic ethics in India and China prevented the spontaneous emergence of modern capitalism (Weber, 1921, pp. 19–21). But the California School, having negated big material differences, also try to show that the business ethics and the business practices in the East were not so different after all.

A consensus as to who is right will not easily be reached. My present contribution is limited. I only want to help to distinguish between different ways of doing history of economic thought, the different conceptions being linked to the different views about economic history and the relationship between the disciplines. I distinguish three conceptions of the history of economic thought, using my own terminology: the positivist, relativist and political. The main results are summarised in Table 1.1. We begin with a first survey.

Table 1.1 Approaches to the history of economic thought

Type	Preferred designation/authors	Epochs	Characteristics of the history of economic theory	Perceptions of economic history	Associated periodisation of economic history	Conceptual framework	Value judgements
Positivistic	History of Economic Theory, History of Economic Analysis, e.g. Schumpeter	since eighteenth century (beginnings in mercantilism)	history of discovery history of progress formation of a theory	the economic problem is a-historical	e.g. (technical) stages (Rostow)	model building, mathematical formulation, analytical reconstruction of theories	ideal of value-free analysis: analysing the practicality of goals
Relativistic	objectivist History of Economic Thought, e.g. Marx (Theories of Surplus Value)	all history of mankind	'progress' not only cumulative, but also substitutive and cyclical	materialistic type: base and superstructure (Marx)	mode of production (esp. antiquity/feudal/capitalist)	materialism claims to derive the genesis of necessary false appearances	theory serves class interest (Marx)
	culturalist History of Economic Thought, e.g. Max Weber (Protestant Ethic)		theories historically relative because of differences in rationality	idealist variant: changing goal orientation	modern capitalism = 'rational' capitalism, protestant thesis	ideal type	theory does not justify values but allows to relate them (Weber)
	'Visual' Theory encompasses 'Rational' Theory		formation of ideology in an institutional context	economic styles (Spiethoff)	features of the economic style	hermeneutics, semantics	evolution of values regarded as immanent in development
Political	History of Political Economy, e.g. Edgar Salin	since state formation, high cultures	entanglement of economy and politics	striving for harmony of politics and economy, 'embedding'	political and cultural, corresponding to the high cultures	philosophical orientation towards the good life	images of the good life; religious ethics
			theory expresses the independence of the economic process	economy becomes political, because social and economic class formation coincide (esp. eighteenth and nineteenth centuries)	'capitalism', 'real socialism'	terms serve political debate	freedom and social justice to be reconciled

2 Approaches to the history of economic thought: an overview

The *positivist* approach is possibly still the most common. Its aim is to provide a history of economic theory. It therefore assumes that economic action can be separated from other forms of human action, that there is consciousness of this separation and that the forms of economic behaviour are sufficiently regular to admit a formalisation and functional representation of the economic variables which depend on human decisions. It is usually assumed that the economic theories so formulated apply to all periods of human history, but there are exceptions to this rule. (The typology proposed here is not free of overlaps.) I should count the economic histories by Mark Blaug (1999), Jörg Niehans (1994) and Joseph Schumpeter (1954) among the positivist approach, with Niehans being perhaps the most radical and most conscious in avoiding overlaps with other approaches. His history begins with the eighteenth century and Cantillon. Even the major early mercantilists are not recognised by him as theorists. He explains that elementary economic insights, such as the recognition of the fact that the different fertility of different lands results in different land values, lack systemic character and thus do not constitute theory. The ambition is to lead up to a history of modern economic theory, with Samuelson as the main protagonist who did much to integrate the different sub-disciplines and to preserve a coherent outlook. Schumpeter's *History of Economic Analysis* was significantly broader in its scope, beginning as it does, with teachings of antiquity and the Middle Ages, but Schumpeter did not find much theory there, and even the theoretical synthesis by the great mercantilists such as Serra only expressed what he called a quasi-system. Schumpeter is famous for his critique of the Ricardian 'vice' which consists in making assumptions relevant only for a special historical constellation and then treating the resulting theory as something general. Schumpeter's general theory is essentially only one, with, as its main support, the Walrasian theory of general equilibrium, which in fact has been considered as the core of economic theory in the second half of the twentieth century by the majority of economists – certainly by the majority of liberal economists – whereas it commands less prestige at present (Schefold, 1986).

The *relativist* approach comprises all attempts to see economic theory and, more generally, economic thought as historically conditioned. One can – and should – include here accounts of ideas, norms and attitudes, which govern economic behaviour, even if there is no conscious separation between the economic sphere and social action in general. 'Economic' then is what we classify as such, on the basis of our interpretation of history. There is no historical limit to such interpretation. *Stone Age Economics* (Sahlins, 1974) once was, deservedly, a popular book which tried to identify the economic peculiarities of primitive cultures. Some economising takes place even in the animal kingdom, because of elementary forms of learning and by virtue of the invisible hand of evolution. We are here interested in more developed and eventually in conscious forms of economic action. I shall distinguish three forms of the relativistic approach: Marxian materialism, Weber's theory of the Protestant ethic and the visual 'theorising' which was a programme of the Youngest Historical School, but, as a practice, much more widespread.

It is not at all easy to substantiate the claim that economic theory should change with historical circumstances and reflect the different traits of different cultures. Are demand and supply not general notions which can be applied in age-old village communities and on the stock exchange? But the historicity of economics becomes more obvious as soon as we consider the state in its relation to the economy (Nau and Schefold, 2002). The forms of the state in what used to be called the high cultures (*Hochkulturen*) vary a great deal. As the cultural contexts vary, the states are financed and spend in different ways on government, administration, war, culture and representation in vastly different forms, which are necessarily connected with the economy and lead to reflections on how to develop the institutions supporting this intercourse of the cultural, the economic and the political. These reflections, even if they appear as fruits of other disciplines such as law or philosophy, deserve to be objects of the history of economic thought. We shall here limit the discussion to the contrast between the ideas of the state, the economy and the community between classical antiquity and modern liberalism of the eighteenth and nineteenth centuries, which is often also called 'classical'. This *political* approach, therefore, can be seen as part of the relativist approach, but it is sufficiently important to be treated as a category of its own.

So far we have only been considering the first three columns of Table 1.1; we now consider the approaches one by one – the rows of the table – taking into account the relationship between the history of economic thought and economic history, seeking in particular to determine which kind of periodisation is appropriate, and discussing the associated conceptual frameworks.

3 The positivist approach

The positivist approach consists in a history of the discovery of theory as a history of progress in theorising, therefore as a history of the accumulation of analytic knowledge and of methodological advances. It is not directly related with positivist economic history, since positivist economic history will use modern forms of economic theory for the explanation of the economic development – to use older theories because they seem to reflect conditions of past periods would mean to subscribe to relativism. This does not exclude a historical perspective on development, to the extent that historical transformations can be represented by means of the concepts of the theory, as changes of taste, as technical progress or as change of, for example, monetary institutions. Accordingly, one will seek to identify phases of economic development by means of stages of technical development as in Rostow (1960). A closer link between economic history and history of economic thought appears in consequence of the change of monetary institutions. As long as the gold standard prevailed, new gold had to be produced in the mines at some cost. Inflation, caused by whatever reason, meant that gold prices of commodities rose and that the purchasing power of gold in terms of commodities fell. Hence an incentive was created to slow down gold production and to use more gold for 'industrial' use, that is, mainly as ornament. If, more specifically, too many gold coins were issued, commodity prices would rise, gold coins would become cheaper in terms of commodities and the better coins would be melted down, whether that was permitted or not. The inflationary tendency thus was corrected. Conversely, deflation would encourage gold production and the monetary use of gold. In terms of the quantity equation, the price level was given by the cost of production of gold, and the level of transactions and the velocity of circulation determined the required amount of gold as money. This endogeneity of the number of coins of precious metal in circulation was observed already by Copernicus (1999 [1519]). But when the stock of precious metal available for monetary use became large, whether a reserve of coins or of specie, and when the value of the gold stock was enhanced by a circulation of redeemable notes, whether circulating or as treasure, the influence of the cost of production of gold on its purchasing power began to wane, the stock dominated the flow and the quantity equation could be read as a quantity theory: the predominant direction of causality now ran from the quantity of the circulating media to the level of prices, and not *vice versa*, as before. This is one of the few examples of how a change in economic history could induce historians of economic thought following the positivist approach to adapt their theory to historical circumstances. They could believe in the quantity theory for their own time, but accepted the cost-of-production theory as valid for past periods and hence recognised the analysis of earlier economists as valid (Niehans, 1994).

I would still regard it as part of the positivist approach, if theories of past authors are interpreted as systematic wholes which are to be represented as such, although the texts have not come down to us in a coherent form, for whatever reason: the author published only part of his system (Marx) or parts have been destroyed (Adam Smith's final synthesis of the *Theory of Moral Sentiments* and the *Wealth of Nations*). The reconstruction of the system can also start from the feeling that the introduction of new concepts could be fruitful for the understanding of old ideas (model-building to represent Ricardo's theory). It has become customary to speak of analytical reconstructions of past theories, if one aims at representing them as deductive systems, employing, where useful and clarifying, also later analytical tools. The art of the historian of economic analysis then is to strike the appropriate balance between a close rephrasing of the original formulation of the theory and its transposition into a modern – often a mathematical – theory. One thus has to situate oneself between historical, indeed philological, accuracy and the elegance and explanatory power of a more modern formulation. Is it appropriate to expound Ricardo's system in terms of the labour theory of value as he did? Should one use curves to explain his vision of diminishing returns in agriculture? Is it licit to explain his system in terms of Sraffa prices with the associated modern terminology (Sraffa, 1951; Kaldor, 1956; Pasinetti, 1974)? Each of these strategies of exposition has its merits and its disadvantages. Each contributes – but each in different way – to our conception of what Ricardo 'really said' and to an understanding of what he 'meant'. With the latter question, one begins to turn towards the relativist approach.

The formation of classical theory provides perhaps the most impressive examples of analytical progress. Its history has been written and rewritten many times;

the role of mathematical tools to represent it in modern form increased step by step from Whewell (1971 [1829]) to Dmitriev (1974 [1904]) and finally to Sraffa (1960) and his followers.

In particular, the gravitation of market prices to natural prices or normal prices has given rise to a variety of analytical reconstructions. It was described by Adam Smith (1976 [1776]) in anecdotal form, much as in earlier mercantilist and cameralist literature. The monarch dies, his faithful subjects wish to express their sorrow by exhibiting black flags. The price of black cloth rises, but it will fall again after the event and return to a level close to the natural price which reflects the cost of production in terms of the natural price of the materials used, the natural wage of labour expended and profits and rents, according to natural rates which Smith postulated, though his theory of those natural rates was not as clear as that of wages. Alfred Marshall (1920 [1890]) had developed the theory of market prices into the model of short-run prices for which marginal cost is equal to the price under competitive conditions. If this does not happen to coincide with average costs, quasi-rents will arise, and if these are positive, new firms will be attracted to this business, or, if the quasi-rents are negative, firms will leave the business, until the price on the market as a whole, equal to marginal cost, will be reduced or elevated to the minimum of average costs. This implies that the short-run supply curve of firms is rising, as the aggregate of all the marginal cost curves, while the long-run supply curve will be horizontal under the convenient assumption that all firms have the same cost curves and that constant returns to scale prevail. This was more than an analytical reconstruction of the Smithian idea: it was an analytical development of it, incorporating classical ideas into a neoclassical scheme, but it did not represent the only possibility of rendering the relationship between market price and normal price more precise (Sraffa, 1925). The idea appears in a different form in modern intertemporal equilibrium theory with given endowments and a distant, but finite time horizon (Schefold, 1997a). Even if preferences are stationary over time, prices will differ from long-run normal costs because of changing endowments over time, and, in particular, because of the accidental composition of initial endowments. But, if certain more technical conditions are met, a convergence towards normal costs and normal prices will result, if preferences and the endowments of non-produced means of production, labour and land, remain stationary from period to period. According to various so-called turnpike theorems, the relative intertemporal prices would gradually tend towards stationary values, if the horizon is sufficiently far away. Yet other models of the gravitation have been formulated in the classical tradition, using so-called crossed dual dynamics to represent growth of the different sectors of the economy according to rates, which depend on the level of prices and profits in each sector, and the prices depend on the discrepancy between quantities of goods supplied and demanded. Convergence does not always result; there can also be limit cycles or even divergence (Political Economy, 1992).

We have already mentioned the labour theory of value as another example of a theory for which analytical reconstructions and extensions have been found. The labour theory of value imposed itself at a time when no other possibility was available to give a clear account of the level of long-run prices in objective terms. To speak of supply and demand was not of much help at a time when supply and demand curves had not yet been invented. Prior to Rau's early introduction of the curves (Rau, 1997; Schefold, 1997b), supply and demand were interpreted as forces which, as Marx (2004 [1894]) put it, ceased to operate when of equal strength, hence they would explain the tendency to, but not the position of, equilibrium. Only Böhm-Bawerk suggested that the 'forces' could be related to the distances from equilibrium. If two groups of children play at tug-of-war, one cannot predict where their rope will stop, once the two groups pull with equal strength, after having first pulled each other backward and forward. This analogy lets us understand why Marx thought that a notion of objective value was required to determine the position of rest. But Böhm-Bawerk chose a different comparison (Schefold, 1991). If a balloon rises, it is exposed to a nearly constant force operating downwards: gravity, and to one operating upwards: lift, and this latter changes with the height attained because of the diminishing pressure of the surrounding air so that the rise of the balloon will stop at a certain level. To show that the amount demanded changed strongly with the prices, the theory of utility and of the possibility of substitution had to be developed. The old concept of effectual demand in Smith meant a given quantity, not a demand curve.

As the concept of supply and demand of the classical (and, prior to them, of the mercantilists) was different from the neoclassical model, so was their concept of the normal price. To calculate long-run prices from a system of interdependent linear equations, as in Sraffa's modern reconstruction of classical theory, was not possible for economists who did not know about linear equation systems, and the neat separation between technical conditions of production and conditions of distribution characteristic for Sraffa's approach had not yet been worked out either. The labour theory seemed simple and obvious, if one assumed production by means of direct labour only, as in the Smithian example of the hunters in a forest where land was free and capital had not yet been accumulated. The application of the labour theory to the general case with capital and land was first based on the treatment of capital goods as embodied labour. It was also based on Ricardo's idea of 'getting rid of rent' by looking at the technique of production used on the marginal land. It included profit in the calculation of prices: in Ricardo's case by elevating or lowering 'value' (meaning the natural price) according to the time it took to 'bring the commodity to market', whereas Marx based his transformation of values into prices on the consideration of different organic compositions of capital. All these procedures can be represented formally by means of linear models; insofar as these seem to provide an analytical reconstruction, but the analytical reconstruction leaves the original conceptions behind, for once the system of normal prices has been formulated in terms of the system of equations, the old approach in terms of the labour theory of value appears to be redundant.

On the other hand, the analytical reconstruction does not capture all aspects of the older theory. Locke used the labour theory of value to defend his theory of property (Schefold, 1993b); Marx (1867) used it to explain his sociological and philosophical conception of alienated work.

We thus find that the history of economic thought is intimately connected with the development of the theory itself. There have been economists like Joan Robinson (1971) in whose work it is occasionally impossible to tell whether the text is history of economic theory or development of the theory. Where analytical history is detached from modern theory, without contextualising it, it becomes a mere history of errors and discoveries, similar to a history of mathematics, which is a matter for specialists, whereas, in context, it becomes related to general history and to the question how people orient themselves in their social life. It then is more similar to a history of philosophy, and history of philosophy simply *is* philosophy.

4 Relativist approaches

And so we arrive at our three variants of the relativist approach, shown in Table 1.1 above. Historical materialism claims both to know how economic forms ('modes of production') evolved in a linear evolution, therefore to possess the true theory of history, and – at least in principle – to be able to derive the ideological representations people make up according to their position in the process. To know economic history, to be able to explain the economic process, thus becomes the condition of cognition: of being able to separate truth and ideology and eventually to act in the interest of the emancipation of mankind. Objective scientific knowledge is the means of overcoming one's own class position. Marx realised only a small part of the programme implied by his historical materialism, and he was well aware of his limitations, but thought that the essential hints had been given in the first volume of *Das Kapital* (see in particular Marx, 1969 [1890], p. 392, on Vico). There were gaps in his theory of capitalism. He had envisaged writing about international trade and the world market, he only had sketches of theories of pre-capitalist modes of production, but his Theories of Surplus Value did contain a rich and still provocative analysis of how classical economics arose and subsequently were transformed into 'vulgar' (neoclassical) theory (Marx, 1861–1863; 1905–1910). The 'false appearances' created by the objective process explained what seemed to him the ideological form of representing the conflict about distribution and accumulation. Being one of the few geniuses who ever deigned to study our lowly subject, he left behind a seemingly infinite mass of hints regarding all other aspects of his large conjecture, like his insights regarding the economics of antiquity where he was closer to the primitivists than to the modernists. He was extremely partisan as a historian of economic thought, especially regarding the German Historical School, which he treated with derision, although he was trying to execute their main idea of building a *historical* theory.

The challenge posed by Marx was taken up by the Youngest Historical School, the generation of Sombart and Weber. The third volume of *Das Kapital*, published by Engels, appeared more than twenty years after the foundation of systematic neoclassical theory by Jevons, Menger and Walras. Hence it was Marx who seemed modern to Sombart (1896), not Menger, and when his socialism gradually gave way to cultural criticism, eventually in a nationalist vein (Sombart, 1934), he continued to use more classical than neoclassical analytical ideas in his theory, which remained (from a formal point of view) rather underdeveloped. Progress was now found to be not linear in economic history and not cumulative in the history of economic thought – there were also cycles – and the material influences in history had to be complemented by social, cultural and religious forces (Sombart, 1928).

Rereading Max Weber (1992), one can be struck by the historical importance he ascribes to the peculiar attitudes developed in a confession which was part of a special variant of the Christian religion, but one can also be surprised by the extent to which he lets material forces rule the roost. 'Rational' capitalism – 'modern' capitalism – presupposes institutions such as wage labour as the only secure basis for a rational allocation of labour; to this extent, the main characteristic of capitalism is the same as in Marx. His ideal types were constructs, like models – though not formulated mathematically. They were constructs, not phenomenological descriptions, not representations based on art and feeling, but, in principle, based on well-defined, unambiguous concepts, like the terms used in jurisprudence, the discipline in which he had his first formation (Schefold, 1992c). He often used counterfactuals. And so his ideal types did not follow one another in a necessary evolution as the modes of production in Marx; history could take surprising turns.

In his conception, the history of economic thought played a role in this only in a very special function: as the history of ethics. Max Weber seems not to have been interested in what people thought about how the economy worked or whether their laws governing taxation were based on a proper understanding of why people could contribute (Weber, 1992). But his analysis of puritanism was an analysis of how the ethics formed which, surprisingly, became the basis for the norms of the behaviour of the modern capitalist and modern professional activity. Conversely, he analysed the history of the world religions in order to demonstrate why capitalism could not originate elsewhere, primarily because of ethical rules limiting nascent capitalist activities, and so his description of, for example, the economic ethics of Confucianism focused on only a particular aspect of what we might call ancient Chinese economic thought (Hu, 1988).

But what do we recognise as economic thought, once we leave the well-trodden path of the history of European and American economic analysis? Even the mercantilists had very little hard economic theory, but a great deal of economic vision and understanding. The same may be said of the scholastics and of the philosophers of antiquity. There were a few concepts such as just price or usury, which are immediately recognisable as related to modern economic concepts, although they were used in the different context of ethical thought. Nevertheless, this ethical thought was, in all essential applications, based on rich visions of the working of the contemporary economies. Almost all modern economists underestimate the significance of such understanding. Only once, 'visual' or 'intuitive' theory became a programme or paradigm again; among economists one generation younger than Max Weber. Edgar Salin (1927) had noted that Sombart's magnum opus *Der moderne Kapitalismus* had chapters with 'visual' theory alternating with chapters with 'rational' theory. When Sombart described the history of discoveries or of colonisation, he would not dwell on single historical facts, but unfolded the logic of development: the adventurous spirit of the discoverers, their rapacious collections of precious metals, the subsequently more systematic exploitation of the mines and the flow of gold and silver back to Europe, where it animated luxury consumption, spread to other countries and led to the great inflation (Sombart, 1928). The corresponding theoretical chapter would explain the supporting monetary theory, based not on a generalised visual description, but on analytical concepts. The idea of the visual theory, on the other hand, could be traced back to Goethe and his synthesising approach to natural phenomena and art. It can be shown for instance that in his accounts of his travels, in particular his Italian journey, his vision of the land dealt not only with phenomena of art and nature, but also with economic facts, be they the advent of mechanisation and its impact on occupation and the forms of life or his observations of economic behaviour and institutions in the different states of Italy, when he saw Venice, Rome or Naples (Schefold, 2012).

The visual approach was a heritage of cameralism. Goethe had been brought up as a lawyer in the cameralist tradition. He was confronted with the revolution of physiocracy, and later with the liberalism of Adam Smith, and he lived on and became a contemporary of early French socialism and the beginnings of the Historical School. He would react to all these influences, he would welcome the liberal spirit, but his genius was in his artful combination of the description of phenomena and his understanding of the logical relations between them, which he rendered in the form of visual theory.

Arthur Spiethoff, of international fame because of his analysis of business cycles, a friend of Edgar Salin, proposed a special form of visual theory: the analysis of economic styles (Spiethoff, 1933). They were characterised in a way similar to Sombart's systems and a homogeneity was postulated as in Weber's ideal types. The characteristics were: (1) the economic spirit, the mentality of the people in an economy demarcated in time and space; it was to have a certain unity. The style was further characterised by (2) the natural and technical conditions, (3) the economic constitution, (4) the social constitution and, finally, (5) a certain economic dynamism. One could see these characteristics as a simplified scheme to compare modern capitalism and mercantilism or feudalism. It was also used to characterise the social market economy after the Second World War with its compromise between efficiency and redistribution (Müller-Armack, 1999 [1947]; Schefold, 1999b), for the compromise was and is based on a mentality and on supporting institutions. What interests me here is the fact that we find a similar approach already in cameralism. My main example is Kaspar Klock who published a voluminous treatise on public finance in 1651 under the title *De Aerario* (2009 [1651]). The second part on public finance was preceded by an entire book as the first part: a description of the countries of the world with their institutions to finance the state, and this he tried to relate to the character of the population, their means of livelihood and, therefore, the economic geography and their social constitution. He summarised his programme, using characteristics, which also happened to number five, and we can compare them to those proposed and used by Spiethoff:

30 Bertram Schefold

Spiethoff (1933):	Klock (2009 [1651]):
1 Economic spirit	1 *Ratio reipublicae*
2 Natural and technical conditions	2 *Populi natura*
3 Economic constitution	3 *Regnorum jura*
4 Social constitution	4 *Populi conditio*
5 Economic dynamics	5 *Reditus regnorum*

Klock thus used (1) Machiavelli's (2005 [1513]) and Botero's (2010 [1596]) notion of the 'reason of state' to comprehend the understanding princes and subjects have of the functioning of their states, he observed (2) how people behaved – indeed, how they looked and worked. He, as a lawyer, paid special attention to the legal system (3), he observed the material condition of the people (4), and he eventually concentrated on his special concern: the financing of the state (5). With this scheme in mind, he set out to capture the extraordinary variety in the world before globalisation had fully taken hold.

Writing during the Thirty Years War, he was mainly concerned with the disintegration of The Holy Roman Empire which he contrasted with the homogeneity and unity of France; he thus perceived advantages – but also problems – of fiscal centralisation. He described the European countries: Spain with its colonies around the globe, which was overextended, protectionist Britain, the relatively democratic Swedish monarchy, the corrupt state trade of the grand duke of Moskovy, the slavery of the Ottoman empire. Each among the many countries served to illustrate some principle. He admired China and how the revenues flew towards the emperor and how his expenditures animated production in the provinces; he thus had visualised the circular flow of income. In Africa, he described Ethiopia, among others, and noticed that they had sugar cane, but did not know how to make sugar. They had hemp, but did not know how to make cloth; he thus related technology, human capital and development. In the second part of his treatise he noted how rents varied with the fertility of the soil; he thus had an understanding of differential rent and used it to explain the principle of taxation: contributions should correspond to earning power. The abstract concepts, which I have used to capture what he had understood, were not yet at his disposal, however. The long process during which the semantics of economic concepts was developed, alongside the corresponding institutions, was still in its beginnings. Klock, when he tried to formulate the principle of personal taxation, was groping towards a concept of personal income, but it was not there yet, and so it was difficult for him to say how the taxation of property and its yield should be combined with the taxation of other incomes and how much room remained to levy excise taxes as well. To this process of the formation of semantic concepts, there corresponds our endeavour as historians of economic thought to get a proper hermeneutic understanding at each stage of the developing intellectual process, which would eventually lead to the formation of modern political economy.

5 The political approach

Political economy is concerned with the values governing the relationships between the economy and the state. One may endeavour to explain the values of others objectively, but often one promotes one's own values instead, and economic thought has been normative most of the time. Ricardo stands out not only as a theorist, but also because he was admired for his impartiality, and so the insight gradually gained ground that one could analyse economic relationships in a disinterested fashion and then use what one had learnt to serve a goal like that of creating the institutions supporting the intercourse of free and independent individuals, capable of providing for their subsistence (Ricardo, 1973). The impartiality of Ricardo was specially praised by Marx. He, by contrast, felt entitled to use the insights gained to serve the goal of socialism. Max Weber became the sternest defender of value-free social and economic research (Weber, 1968 [1904]). We have counted Marx and Weber together as relativists in the history of economic thought: relativism compels us to reflect on the values of others and our own; it educates us to separate historical values and facts, but it also invites us to identify with different goals. Even pure theory can blind the theorist for values which inadvertently creep in. Those whom we have called positivists, though today certainly mostly inclined towards the ideal of value-free science, are predominantly liberals, whose teaching embodies specific values such as the autonomy of the individual regarding the choice of consumption as the basis for maintaining the principle of Pareto efficiency which is therefore not entirely value-free (Wicksell, 1913), though impartial in that all individuals are treated as equals, regardless of whether they are rich or poor, and without considering their contribution to social life outside the market.

Perhaps it is fair to say that the positivists do not disregard values, but try to render them explicit and to explain why the pursuit of goal x might diminish one's possibilities to achieve goal y. This was also Weber's attitude, with the difference, however, that he saw a much richer variety of goals pursued in past societies and in the different strata of social life; the different rationalities were needed to characterise the different social and economic forms encountered in history. Visual theory went one step further: values were immanent in social evolution; it generated norms.

The historical school saw the evolution of values, hoping for moral betterment, as part of social development. I take the liberty of proposing my own modern example of the genesis of norms: the great depression led to Keynes' 'General Theory', hence to the measurement of GDP and of unemployment (as opposed to the traditional mere counting of the poor), and the norm of full employment began to impose itself as a result of the perception of a new reality (sudden increase of mass unemployment), of a new conceptualisation to explain it, of a new semantic to discuss it, and of a feeling of solidarity. From then on, measuring unemployment implied that unemployment in itself was a negative occurrence, something that ought not to happen. Crises had been regarded as calamities and the unemployed had been pitied before, but economic policy in the nineteenth and the early twentieth centuries did not attempt to avoid the downturn, let alone to create employment on a large scale; the state was content to mitigate the consequences by monetary policy and social insurance. Now Keynes claimed to have shown that the boom could be eternalised and that, if a slump occurred all the same, full employment could be restored. Once it was thought that it could be done, it was felt that it had to be done. New norms thus arise out of combinations of old ones; their transformations accompany the process of development, as the historical school had observed (Glaeser, 2014). Weber did not deny that norms changed, but he rejected any claim to decide scientifically which norms should be accepted. The political approach to the history of economic thought faces the fact that, as soon as society begins to build complex institutions endowed with power, to regulate the life and the material reproduction of its members, grouped in families, it becomes inevitable also to regulate the economic support of those institutions, to discuss those regulations and hence not only to act, but also to speak and to *think* economically, approving or disapproving of the norms, whether one is Hammurabi's scribe or an employee of the European Central Bank.

The political approach is a special form of relativism. It focuses on the state: as the main expression of social conditions, as the main institution shaping cultural development, as the focus of political action and hence as the economic institution which is historically most specific, more than the organisation of the markets and even of the households. One discusses here how the state and taxation were treated by the physiocrats, by Smith and Ricardo, or later by Mill, Marshall and Keynes. Marx regarded this topic as demanding and difficult and he never got round to dealing with it systematically in his mature work. I shall limit myself to two well-known aspects: the embeddedness of the Athenian economy in antiquity and how disembeddedness becomes a theme in the modern world (Polanyi, 1957).

As a matter of fact, embeddedness is a question of degree, and the contrast between aims and institutions, which reflect the coherence of the community, and forces, which are autonomous and seem to threaten it, can be seen in characteristic contrasts, which the Athenian philosophers and orators observed (Plato, 2000).

The Aristotelian conception of a good life as the aim of the household is generally known. Like the virtues, it is a middle between extremes, here between poverty and plenty, hence it requires modest, limited means of livelihood for its realisation, and there are natural arts of acquiring these means, whereas wealth-getting for its own sake, chrematistics, is not governed by the aim of leading the good life. The corresponding means of acquisition such as trade and, in particular, usury, are seen as a threat to the community. Although Aristotle does not propose to defend them, he knows and admits that these practices, to some extent, are necessary for the state (Schefold, 1989). The same contrast appears in Xenophon. In his *Oikinomikos*, the central figure of the dialogue, Ischomachos, praises the modest life on the land, agriculture and gardening, as natural forms of acquisition, he trusts his wife with the overseeing of this large estate with many dependants, but in the end he admits, questioned by Socrates, that he deals in such estates, buying them when they are in bad order, with the intention of improving and eventually of selling them for a profit (Schefold, 1998).

The communitarian spirit of the citizens was tested with the liturgies, the formally voluntary donations to the state by rich citizens. The obligation to give was of a moral nature. To have given added to one's reputation; social pressure made it inevitable to contribute to some extent. Public finance in fourth-century Athens and elsewhere in Greece did not depend on donations alone. There were harbour taxes, there were gains from coining money, occasionally, there were forced loans and many other techniques. These were described in the pseudo-Aristotelian *Oeconomica* (Kyrkos and Baloglou, 2013; Aristotle, 2006), a book which, by the way, was also studied by Kaspar Klock (2009 [1651]) who commentated that similar devices were used in his own time.

The citizens were supposed to give in rough proportion to their possessions. The system of liturgies thus led to a curious distinction between two kinds of capital: between 'visible' and 'invisible' riches (Salin, 1963). Visible riches were the house and the land, the olive trees or the ships that someone owned; this kind of wealth could be seen and assessed by other citizens who were anxious that the rich should give, since they had given and wanted the weight of the state to be shared. But the loans, which someone had made, were not visible, and persons who had lent possessed 'invisible' riches. The contrast played a role in the text of the orators, for example in Lysias (2013), where citizens, who had a civilian cause to defend, would boast that they had made big contributions from their visible riches in order to impress the judges, and so they also would pretend not to possess much in terms of invisible riches.

The historian of economic thought needs to know institutions such as the liturgies in order to understand the texts about them; they play a role, more often implicitly than explicitly, in Aristotle and Xenophon. The Athenian system of public finance thus was embedded in a peculiar social framework. 'Embeddedness' did not mean that there was only altruism and no market for commodities, and it certainly did not mean that there was no profit motive operating, but that the institutions were such as to require people to act in personal responsibility according to moral and political standards, because the state and hence the economy could not function without such constraints. Thus, well-born young Athenians were, for instance, under social pressure to stick to agriculture rather than to turn to financial activities. That the rules were not always adhered to is no proof that they were without material consequences, let alone that they did not exist.

Another sector in which such personal accountability played an important role was banking. There was no bank as an abstract juridical entity: there was only the banker. How could he be entrusted with money when he became old? Would his heirs honour his obligations? A solution was for the banker to appoint his main slave, who had been his administrator, as his heir, to set him free in his will, but to stipulate also that he should marry the widow and so become part of Athenian society (Schefold, 2014). As a consequence of institutions ensuring the continuity of the bank as a legal entity, a personal continuity was created. This was described by the orator Demosthenes. Temples could also act as banks, lending to cities in particular, and they had the advantage of being lasting institutions.

Disembeddedness in the modern period does not mean that there were no institutions for the integration of society left, but that the emphasis now is on letting the autonomous forces free, and the social institutions are to serve them. This is expressed in the texts, most obviously in the case of Adam Smith and the founders of liberalism. But it is also true, though with a qualification, for mercantilism as a preparatory stage. Examples are Petty's proposed policies for the mobilisation of the labour force in order to facilitate production (Schefold, 1992b) or the concern of the cameralists such as Justi (Schefold, 1993a). He postulated that the state should provide the infrastructure, building canals and roads, but that the prince should also attract merchants and hence should build theatres. Consecutive changes in the institutions of public finance can be interpreted as adaptations to the growing autonomy of the economic actors (Schumpeter, 1953). The feudal lord and his villeins stood in a relationship of mutual direct personal dependence. Tax collection had to provide the prince with new powers such as the possibility to maintain an army of mercenaries, and these taxes shifted from methods which restricted freedoms, such as bridge tolls, towards income taxes, which do not interfere with the movement of people, but are more efficient for raising a surplus (Mann, 1930).

And yet, despite the liberal reliance on the autonomy of the economic process, specific social forms continued to be necessary for the functioning of probably most economic mechanisms. Liberal theory perhaps sometimes forgot that it was advocating values, because it arose in monarchic societies, but assumed the equality of citizens as economic subjects. It was convenient to think of the economic sphere as independent from the political framework; conflicts with the latter were avoided by insisting on economic efficiency. One tended to overlook the social bond supporting the liberal system. An extreme example is provided by Edgar Salin (1932) who thought that even the gold standard prior to the First World War depended on the social form of bourgeois society. The working of the gold standard is the prime example of an anonymous, self-regulating mechanism. But Salin thought that it was a matter of honour for European central banks to keep the parity of their currency to the pound, and it was equally a matter of honour for the Bank of England to stick to the price of gold. The gold standard worked less and less well, when it was interpreted only as a mechanism. This was Keynes's view in his *A Tract on Monetary Reform* (Keynes, 1923), and, with the change of perspective on the gold standard, came its transformation and eventually its abandonment under adverse circumstances, until President Nixon felt no shame – and was not afraid of American opinion – when he unilaterally let the system of Bretton Woods collapse.

6 Perspectives for the history of economic thought

I have tried to show that the history of economic thought can be seen as a wider undertaking than as a history of economic analysis, and I have provided my view of the perspective that emerges. It involves a more complex understanding of the relationship between economic history and history of economic thought; the latter becomes a history of what was once designated as the economic spirit, but the economic spirit is not simply a combination of a principle of satisfaction and a principle of acquisition, of need and of greed, and it is more than a mentality in the sense of habitual behaviour, since it involves the understanding people have of how the economy works, hence of the concepts they use to comprehend what we call economic phenomena, and in forming such concepts, they develop the economy. Two projects of mine, one completed, the other in preparation, may help to exemplify this endeavour. I have collected the views of a number of known historians and historians of economic thought on the relationship between their disciplines (Schefold, 2009b). Werner Plumpe (2009) emphasised the relationship between economic history and historical semantics in the history of economic thought. Kurt Dopfer (2009) saw the relationship between the disciplines in an evolutionary perspective. Jean Cartelier (2009) tried to determine the contribution by which economics became a science (physiocracy). Edward Nell (2009) related the origin of economic theory and the emergence of capitalism. Carlo Poni (2009) studied how the writers of the *Encyclopédie* of Diderot and d'Alembert came to extract the scientific content of the implicit knowledge of artisans and how handicraft thus was split and transformed into scientifically supported technical production on the one hand and art on the other. Heinz Rieter (2009) examined the monetary policy of the Deutsche Bundesbank and found that, one to two generations ago, it used a broader understanding of the maintenance of the currency than today and how it adopted a narrow view of focusing on the price level only with monetarism. There were also two contributions on the economics of antiquity by Peter Herz (2009) and Erik Schliesser (2009); these are not summarised here, since antiquity has been discussed above.

The examples show that different researchers see the relation between economic history and the history of economic thought in quite different ways; their interpretations are on the whole complementary, rather than alternatives. The project also illustrates the breadth of the history of economic thought, if this is interpreted in the wider sense which I have tried to defend. I hope that this view, if adopted by others, will help to revive the discipline as an endeavour of cultural importance, given that a more conventional history of economic thought is being questioned and the chairs are being converted and dedicated to 'more useful' specialisations such as finance.

There is yet another aspect to be considered. I now see it as a major task to transcend the focus on the economics of the Occident. For some kind of visual theory of the economy is present not only in the Middle Ages and in antiquity, but in all cultures, especially those involving state building and the financing of public enterprise, for these are not possible without some reflections on the economic possibilities for centralising power. I incorporated three oriental authors in my series *Klassiker der Nationalökonomie*: Ibn Khaldun with his *Muqqadima* (we published the facsimile of an autograph of circa 1400; Schefold, 2000), the *Dialogue on Salt and Iron* (written in the first century, Han Dynasty, facsimile of a Chinese woodprint edition of the sixteenth century; Schefold, 2002a) and Miura Baien's *Kagen* (*Tract on Value*) (facsimile of Baien's manuscript; Miura Baien lived 1723–1789 in Japan; Schefold, 2001). Each facsimile was accompanied by a translation and several interpretations by specialists of the corresponding culture, but also by my own introductions in which I tried to compare these major representations of the Arabian, the Chinese and the Japanese traditions with Western economic thought.

The logical extension of this prior work would be to do research on the economic thought of the world cultures, in analogy with Max Weber's writings on the ethics of the world religions (Weber, 1921). His aim was to show that modern capitalism could arise only in Europe and its colonies, because of a unique economic and cultural development in which the emergence of Protestantism was the decisive factor, making a modern capitalism possible, as opposed to other forms of capitalism, such as that of the late Middle Ages in Italy, in antiquity or in mercantilism. In the papers on the ethics of the world religions he wanted to show, conversely, that others had developed high levels of culture and complex economic forms, but not rational capitalism. Whether a comparison, of Indian, Chinese, Japanese, Arabic, Ottoman, and possibly other traditions of economic thought with the European tradition, will lead to a similar distinction or whether, conversely, all pre-modern forms of economic thought resemble each other in some way, is not clear to me at present.

As mentioned in the beginning, there have been attempts in economic history to contradict the Max Weber thesis by asserting that similar levels of economic development had been reached in the major cultures in the early eighteenth century, suggesting that the outbreak of the industrial revolution in Great Britain was something of an accident. This thesis, associated with a 'California School of economic history', referred to above, may in part have become popular, because it fits with what would seem politically correct in a period of globalisation. Against this, I should argue that it is perhaps the greater honour to have developed a different culture, not entirely commensurable with the West, than to be similar, but to have fallen behind. And it seems clear that major representatives of those cultures were fully aware of profound differences at the time when the clash of cultures occurred in the nineteenth century. Japan affords perhaps the most important example, having been closed off from the West most effectively until the middle of the nineteenth century and then having made the transition and having industrialised much faster than others. Fukuzawa Yukichi, the most important intellectual of the Meiji Period because of his many books and writings about the differences between Western and Japanese thought – including economic thought – wrote succinctly:

> If one compares the Confucianism of the Orient with the civilisation of the Occident one realises that two points are missing in the Orient: physics in the material sphere and the idea of independence in the spiritual sphere. Hence there would be little hope for Japan to become an equal of the Western powers by means of a mere opening of the country.
>
> (Fukuzawa, 1971, p. 248)

He stressed what the East was lacking, not what it was able to give. Perhaps the time has come for the West not only to learn *about* the East, but to learn *from* the East.

There have been complaints about the growing number of economists who think that the history of economic thought is an old subject, which does not have to be pursued any longer, and that the teaching of the subject has been diminished. It seems to me that the major tasks are still ahead of us. If the research is extended convincingly, it will become possible to extend the teaching as well.

Note

1 This paper, based on Schefold (2009b), was first presented in English at the AISPE Conference in Florence, 21–24 February 2013. I should like to thank Monika Poettinger and the other organisers of the conference for the opportunity to develop ideas, which have been at the core of my teaching for four decades, in front of a mixed audience of historians of economic thought and economic historians.

References

Aristotle (2006): Oikonomika. Schriften zu Hauswirtschaft und Finanzwesen. Übersetzt und erläutert. In: R. Zoepffel (ed.), *Aristoteles. Werke in deutscher Übersetzung*. Berlin: Akademie Verlag.

Blaug, M. (1999): *Economic Theory in Retrospect*, 5th ed. Cambridge: Cambridge University Press.

Botero, G. (2010 [1596]): *Le Relationi Universali Di Giovanni Botero Benese*. Whitefish, MT: Kessinger Publishing.

Cartelier, J. (2009): Tableau économique in the France of Louis XV: The Invention of Economics as a Science. *Jahrbuch für Wirtschaftsgeschichte*, vol. 50, no. 1, pp. 76–102.

Copernicus, N. (1999 [1519]): Ökonomische Schriften, Nr. 2 (Münzdenkschrift). In: H. M. Nobis (ed.), *Opera minora. Die humanistischen, ökonomischen und medizinischen Schriften. Texte und Übersetzungen. Nicolaus Copernicus Gesamtausgabe*. Berlin: Akademie Verlag, pp. 128–134.

Dmitriev, V. K. (1974 [1904]): *Economic Essays on Value, Competition and Utility*, ed. by D. M. Nuti. Cambridge: Cambridge University Press.

Dopfer, K. (2009): Wie viel Geschichte braucht die Ökonomie? Das Verhältnis von Theorie und Geschichte in evolutionstheoretischer Interpretation. *Jahrbuch für Wirtschaftsgeschichte*, vol. 50, no. 1, pp. 53–76.

Ermis, F. (2013): *A History of Ottoman Economic Thought: Developments Before the 19th Century*. London: Routledge.

Finley, M. I. (1973): *The Ancient Economy*. Berkeley: University of California Press.

Frank, A. G. (1998): *ReOrient: Global Economy in the Asian Age*. Berkeley: University of California Press.

Fukuzawa, Y. (1971): *Eine autobiographishe Lebensschilderung*, ed. by G. Linzbichler. Tokyo: Die Japanisch-Deutsche Gesellschaft.

Glaeser, J. (2014): *Der Werturteilsstreit in der deutschen Nationalökonomie. Max Weber, Werner Sombart und die Ideale der Sozialpolitik*. Marburg: Metropolis.

Goldstone, J. A. (2000): The Rise of the West, or Not? A Revision to Socio-economic History. *Sociological Theory*, vol. 18, no. 2, pp. 175–194.

Herz, P. (2009): Oikonomia und Politik bei Aristoteles. Der oikos als Grundlage des staatlichen Lebens. *Jahrbuch für Wirtschaftsgeschichte*, vol. 50, no. 1, pp. 177–194.
Hu, J. (1988): *A Concise History of Chinese Economic Thought*. Beijing: Foreign Languages Press.
Kaldor, N. (1956): Alternative Theories of Distribution. *Review of Economic Studies*, vol. 23, no. 2, pp. 83–100.
Keynes, J. M. (1923): *A Tract on Monetary Reform*. London: MacMillan.
Klock, K. (2009 [1651]): *Tractatus juridico-politico-polemico-historicus de Aerario . . .* , ed. by B. Schefold. Hildesheim: Olms Verlag.
Kyrkos, B. A. and Baloglou, C. P. (2013): *Oeconomica. Introduction, Translation and Commentaries*. Athens: Herodotes.
Lessius, L. (1999): *De iustitia et iure caeterisque virtutibus cardinalibus Libri IV*. Düsseldorf: Verlag Wirtschaft und Finanzen.
Lysias. (2013): *Reden*, ed. by K. Brodersen. Darmstadt: Wissenschaftliche Buchgesellschaft.
Machiavelli, N. (2005 [1513]): *Il Principe*. Turin: Einaudi.
Maddison, A. (2007): *Chinese Economic Performance in the Long Run, 960–2030 AD*, 2nd ed. Paris: OECD Publishing.
Mann, F. K. (1930): *Die Staatswirtschaft unserer Zeit. Eine Einführung*. Jena: Fischer.
Marshall, A. (1920 [1890]): *Principles of Economics*. London: MacMillan.
Marx, K. (1861–1863): Manuskript 1861–1863. In: *Marx-Engels-Gesamtausgabe (MEGA)*. Berlin: Akademie der Wissenschaften, 1976–82, vol. 2/3, pp. 1–6.
Marx, K. (1867): Das Kapital. Kritik der politischen Ökonomie. Erster Band (1. Auflage). In: *Marx-Engels-Gesamtausgabe (MEGA)*. Berlin: Akademie der Wissenschaften, 1983, vol. 2.5.
Marx, K. (1905–1910): *Theorien über den Mehrwert, 3 Volumes (1905–1910)*, ed. by K. Kautsky. Stuttgart: Dietz.
Marx, K. (1969 [1890]): *Das Kapital. Kritik der politischen Ökonomie*. Erster Band (nach der vierten, von F. Engels hrsg. Auflage). Berlin: Dietz.
Marx, K. (2004 [1894]): Das Kapital. Kritik der politischen Ökonomie. Dritter Band. In: F. Engels (ed.), *Marx-Engels-Gesamtausgabe (MEGA)*. Berlin: Akademie der Wissenschaften, 2004, vol. 2.15.
Müller-Armack, A. (1999 [1947]): *Wirtschaftslenkung und Marktwirtschaft*. Düsseldorf: Verlag Wirtschaft und Finanzen.
Nau, H. and Schefold, B. (eds.) (2002): *The Historicity of Economics. Continuities and Discontinuities of Historical Thought in 19th and 20th Century Economics*. Berlin, Heidelberg: Springer.
Nell, E. J. (2009): On the History of Economic Theory and the Emergence of Capitalism. *Jahrbuch für Wirtschaftsgeschichte*, vol. 50, no. 1, pp. 103–134.
Niehans, J. (1994): *A History of Economic Theory: Classic Contributions, 1720–1980*. Baltimore, MD: Johns Hopkins University Press.
Pasinetti, L. L. (1974): *Growth and Income Distribution. Essays in Economic Theory*. Cambridge: Cambridge University Press.
Plato (2000): *Der Staat. Politeia*, ed. by T. Szlezák. Berlin: Akademie Verlag.
Plumpe, W. (2009): Ökonomisches Denken und wirtschaftliche Entwicklung. Zum Zusammenhang von Wirtschaftsgeschichte und historischer Semantik der Ökonomie. *Jahrbuch für Wirtschaftsgeschichte*, vol. 50, no. 1, pp. 27–52.
Polanyi, K. (1957): *The Great Transformation*. Boston, MA: Beacon Press.
Political Economy (1990): Special Issue: Convergence to Long-Periods Positions. Proceedings of the workshop at Certosa di Pontignano 1990. *Political Economy. Studies in the Surplus Approach*, vol. 6, no. 1–2.

Pomeranz, K. (2000): *The Great Divergence: China, Europe, and the Making of the Modern World Economy*. Princeton, NJ: Princeton University Press.

Poni, C. (2009): The Worlds of Work: Formal Knowledge and Practical Abilities in Diderot's Encyclopédie. *Jahrbuch für Wirtschaftsgeschichte*, vol. 50, no. 1, pp. 135–150.

Rau, K. H. (1997): *Lehrbuch der politischen Ökonomie (1826–1837)*, ed. by B. Schefold. Hildesheim: Olms Verlag.

Ricardo, D. (1973): Biographical Miscellany. In: P. Sraffa (ed.), *The Works and Correspondence of David Ricardo*, vol. 10. Cambridge: Cambridge University Press, 1973.

Rieter, H. (2009): Die währungspolitische Maxime der Deutschen Bundesbank aus ideengeschichtlicher Sicht. *Jahrbuch für Wirtschaftsgeschichte*, vol. 50, no. 1, pp. 151–176.

Robinson, J. (1971): *Economic Heresies: Some Old Fashioned Questions in Economic Theory*. New York: Basic Books.

Rostow, W. W. (1960): *The Stages of Economic Growth: A Non-Communist Manifesto*. Cambridge: Cambridge University Press.

Sahlins, M. (1974): *Stone Age Economics*. Berlin: De Gruyter.

Salin, E. (1927): Hochkapitalismus. Eine Studie über Werner Sombart, die deutsche Volkswirtschaftslehre und das Wirtschaftssystem der Gegenwart. *Weltwirtschaftliches Archiv*, vol. 25, pp. 314–344.

Salin, E. (1932): *Wirtschaft und Staat, drei Schriften zur deutschen Weltlage*. Berlin: Hobbing.

Salin, E. (1963): Kapitalbegriff und Kapitallehre von der Antike zu den Physiokraten. In: E. von Beckerath, *Lynkeus: Gestalten und Probleme aus Wirtschaft und Politik*. Tübingen: Mohr, pp. 153–181.

Schefold, B. (1986): Schumpeter as a Walrasian Austrian and Keynes as a Classical Marshallian. In: H. J. Wagener and J. W. Drukker (eds.), *The Economic Law of Motion of Modern Society. A Marx-Keynes-Schumpeter Centennial*. Cambridge: Cambridge University Press, pp. 93–111.

Schefold, B. (1988): Karl Bücher und der Historismus in der Deutschen Nationalökonomie. In: N. Hammerstein (ed.), *Deutsche Geschichtswissenschaft um 1900*. Stuttgart: Steiner, pp. 239–267.

Schefold, B. (1989): Platon und Aristoteles. In: J. Starbatty (ed.), *Klassiker des ökonomischen Denkens*. Munich: Beck-Verlag, pp. 15–55.

Schefold, B. (1991): Zur Neuausgabe von Böhm-Bawerks 'Positive Theorie des Kapitales'. In: *Vademecum zu einem Klassiker der Kapitaltheorie*. Kommentar zur Faksimile-Ausgabe der 1889 erschienenen Erstausgabe von Böhm-Bawerk, Eugen von: *Positive Theorie des Kapitales*. Düsseldorf: Verlag Wirtschaft und Finanzen.

Schefold, B. (1992a): Review of: Antiquity and Capitalism. Max Weber and the Sociological Foundations of Roman Civilization (by J. R. Love; London: Routledge, 1991). *The Manchester School of Economic and Social Studies*, vol. 40, pp. 208–210.

Schefold, B. (1992b): Einleitung zur 'Political Arithmetick' von William Petty. In: *Vademecum zu einem Klassiker der angewandten Nationalökonomie*. Kommentar zur Faksimile-Ausgabe der 1690 erschienenen Erstausgabe von Petty, William: *Political Arithmetick*. Düsseldorf: Verlag Wirtschaft und Finanzen.

Schefold, B. (1992c): Max Webers Werk als Hinterfragung der Ökonomie. Einleitung zum Neudruck der 'Protestantischen Ethik' in ihrer ersten Fassung. In: *Vademecum zu einem Klassiker der Geschichte ökonomischer Rationalität*. Kommentar zur Faksimile-Ausgabe der 1905 erschienenen Erstdrucke von Weber, Max: *Die Protestantische Ethik und der 'Geist' des Kapitalismus*. Düsseldorf: Verlag Wirtschaft und Finanzen.

Schefold, B. (1993a): Glückseligkeit und Wirtschaftspolitik: Zu Justis 'Grundsätze der Policey-Wissenschaft'. In: *Vademecum zu einem Klassiker des Kameralismus*. Kommentarband zur Faksimile-Ausgabe der 1756 erschienenen Erstausgabe von Justi, Johann Heinrich Gottlob von: *Grundsätze der Policey-Wissenschaft*. Düsseldorf: Verlag Wirtschaft und Finanzen.

Schefold, B. (1993b): John Locke: Ein ökonomisch engagierter Philosoph. In: *Vademecum zu einem Klassiker der merkantilistischen Geldtheorie*. Kommentar zur Faksimile-Ausgabe [London 1692] von Locke, John: *Some Considerations of the Consequences of the Lowering of Interest, and Raising the Value of Money*. Düsseldorf: Verlag Wirtschaft und Finanzen.

Schefold, B. (1994): Antonia Serra: der Stifter der Wirtschaftslehre? In: *Vademecum zu einem unbekannten Klassiker*. Kommentar zur Faksimile-Ausgabe der 1613 erschienenen Erstausgabe von Serra, Antonio: *Breve Trattato delle cause, che possono far abbondare li regni d'oro e argento*. Düsseldorf: Verlag Wirtschaft und Finanzen.

Schefold, B. (1997a): Classical Theory and Intertemporal Equilibrium. In: *Normal Prices, Technical Change and Accumulation*. London: MacMillan, pp. 425–501.

Schefold, B. (1997b): Einleitung. In: B. Schefold (ed.), *Rau, K.: Lehrbuch der politischen Ökonomie (1826–1837)*. Hildesheim: Olms Verlag, Historia Scientiarum, vol. 1, pp. I–LIII.

Schefold, B. (1998): Xenophons *Oikonomikos*: Der Anfang welcher Wirtschaftslehre? In: *Vademecum zu einem Klassiker der Haushaltsökonomie*. Kommentarband zum Faksimile-Nachdruck der 1734 erschienenen Ausgabe von Xenophon: *Oikonomikos*. Düsseldorf: Verlag Wirtschaft und Finanzen.

Schefold, B. (1999a): Leonhard Lessius: Von der praktischen Tugend der Gerechtigkeit zur Wirtschaftstheorie. In: *Vademecum zu einem Klassiker der spätscholastischen Wirtschaftsanalyse*. Kommentarband zum Faksimile-Nachdruck der 1605 in Leuven erschienenen Erstausgabe von Lessius, Leonardus: *De iustitia et iure caeterisque virtutibus cardinalibus Libri IV*. Düsseldorf: Verlag Wirtschaft und Finanzen.

Schefold, B. (1999b): Vom Interventionsstaat zur Sozialen Marktwirtschaft: Der Weg Alfred Müller-Armacks. In: *Vademecum zu einem Klassiker der Ordnungspolitik*. Kommentarband zum Faksimile-Nachdruck der 1947 erschienenen Erstausgabe von Müller-Armack, Alfred: *Wirtschaftslenkung und Marktwirtschaft*. Düsseldorf: Verlag Wirtschaft und Finanzen.

Schefold, B. (2000): Aufstieg und Niedergang in der Wirtschaftsentwicklung. Ibn Khalduns sozioökonomische Synthese. In: *Vademecum zu dem Klassiker des arabischen Wirtschaftsdenkens*. Kommentarband zum auszugsweisen Faksimile-Nachdruck der 1401/02 entstandenen Handschrift von Ibn Khaldun: *Muqaddima*. Düsseldorf: Verlag Wirtschaft und Finanzen.

Schefold, B. (2001): Ein Leitbild für die Tokugawa-Zeit: Miura Baiens 'Kagen'. In: *Vademecum zu einem japanischen Klassiker des ökonomischen Denkens*. Kommentarband zum Faksimile-Nachdruck der zwischen 1773 und 1789 entstandenen Handschrift Baien, Miura: *Kagen*. Düsseldorf: Verlag Wirtschaft und Finanzen.

Schefold, B. (2002a): Dauer im Wechsel. Das Selbstverständnis der chinesischen Wirtschaftswelt. In: *Vademecum zu dem Klassiker der chinesischen Wirtschaftsdebatten*. Kommentarband zum Faksimile des 1501 erschienenen Drucks (Hongzhi 14) von Huan Kuan: *Yantie lun*. Düsseldorf: Verlag Wirtschaft und Finanzen.

Schefold, B. (2002b): Nachwort. Ein Kanon und seine Wirkung. In: A. Heertje (ed.), *Vademecum zu einem Klassiker der Physiokratie*. Kommentarband zum

Faksimile-Nachdruck der 1763 erschienenen Erstausgabe von Mirabeau, Victor Riquetti Marquis de und François Quesnay: *Philosophie rurale, ou Economie générale et politique de l'agriculture*, Klassiker der Nationalökonomie, Düsseldorf: Verlag Wirtschaft und Finanzen, pp. 115–125.

Schefold, B. (2009a): Die 'Klassiker der Nationalökonomie'. Gedanken des Herausgebers der Reihe zur Zusammenstellung des Kanons. In: C. Scheer (ed.), *Ideen, Methoden und Entwicklungen der Geschichte des ökonomischen Denkens*. Berlin: Duncker und Humblot, pp. 99–116.

Schefold, B. (2009b): Geschichte der Wirtschaftstheorie und Wirtschaftsgeschichte: Einleitung. *Jahrbuch für Wirtschaftsgeschichte*, vol. 50, no. 1, pp. 9–25.

Schefold, B. (2009c): Max Weber: Abriß der universalen Sozial- und Wirtschaftsgeschichte. Mit- und Nachschrift 1919–1920, Einführung von Bertram Schefold in Zusammenarbeit mit Joachim Schröder (Forthcoming).

Schefold, B. (2012): Goethe and Visual Theory. In: V. Hierholzer and S. Richter (eds.), *Goethe and Money. The Writer and Modern Economics*. Freies Deutsches Hochstift: Frankfurt, pp. 78–94.

Schefold, B. (2013): Review of: The Economies of Hellenistic Societies, Third to First Centuries BC (ed. by Z. H. Archibald, J. K. Davies and A. Gabrielsen; Oxford: Oxford University Press, 2011). *The European Journal of the History of Economic Thought*, vol. 20, no. 1, pp. 150–158.

Schefold, B. (2014): Antiquity. In: G. Faccarello and H. D. Kurz (eds.), *Handbook of the History of Economic Analysis*. Aldershot: Edward Elgar, forthcoming.

Schliesser, E. (2009): Prophecy, Eclipses and Whole-Sale Markets: A Case Study on Why Data Driven Economic History Requires History of Economics. A Philosopher's Reflection. *Jahrbuch für Wirtschaftsgeschichte*, vol. 50, no. 1, pp. 195–206.

Schumpeter, J. A. (1953): Die Krise des Steuerstaates. In: *Aufsätze zur Soziologie*. Tübingen: Mohr, pp. 1–71.

Schumpeter, J. A. (1954): *History of Economic Analysis*. London: Allen and Unwin.

Serra, A. (2011 [1613]): *A Short Treatise on the Wealth and Poverty of Nations*, edited by S. A. Reinert. London: Anthem Press.

Smith, A. (1976 [1776]): *An Inquiry into the Nature and Causes of the Wealth of Nations*. Oxford: Clarendon Press.

Sombart, W. (1896): *Sozialismus und soziale Bewegung im 19. Jahrhundert*. Jena: Fischer.

Sombart, W. (1928): *Der moderne Kapitalismus. Historisch-systematische Darstellung des gesamteuropäischen Wirtschaftslebens von seinen Anfängen bis zur Gegenwart, Three Volumes*. Berlin: Duncker und Humblot.

Sombart, W. (1934): *Deutscher Sozialismus*. Charlottenburg: Buchholz und Weisswange.

Spiethoff, A. (1933): Die Allgemeine Volkswirtschaftslehre als geschichtliche Theorie. Die Wirtschaftsstile. In: *Festgabe für Werner Sombart zur siebenzigsten Wiederkehr seines Geburtstages 19. Jänner 1933*. Munich: Duncker und Humblot, pp. 51–84.

Sraffa, P. (1925): Sulle relazione fra costo e quantità prodotta. *Annali di Economia*, vol. 2, pp. 277–328.

Sraffa, P. (1951): Introduction. In: P. Sraffa (ed.), *The Works and Correspondence of David Ricardo*. Cambridge: Cambridge University Press, vol. 1, pp. xii–lxii.

Sraffa, P. (1960): *Production of Commodities by Means of Commodities: Prelude to a Critique of Economic Theory*. Cambridge: Cambridge University Press.

Vidal-Naquet, P. and Austin, M. (1977): *Economic and Social History of Ancient Greece: An Introduction*. Berkeley: University of California Press.

Weber, M. (1921): *Die gesammelten Aufsätze zur Religionssoziologie*, 3 vol. Tübingen: Mohr.

Weber, M. (1968 [1904]): Die 'Objektivität' sozialwissenschaftlicher und sozialpolitischer Erkenntnis. In: *Gesammelte Aufsätze zur Wissenschaftslehre*. Tübingen: Mohr, pp. 146–214.

Weber, M. (1992): *Die Protestantische Ethik und der 'Geist' des Kapitalismus*, ed. by B. Schefold. Düsseldorf: Verlag Wirtschaft und Finanzen.

Whewell, W. (1971 [1829]): *Mathematical Exposition of Some Doctrines of Political Economy*. New York: Kelley.

Wicksell, K. (1913): Vilfredo Pareto's Manuel d'Economie Politique. *Zeitschrift für Volkswirtschaft, Sozialpolitik und Verwaltung*, vol. 22, pp. 132–151.

Wolters, F. (1922): Colbert. In: E. Marcks and K. A. von Müller (eds.), *Meister der Politik. Eine weltgeschichtliche Reihe von Bildnissen*. Stuttgart, Berlin: Deutsche Verlagsanstalt, vol. 2, pp. 1–38.

2 Economic facts, theoretical beliefs and the 'double movement'

Claus Thomasberger

1 Introduction

The vision of the relation between facts and thought, which prevails in economic theory and historical research does not only influence the answers to the question of how fruitful the introduction of economic history into the study of the history of economic thought and vice versa is, it also has a history of its own. This chapter focuses on a range of interpretations of this relationship that were underlying economic theories in the nineteenth and twentieth centuries.

2 Facts and thought: economic theories in the nineteenth century

The social and economic sciences of the nineteenth century relied on the assumption that facts and thought can be (and should be) separated. David Ricardo, Jean Baptiste Say and their followers regarded the laws of economics not only as laws, which were similar to natural laws, they also supposed that the social and economic laws could be derived *directly* from the laws of Nature.

2.1 David Ricardo

Comparing Ricardo with Adam Smith, the difference between both approaches becomes immediately evident. Smith's approach was still part of the eighteenth century. He considered political economy a *human science*. Ricardo, instead, relies directly on the laws of Nature. Smith used notions such as 'natural progress of opulence', 'natural price', 'natural freedom', 'natural rates of wages, profit, and rent' to indicate the evolution of human civilization. Ricardo employs the same terms in order to demonstrate that the economic laws are beyond human command.

Obviously, historical incidents do play a role here. The industrial revolution and the problem of poverty within the increasing wealth needed an explanation. Thomas R. Malthus and David Ricardo turned to the laws of Nature in order to make sense of the market mechanism. Poverty is explained as the result of laws, which are *not* human laws. The Malthusian law of population is ultimately grounded in two biological laws, the fertility of man and the fertility of the soil. Ricardo, accepting the framework, builds the law of distribution, 'the principal problem in Political Economy' (Ricardo, 1984 [1817], p. 3) directly on the inexorable laws of Nature.

Clearly, the belief in economic laws that are beyond human control does not prevent Ricardo from exerting influence on the economic realities *in praxis*. He uses his theoretical ideas when he fights for a reform of the monetary system and for the abolishment of the Speenhamland laws. Furthermore, he builds on his insights when, as a member of the House of Commons, he advocates free trade and the abolishment of the Corn Laws. At the same time, he denies that political interventions can have an impact on economic *theory*. The economic laws as such are considered facts, which are beyond human control, just like the 'law of gravity' or the 'law of conservation of energy'. Ricardo sticks to the idea that economic laws are independent of any kind of theoretical dispute or political intervention, and that no government and no political action can abolish the 'iron law of wages', the law of accumulation, or the law of the falling rate of profit.

2.2 John S. Mill

In later years John S. Mill takes up this contradiction. In his famous fifth essay, 'On the Definition of Political Economy and on the Method of Investigation Proper to It', he introduces the distinction between 'science' and 'art'. 'Science', following the logic of natural sciences, regards the economic laws as facts. 'Art' reflects the insight that social and economic relations are a result of human action. It assumes that these relations are manmade and that they can be changed.

> [The] ideas of *science* and *art* [. . .] differ from one another as the understanding differs from the will [. . .]. The one deals in facts, the other in precepts. Science is a collection of *truths*; art a body of *rules*, or directions for conduct. The language of science is, This is, or, This is not; This does, or does not, happen. The language of art is, Do this; Avoid that. Science takes cognizance of a *phenomenon*, and endeavours to discover its *law*; art proposes to itself an *end*, and looks out for sneaks to affect it [. . .]. The science of mechanics, a branch of natural philosophy, lays down the laws of motion, and the properties of what are called the mechanical powers. The art of practical mechanics teaches how we may avail ourselves of those laws and properties, to increase our command over external nature.
>
> (Mill, 1844, pp. 88–89)

However, Mill remains a thinker of the nineteenth century. It is 'science' which is granted the primacy; 'art' has to follow. As in the natural world, the scientific knowledge is regarded as a precondition of any kind of intervention, not the other way round. In other words, John S. Mill, too, holds onto the idea that, at least in the realm of 'science', the facts are independent of theoretical reasoning. He, too, supposes that the worldviews and theoretical insights of political economy do not have influence on the facts. Social reality is taken as given and independent of social theory. The task of theory is to adapt to the facts, to describe facts and to give a picture of the facts. Mill keeps the idea that the laws of economics or sociology cannot be changed by political intervention.

The scientist sees himself as an *observer*, and not as a *participant*, in society. He believes in the epistemological assumption that social and economic reality is separated and independent of theoretical thinking. Still, some kind of 'correspondence theory of consciousness' prevails. Political economy claims that its categories and laws correspond to the actual state of affairs.

2.3 Karl Marx

During the nineteenth century Karl Marx was, perhaps, the most important critic of the 'naive naturalism' of the classical political economy. He started from the acknowledgement that there is a fundamental difference between society and nature: It is man who creates society. Man creates his consciousness, and man makes history. Social and economic laws, therefore, have to be grounded in human behaviour and reasoning. They are different in character from natural laws insofar as they express relations between persons. In other words, if social theories treat social laws in a way *as if they were laws of Nature*, it needs some kind of *justification* and cannot be taken for granted. At last, we cannot naively apply the methodology of natural sciences because of the human origins of all social relations.

Nonetheless, Marx underlines the idea that markets, prices, power, etc. are not a result of human intention, though they are an outcome of human action. Indeed, he regards the economic laws of the bourgeois society as laws, which are *neither* rational *nor* human. They are *like* facts. The laws of the capitalist economy are inhuman, just *like* nature.

By sticking to the idea of an objective economic system, Marx remains imprisoned in the intellectual world of the nineteenth century. Instead of challenging the economic determinism, he asks for a *justification* for treating social laws in a way as if they were laws of Nature. Additionally, Marx pretends to *offer* such a justification: Reification and fetishism are the keywords.[1] Marx regards reification as a condition of the modern bourgeois world. Here, and only here, social relations assume the shape of a relation between things. In the 'German Ideology' he ascribes reification to the level of division of labour and private property. Later, in the 'Capital' he develops the ideas further and refers to the commodity form of the labour product. Man is caught in a fictitious world of things.[2] According to Marx's vision man lives in a self-made prison of economic and social facts without having a chance to free himself of his chains as long as the bourgeois world prevails.

It is important to understand that, by providing a justification, Marx criticizes and, at the same time, reinforces the belief in economic determinism and the interpretation of economic categories and laws in terms of facts, which are outside human control. On the one hand he criticizes capitalism because the reification of social relations is incompatible with free society. However, he believes in the validity of economic laws and reified categories *within the bourgeois society*.[3]

Not human ideas, but the economic laws and the contradictions of the bourgeois society are regarded as the driving forces of capitalism. Consequently, he minimizes the possible influence of the application of his own theory. The discovery of the laws of society's movement can only 'shorten and lessen the birth-pangs' of a new society, he states. But it 'can neither clear by bold leaps, nor remove by legal enactments, the obstacles offered by the successive phases of its normal development' (Marx, 1887 [1867], Preface to the First German Edition).[4]

Marx recognizes the interdependency between material life-process and consciousness. Moreover, he identifies that the bourgeois society supposes a worldview, in which economic deterministic ideas prevail and the 'categories of bourgeois economy' are taken for granted. Nevertheless, he falls back in some version of economic determinism. Marx remains part of the nineteenth century's intellectual world insofar as he accepts the assumption that there is a pure theory of society that is independent of any kind of conscious social or political intervention.

3 Facts and thought: theories in the twentieth century

The vision of the relationship between facts and thought changes completely after the First World War and the Bolshevik Revolution. Both events end the belief in economic laws of social development. The change is evident in political science, sociology and in the realm of political economy. Recall Gramsci's characterization of the Bolshevik Revolution as 'the revolution against Karl Marx's *Capital*', because it 'consists more of ideologies than of events' (Gramsci, 1917). Liberal political economy cannot elude the change in the vision of the world. Yet, paradoxically enough, their protagonists do not consider the end of the belief in economic determinism a liberating insight. They are frightened by the idea of a world that is not ruled by economic and social laws. Additionally, they aspire to play down the impact of theoretical ideas on economic and social reality. By analysing the approaches of Keynes and Hayek, this chapter tries to show what the implications of such an approach are. In the final section a comparison of both approaches to the analysis of Karl Polanyi will be presented.

3.1 John M. Keynes

You all are aware of John M. Keynes' famous statement at the end of the *General Theory* that

> the ideas of economists and political philosophers, *both when they are right and when they are wrong* are more powerful than is commonly understood. Indeed, the world is ruled by little else [. . .] I am sure that the power of vested interests is vastly exaggerated compared with the gradual encroachment of ideas [. . .]. Soon or late, it is ideas, not vested interests, which are dangerous for good or evil.
>
> (Keynes, 1936, p. 383)

Indeed, Keynes is an interesting case in this context because by highlighting the relevance, not only of political decisions but also of the 'expectations' of entrepreneurs and households, he recognizes tacitly the importance of economic theories for the functioning of the market mechanism, for investment, for effective demand and for employment. Surely, Keynes is convinced that the theories of the classical school were fictitious and utopian. Moreover, he knows that the theories of the classical school played a key role in the development of the Great Depression. Without austerity in the middle of a recession, the impairment of international trade, i.e. misleading policy advice, the depression would never have developed the way it did. The economic history of the twentieth century cannot be explained in full without taking into consideration leading worldviews, economic theories and their effects on the economic affairs. What is more: Keynes is convinced that the faith of western civilization after the Second World War will depend largely on a fundamental change in economic thinking.

If one takes seriously this insight, it becomes obvious that the relation between facts and theory is more complicated than the economists of the nineteenth century had assumed. Theory cannot simply adapt to the facts, it cannot describe given facts or give a picture of the facts. Akerlof and Shiller speak out the implications. If the term 'theories' is substituted for 'stories' in the following paragraph, they declare:

> What if the *theories* themselves move markets? What if these *theories* of over explanation have real effects? What if they themselves are a real part of how the economy functions? Then economists have gone overboard. The *theories* no longer merely explain the facts; *they are the facts*.
> (Akerlof and Shiller, 2010, p. 54; emphasis added)

Nevertheless, Keynes does not think through the implications of this insight for the understanding of the market system. Instead, he upholds the *belief* in facts and tries to circumvent the difficulty by a methodological device. At first he introduces the distinction between 'independent variables' and 'given factors'. Later he admits that the division of 'the two groups of given factors and independent variables is, of course, quite arbitrary from any absolute standpoint'. And finally he assumes that, even if the three fundamental psychological factors (psychological propensity to consume, the attitude to liquidity and the expectation of future yield from capital assets) are regarded as independent variables, 'our final task might be to select those variables which can be deliberately controlled or managed by central authority in the kind of system in which we actually live' (Keynes, 1936, p. 247). He neglects the fact that economic theories do not only have an influence on the behaviour of the 'central authorities', but also on the 'propensity to consume', 'state of expectations' and the 'state of confidence'.

Therefore, the role that contrasting economic theories, misguiding models and fictitious notions play in the formation of expectations remains unclear.[5] Also: Keynes never asks the question of what it means if misleading theories 'rule the world'. He never *analyses* the consequences of the fictitious ideas of the classical school for the nineteenth century. Instead, he concentrates on his own ability to *change* 'the way the world thinks about economic problems'.[6] Finally, he contributes and succeeds in influencing economic realities after the Second World War, whereas the central questions remain open. What are the consequences, if fictitious ideas 'rule the world'? What does it mean, if not the material world, but ideas, beliefs and theories – *when they are right and when they are wrong* – are a driving force of social and economic change?

3.2 Friedrich A. Hayek

It is interesting to see that Hayek, even if he is working within a completely different theoretical tradition, faces the same problems as Keynes. He, too, has to recognize that in the social and economic sciences there are no facts that are independent of human thinking and behaviour. And he comes to a conclusion that is quite close to the statement of Akerlof and Shiller quoted above: 'So far as human actions are concerned the things are what the acting people think they are' (Hayek, 1969 [1941–1943], p. 27). How does Hayek arrive at this conclusion?

In *The Counter-Revolution of Science* he describes the difference between social and natural sciences in the following way:

> The special difficulties of the social sciences, and much confusion about their character, derive precisely from the fact that in them ideas appear in two capacities, as it were, as part of their object and as ideas about that object. While in the natural sciences the contrast between the object of our study and our explanation of it coincides with the distinction between ideas and objective facts, in the social sciences it is necessary to draw a distinction between those ideas which are constitutive of the phenomena we want to explain and the ideas which either we ourselves or the very people whose actions we have to explain may have formed about these phenomena and which are not the cause of, but theories about, the social structures. This special difficulty of the social sciences is a result, not merely of the fact that we have to distinguish between the views held by the people which are the object of our study and our views about them, but also of the fact that the people who are our object themselves not only are motivated by ideas but also form ideas about the undesigned results of their actions.
>
> (Hayek, 1969 [1941–1943], p. 36)

The social and economic sciences cannot follow the model of natural sciences, he concludes. Any attempt in this direction he criticizes as 'scientism', 'scientistic' prejudice or the 'engineering type of mind'. The reason is that there are no social and economic facts that are not grounded in human behaviour and reason. His teacher, Ludwig Mises, had declared already in 1922: 'Neither God nor a mystical "Natural Force" created society, it was created by mankind. Whether society shall continue to evolve or whether it shall decay lies [. . .] in the hand of man" (Mises, 1951 [1922], p. 515). 'Human society is an issue of the mind. Social co-operation must first be conceived, then willed, and then realized in action. *It is ideas that make history, not the "material productive forces"* (p. 509; emphasis added).[7] The recognition of the human origin of all economic realities is only the starting point. If ideas rule the world, where do the ideas come from? Mises' answer is straightforward when he states: 'The masses do not think. But just for this reason they follow those who do think. The intellectual guidance of humanity belongs to the very few who think for themselves' (p. 508). The social and economic sciences themselves play a key role.

Hayek follows his teacher and colleague and relies on the influence of the economic sciences. According to Hayek, it is the task of science to change the ideas, which the acting people – the object of the studies – form about their social world. The social and economic sciences should not take these ideas as given, but constitute new pictures, modify the models and adjust the theories and thus contribute to the change of the existing worldviews. The concern of science, he states,

> is not what men think about the world and how they consequently behave, but what they *ought to* think. The concepts which men actually employ, the way in which they see nature, is to the scientist necessarily a provisional affair and his task is to *change* this picture, to *change* the concepts in use.
> (Hayek, 1969 [1941–1943], p. 22)

In Hayek's view of social and economic sciences, not only does the distinction between facts and opinions vanish. It becomes the most important task of the sciences to influence the opinions of their objects and, by doing so, the facts. Hayek and his followers do not consider themselves primarily as observers, but as *participants* (or perhaps, even better: *protagonists*) of the social transformation. They see themselves as the elite, which leads the masses. At the founding meeting of the Mont Pelerin Society Hayek underlines (in respect to the public understanding of economic and social reform):

> Public opinion on these matters is the work of men like ourselves, the economist and political philosophers of the past few generations, who have created the political climate in which the politicians of our time must move [. . .]. It is from this long-run point of view that we must look at *our task*.
> (Hayek, 1980 [1949], p. 108; emphasis added)

In Hayek's view the self-regulating market system is not a fact. Instead, its creation and the extension of the market system are considered as a goal to be achieved, as *their mission*.

However, in Hayek's approach we find the same unwillingness to recognize the implication of this insight, which we have already seen in Keynes' approach. Hayek knows that the ideas formed by economic actors about society are a product of intellectuals and scientists. Yet, he attempts to hold onto the idea of an objective social reality that is independent of the influence of theories. Taking these insights seriously would mean to accept that in the social and economic sciences there are no facts, which are not influenced by theoretical reasoning. The difference between the social and the natural sciences is not only that in the former the facts are opinions. The crucial point is that these 'fact-opinions' are not independent of the ideas developed by social and economic scientists. The latter cannot ignore that their object of investigation, as distinguished from the object of the natural sciences, is a result of human ideas and action, which are not independent of theoretical beliefs, worldviews and interpretations. The apple falls from the tree whatever man thinks about the law of gravity. However, the development of stock prices is not independent of the theories applied by the actors when they form expectations, based on which they buy and sell company shares.

With all that, it is not meant that the single scientific work or a single scientist has a direct and traceable influence on a single actor. More important is that the social and economic sciences contribute to the creation of a social climate, a dominating worldview, which becomes characteristic for an epoch. Both Keynesianism and Neo-liberalism exert (or have exerted) this kind of influence, but neither Keynes nor Hayek is willing to accept the consequences. Both economists escape into the realm of methodological considerations so as to legitimate an approach, which holds onto the idea of scientific facts that are independent of their own research.

In order to safeguard the idea of economic facts, Hayek attempts to define a dividing line between 'motivating or constitutive opinions' and 'provisional theories', 'popular abstractions':

> It is very important that we should carefully distinguish between the motivating or constitutive opinions on the one hand and the speculative or explanatory views which people have formed about the wholes; confusion between the two is a source of constant danger. It is the ideas which the popular mind has formed about such collectives as 'society' or the 'economic system,' 'capitalism' or 'imperialism,' and other such collective entities, which the social scientist must regard as no more than provisional theories, popular abstractions, and which he must not mistake for facts. That he consistently refrains from treating these pseudo-entities as 'facts,' and that he systematically starts from the concepts which guide individuals in their actions and not from the results of their theorizing about their actions, is the characteristic feature of that methodological individualism which is closely connected with the subjectivism of the social sciences.
>
> (Hayek, 1969 [1941–1943], pp. 37–38)

But this division is fictitious. The idea of *constitutive* opinions (as distinguished from *explanatory* views) is by itself nothing else than a theoretical construct, invented by Hayek in order to hold onto the idea of scientific facts, which are beyond the influence of science. No real human being is motivated by ideas that are independent of meaningful worldviews. Human action and meaning cannot be separated. There is, and there can be, no motive, no interest, and no guideline, which is not legitimated by a vision of a person's position in the world.

In a certain sense Hayek admits that this dividing line is a fictitious theoretical construct that has to be drawn differently depending on the object under consideration. In a footnote he adds:

> In some contexts concepts which by another social science are treated as mere theories to be revised and improved upon may have to be treated as data. One could, e.g., conceive of a 'science of politics' showing what kind of political action follows from the people holding certain views on the nature of society and for which these views would have to be treated as data. But while in man's actions towards social phenomena, i.e., in explaining his political actions, we have to take his views about the constitution of society as given, we can on a different level of analysis investigate their truth or untruth.
> (Hayek, 1969 [1941–1943], p. 211, fn. 31)

What does it mean that we have to recognize that in the social and economic sciences there are no facts that are independent of scientific ideas and theories? Keynes and Hayek are thinkers of the twentieth century. In contrast to Ricardo, say, or Mill, both see that there are no 'objective facts', but they try to circumvent the insight. By pushing aside the question and treating it in terms of a methodological consideration, they pretend to escape. Hayek adheres to the *belief* in 'facts', but this is an illusion because 'facts' cannot be constructed artificially by defining a dividing line between constitutive opinions and explanatory views.

Hayek and his followers refuse to analyse the consequences of the neoliberal theories on the economic and social reality after the deconstruction of Keynesianism. Furthermore, they are not prepared to take responsibility for the outcome. The crucial questions remain open: What does it mean if we have to recognize that, in the social and economic sciences, the object of investigation is influenced by human ideas, theoretical beliefs, and world views? What are the consequences, if we accept that theoretical ideas have to be considered part of social reality? What are the implications, if the social scientists and political economists are not only observers, but also *participants* in social life? What remains from the corresponding vision of truth, if, at least in the realm of social theory proper, there is (and can be) no theoretical conjecture which simply adapts to the 'facts', which describes 'facts', and which gives a true picture of the 'facts' without influencing the 'facts' at the same time?

I am not able to answer these questions in the context of this chapter. Some of them I have faced on another occasion (Thomasberger, 2012). Today, instead, I will limit myself to concentrating on the implications.

What follows from the insight that there are no 'objective facts' (i.e., no facts that are not influenced by theoretical considerations) for the study of economic history? And what are the consequences for the analysis of the history of economic thought? I will try to answer these questions by referring to the work of Karl Polanyi because the latter, in contrast to Keynes and Hayek, poses the questions: What follows, if the actors believe in economic facts? What are the consequences, if misleading and fictitious economic theories 'rule the world'? At the centre of Polanyi's research is the history of the civilization of the nineteenth century. Nonetheless, the most important insights of his work go beyond the analysis of the 'civilization of the nineteenth century'.

3.3 Karl Polanyi

The starting point of Polanyi's approach can be traced back to an article titled 'The crisis of our vision of the world' which Polanyi published immediately after the First World War. The pivotal point is expressed in the following passage:

> The breakout of the World War has been the turning point for all capitalist and therewith Marxist thinking [. . .]. The omnipresent economic interests [. . .] proved to be bare economic superstition and blank chimera. It became clear that not the material world, but the *idea* of this material world is the driving force, however wrong and erroneous this idea may be.
> (Polanyi, 1919, p. 461; transl. by the author)

Polanyi never accepted the naturalist viewpoint, which is implicit in the reasoning of the classical political school of Ricardo and his followers. Even if the Speenhamland Law may not have exerted the strong influence on the elaboration of economic theories at the beginning of the nineteenth century, which he supposes, the important point is that he does not accept any justification for considering social laws as laws that are beyond man's control. If man is the originator of society, the social institutions – self-regulating or not – are the outcome of human reasoning and acting. In other words: Polanyi insists that it is not economic facts, but the *belief* in such facts, that is the key to understanding not only the civilization of the nineteenth century, but also social institutions in general. 'Institutions are embodiments of human meaning and purpose', summarizes his position (Polanyi, 2001 [1944], p. 262). Polanyi does not deny that human consciousness, ideas, and social theories may be limited by the technological knowledge and by the 'relations of production', but he maintains that they are not determined (not even in the last instance) by objective (material) facts. If it is correct that under the condition of the modern world prices, markets and economic laws take on an objective character, the reason is the peculiar vision of the world, which considered the laws of economics beyond human influence.

It is not possible to go into the details of Polanyi's analysis on this occasion. Everybody who is interested in economic history is familiar with his work. Therefore, I want to concentrate on one aspect. The crucial message of Polanyi's most influential book, *The Great Transformation,* is: Economic laws determined the nineteenth-century civilization because people *believed in* the existence of such laws. There were, there are and there can be no economic laws *as such*. What made the civilization of the nineteenth century an economic civilization was the *belief in* the existence of economic laws.

What are the consequences of the idea that the world in the nineteenth century was not ruled by economic facts, but by the *belief* in economic facts? The crucial point is that Polanyi takes the 'belief in economic determinism' (Polanyi, 1947) seriously, that is, he regards ideas, theoretical beliefs and worldviews as part of social reality. Under the International Gold Standard, speculation could have a stabilizing effect only because the actors *believed* in the maintenance of the gold parity. In the civilization of the nineteenth century the economic classes do play a key role because people defined themselves in economic terms. In other words: If man believes in the objective existence of economic laws, these laws will become real. If man takes the autonomy of the economy and the institutional separation of the economic sphere from the rest of society for granted, the market system will function largely as a self-regulating system in which the economic motives of man, self-interest, and the essentially economic motivation of human behaviour prevail. In a certain sense Polanyi's interpretation anticipates what Robert Merton calls the 'Thomas theorem': 'If men define situations as real, they are real *in their consequences*' (Thomas and Thomas, 1928, p. 572; emphasis added). The assertion that beliefs or definitions of a situation are real in their consequences does not necessarily mean that they are able to realize their intentions.[8] Misleading, fictitious and utopian ideas can never be realized in full. These will produce results that are in conflict with the intentions of the actors. Nevertheless, whatever the outcome is, the ideas shape social and economic reality.

Supporters of the correspondence theory of truth might expect that fictitious and misleading ideas or theories are irrelevant because they do not work and/or, sooner or later, they will be weeded out, yet Polanyi shows that this idea is much too simple. In the field of tacit assumptions, utopian ideas about social ideals, and worldviews there is no process of falsification, no weeding out of wrong ideas, and no automatic convergence in direction of truth. It is erroneous to think that economic disasters, breakdowns or crises can help to overcome the liberal utopia. Reality *as such* can neither prove nor refute a belief. Decisive is the *interpretation* and *explanation* of the occurrences, by the scientific models and the theories.

Society is different from science. Unintended negative consequences do not falsify worldviews. Polanyi shows that the 'liberal utopia', supported by misleading theories and the belief in economic facts, have ruled the world in the nineteenth century. The utopian ambitions cannot prevent the liberal credo from becoming *real in its consequences*. They cannot prevent the actors from attempting to stick to their beliefs. Furthermore, they cannot avoid the results from diverging from the intentions. The people affected most will try to protect themselves and society against the negative consequences of the utopian endeavour. The outcome is what Polanyi calls *double movement*: On the one hand the liberal political forces are effective in their attempt to push forward the impossible, on the other hand the counter movement tries to fight against the negative outcome of the initiative of the first. Therefore, there is no symmetry. The liberal project disposes of a more or less coherent idea. The counter movement is often spontaneous, unstructured and heterogeneous. Finally, both are necessary components of the nineteenth-century civilization.

This chapter cannot enter into the question of how Polanyi examines the social transformation, which the double movement brings about. The important point for our analysis is that the misleading character of the classical doctrine has the consequence that the civilization of the nineteenth century could not have existed without the protection of the counter movements. Therefore, the counter movement against the expansion of the market process has to be considered an *integral part* of the nineteenth-century civilization as much as the liberal credo itself. The belief in economic determinism and the protection against the negative consequences are the two pillars on which the civilization of the nineteenth century rests.

> The double movement [. . .] can be personified as the action of two organizing principles in society, each of them setting itself specific institutional aims, having the support of definite social forces and using its own distinctive methods. The one was the principle of economic liberalism, aiming at the establishment of a self-regulating market, relying on the support of the trading classes, and using largely laissez-faire and free trade as its methods; the other was the principle of social protection aiming at the conservation of man and nature as well as productive organization, relying on the varying support of those most immediately affected by the deleterious action of the market – primarily, but not exclusively, the working and the landed classes – and using protective legislation, restrictive associations, and other instruments of intervention as its methods.
> (Polanyi, 2001 [1944], pp. 138–139)

4 Implications and consequences

What are the consequences of the insight that in the realm of social and economic sciences there are no facts that are independent of theoretical beliefs? What should we think of the attempt to hold onto the idea of an objective social reality that is independent of the influence of theories? What follows from this insight for the study of economic history on the one hand and for the research in the field of the history of economic thought on the other hand? The immediate consequence is that the insight opens new research areas that until now have been ignored or neglected.

Beginning from the point of view of economic history: If the economic history of the nineteenth century cannot be understood without taking into account fictitious theories, shouldn't this be true for other epochs, too? The idea may be of particular relevance for the analysis of the twentieth century (but not only). Is it possible to develop a better understanding of the interwar period and the Great Depression if we take into account the theoretical beliefs which influenced both the actions of the private sector and political authorities? Up to what point did Keynesian ideas shape the economic and social reality after the Second World War? How effective were the intentions of some Chicago economists to destroy the Bretton Woods system? What is the role of different traditions (Austrian School, Freiburg School, Chicago School of Economics) in what we may call the 'neo-liberal counterrevolution'? Or more concrete: What role did different economic theories play in the making of the European Union? How much did monetarist ideas influence the setup of the European Central Bank? Up to what point does the 'incomplete' European Monetary Union have to be regarded as a neo-liberal experiment, as the result of some influential theories of the 1980s and 1990s? And we should not forget the impact of the counter movement. How did the attempts to protect the living conditions against the unintended, destructive consequences of utopian theoretical ideas shape economic realities in different countries? Polanyi examines the Great Depression as a consequence of the impact of counter movements which, in order to protect society, undermined the functioning of the International Gold Standard. Do we have to take into account similar influences, if we want to understand the outbreak of the financial crisis of 2008/09 and the Great Recession? What about the protective responses of the countries to the Asian crisis a decade earlier? What about their influence on the 'global imbalances'? Is it possible to develop a more profound understanding of the transformation of society after the Second World War, if we try to analyse it in terms of a double movement?

The insight that in the realm of social and economic sciences the facts are not independent of theoretical beliefs should be seen as a challenge from the point of view of the history of economic thought, too. If the impact of theories on economic reality is important, the studies of the history of economic thought cannot only reconstruct past theories analytically and/or disclose the continuous and cyclical reappearance of the same ideas in time. Further questions should be considered. Where does the idea of a double movement have its origins? Polanyi refers to liberal writers such as Spencer, Sumner, Mises and Lippmann. Are there other writers who build on this idea? How do they draw the influence of theoretical beliefs? What are the reasons for the attempt to adhere to the belief of economic 'facts'? Are there intrinsic reasons, which motivate researchers in the field of economics to follow the model of natural sciences? If theories do keep to the idea of 'objective facts', neglecting their impact, what influence does this have on the theories? Or, from the opposite side: If economists and political philosophers, as Hayek teaches, create the political climate or the 'style' of an epoch, how do they reflect about their own position in society? How do different theories come to terms with their influence on reality? Does the consciousness of their practical impact on economic, monetary, and financial institutions direct theoretical reasoning? Do they protect their theories from being falsified by the events that they bring about – and, if yes, how? There is one small but brilliant example. When some years ago Paul Krugman declared that 'monetarism is now widely regarded as a failure' (Krugman, 2007), the reaction followed immediately, in the form of a redefinition of what the major legacy of Friedman and of monetarism is, by Edward Nelson and Anna J. Schwartz (2008, p. 3). Was that an exceptional misstep? Or are we aware of other examples of this kind? And more than that: Do the scientists live up to their responsibility? Are they prepared to take responsibility if things go wrong and if the results are not in line with the expectations and promises?

Notes

1 Karl Polanyi is right when he considers the 'theory of the fetish character of commodities [. . .] as the key to Marx's analysis of the capitalist society' (Polanyi, 2005 [undated], p. 260).
2 And he explains: As in the religious world where 'the productions of the human brain appear as independent beings endowed with life, and entering into relation both with one another and the human race. So it is in the world of commodities with the products of men's hands. This I call the Fetishism which attaches itself to the products of labour, so soon as they are produced as commodities' (Marx 1887 [1867], ch. 1, sect. 4, 'The Fetishism of Commodities and the Secret thereof').
3 'The categories of bourgeois economy [. . .] are forms of thought expressing with social validity the conditions and relations of a definite, historically determined mode of production' (Marx 1887 [1867], ch. 1, sec. 4, 'The Fetishism of Commodities and the Secret thereof').
4 In the German original he is even more explicit, using the term 'natural phases of development' (naturgemäße Entwicklungsphasen).
5 This weakness was exploited later by the 'rational choice theory' which simply substituted 'rational' expectations for the Keynesian 'adaptive' expectations.
6 Keynes was optimistic about the advancement of *his own ideas*: 'I believe myself to be writing a book on economic theory which will largely revolutionize not, I suppose, at once – but in the course of the next ten years the way the world thinks about economic problems [. . .]. I don't merely hope what I say, in my own mind I'm quite sure' (Keynes, 1973 [1935], pp. 492–493).
7 In perhaps his most important book *Human Action*, he underlines again, 'Society is a product of human action. Human action is directed by ideologies. Thus society and any concrete order of social affairs are an outcome of ideologies' (Mises, 1996 [1940], p. 188).
8 Merton's category 'self-fulfilling prophecy' is more limited insofar as it supposes some kind of confirmation of the false definition. 'A self-fulfilling prophecy is, at the beginning, a *false* definition of the situation evoking a new behavior which makes the original false conception come *true*. The specious validity of the self-fulfilling prophecy perpetuates a reign of error' (Merton, 1963 [1948], p. 423).

References

Akerlof, G. A. and Shiller, R. J. (2010): *Animal Spirits: How Human Psychology Drives the Economy, and Why it Matters for Global Capitalism*. Princeton, NJ: Princeton University Press.

Gramsci, A. (1917): La rivoluzione contro il 'Capitale'. In: *Avanti!*, 24 November (English transl. by Marxist Internet Archive; http://marxism.halkcephesi.net/Antonio%20 Gramsci/1917/12/rev_against_capital.htm).

Hayek, F. A (1969 [1941–1943]): *The Counter-Revolution of Science. Studies on the Abuse of Reason*. New York: The Free Press of Glencoe.

Hayek, F. A. (1980 [1949]): 'Free' Enterprise and Competitive Order. In: *Individualism and Economic Order*. London, Chicago: The University of Chicago Press, pp. 107–118.

Keynes, J. M. (1973 [1935]): Letter to George Bernard Shaw, 1st January. In: J. M. Keynes, *The General Theory and After*. London: Macmillan, pp. 492–493.

Keynes, J. M. (1936): *The General Theory of Employment, Interest and Money*. London: Macmillan.

Krugman, P. (2007): Who was Milton Friedman? *The New York Review of Books*, 15 February.
Marx, K. (1887 [1867]): *Capital. A Critique of Political Economy*. Moscow: Progress Publishers (transl. by S. Moore and E. Aveling; http://www.marxists.org/archive/marx/works/1867-c1/index.htm).
Merton, R. K. (1963 [1948]): The Self-Fulfilling Prophecy. In: R. K. Merton, *Social Theory and Social Structure*. New York: The Free Press of Glencoe, pp. 421–438.
Mill, J. S. (1844): *Essays on Some Unsettled Questions of Political Economy*. London: Batoche Books.
Mises, L. (1951 [1922]): *Socialism, An Economic and Sociological Analysis*, transl. by J. Kahane. New Haven, CT: Yale University Press.
Mises, L. (1996 [1940]): *Human Action, A Treatise on Economics*. San Francisco, CA: Fox and Wilkes.
Nelson, E. and Schwartz, A. J. (2008): *The Impact of Milton Friedman on Modern Monetary Economics*. Federal Reserve Bank of St. Louis Working Paper Series, WP 2007-048D.
Polanyi, K. (1919): Weltanschauungskrise. *Neue Erde*, vol. 1, no. 31/32, pp. 458–462.
Polanyi, K. (1947): On the Belief in Economic Determinism. *Sociological Review*, vol. 39, no. 1, pp. 96–102.
Polanyi, K. (2001 [1944]): *The Great Transformation*. Boston, MA: Beacon Press.
Polanyi, K. (2005 [undated]): Christentum und wirtschaftliches Leben. In: K. Polanyi, *Chronik der großen Transformation III: Menschliche Freiheit, politische Demokratie und die Auseinandersetzung zwischen Sozialismus und Faschismus*, ed. by M. Cangiani, K. Polanyi-Levitt and C. Thomasberger. Marburg: Metropolis, pp. 252–264.
Ricardo, D. (1984 [1817]): *On the Principles of Political Economy and Taxation*. London, Melbourne: Everyman's Library.
Thomas, W. I. and Thomas, D. (1928): *The Child in America*. New York: Knopf.
Thomasberger, C. (2012): *Das neoliberale Credo*. Marburg: Metropolis.

3 Economic knowledge and value judgments

Michele Cangiani

1 From facts to values, and back

Max Weber affirms that, in the "modern situation" of society, problems typically acquire a "*political-social* character," in the sense that solutions are neither traditionally nor technically given. Moreover, problems and aims are themselves to be worked out. Therefore, we are "allowed, indeed *obliged to dispute* on value principles" (Weber, 1968, p. 153). "Choices have to be made," Warren J. Samuels writes almost a century later; and "making choices compels recourse to some criteria of choice," to some "valuational principle," which "itself involves choice," and, obviously, is never definitive (Samuels, 1998, pp. 127–128).

The diffusion of individual economic activities, so methodically and "professionally" performed as to become an end in themselves, is, according to Weber, the decisive factor of the secular process of "rationalization." Not only economic activities, but all kinds of social activity tend to follow norms of their own, thereby differentiating from each other. Thus the world loses the religious or, at least, traditionally given sense it used to have: it appears now, as Weber says, "disenchanted," and open to human free choices – choices that humans are not free not to make.

This epochal issue constitutes a starting point for modern political philosophy. How can society function, and how ought its institutions to change? Social sciences having arisen out of the need to reply to this question, indeed to face this problem, their practical relevance is obvious. Weber's assiduous and deep reflection on the distinction and relationship between *values* and the ascertainment of *facts* through scientific procedures is motivated by the inevitable link between social knowledge and political choices. On the one hand, practical problems and value judgments not only trigger and steer scientific knowledge, thereby defining its boundaries, but they also constitute the "interest" pressing for revising and widening knowledge. On the other hand, both scope and freedom of choice depend, in fact, on the knowledge of its conditions, constraints, and consequences. Furthermore, motives and values themselves deserve to be better known, in the first place by the persons whose attitudes and behavior they influence. We could say, in short, that Weber asserts the need to conceptually distinguish between scientific knowledge and political choice (implying value judgments) in order to allow better opportunities and performances to both, which, as a matter of fact, are constitutively linked to one another.

Interestingly enough, in Weber's methodological essays a favorite instance he gives of confusion between facts and values is the tendency of economics to accept "certain practical positions" as obvious facts and as elements of theory. Those positions actually constitute a part of reality, but are cultural, conventional, institutional facts: and the specific function of science – Weber maintains – should be "that of transforming what is traditionally obvious into a problem" (Weber, 1968, p. 502).

Normally, Weber observes, economic science confines itself to the limited task of working out "patterns of rational behavior," through an "ideal-typical reproduction of the competitive mechanism of prices." Thus the decisive factor determining that behavior is to be found in the "objective situation" of the market, in which individuals "can only choose between two alternatives: a 'teleological' adaptation to the 'market' or economic decay" (Weber, 1968, p. 140). In this connection, Weber recalls a basic methodological principle: economic analysis does not discover natural and/or psychological laws, but elaborates models concerning the *institutional organization* of economic activity. So economic facts can be represented. He adds then a fundamental caution: economics usually considers facts as such, as given phenomena, while the institutional and historical reality of the organization to which they belong is excluded from the scope of knowledge. Weber's statement that economics does not exhaust economic reality, and even less social reality, has also this sense; any improper generalization of its "ideal-typical reproduction" of the economic conduct amounts to a confusing interpolation of factual analysis with value judgments. Weber maintains, for instance, that the error of "Manchesterism" consists in "the belief in the existence of a purely economic order to be established, and in the possibility to deduce or to gauge that order on the basis of the existing economy" (Weber, 1909, p. 617).

Problems concerning "how reality should be" must be dealt with as such; they cannot be reduced, for example, to "problems of 'productivity' in the sense of economic technology," Weber affirms at a meeting of the *Verein für Sozialpolitik*. He continues by observing that this association was founded with the purpose of opposing

> the prejudice of certain scientific circles, that a science whose object is the desire of gain as the basic motive of social life should as well consider that desire as the only *valuation standard* of things or processes or human deeds.
> (Weber, 1924, p. 421)

Not only, for instance, can productivity be "economically" considered either as the ratio between the quantity of product and the quantity of labor, or as the measure of "profitability according to the entrepreneur's bookkeeping": but "subjective opinions about what is *ethically* permitted or what is 'useful for the *general* good'" not only cannot be quantitatively measured, but constitute a different kind of issue (p. 423).

Some years later, in his essay of 1917 on the meaning of "value-freedom," Weber develops and exemplifies this methodological position. The necessity is recalled to define precisely the problem we want to deal with, and so the object of the analysis. Take, he says, the problem of "'economic' progress towards a relative *optimum* in providing for wants, on the basis of given disposable means": this problem, to the extent that it is an "economic" problem, is defined (also in the sense of bounded) by the fact that wants and means are given, and "some sort of economic order" too is given (Weber, 1968, p. 527).

It is within a given economic order that, if prices tend to fall below costs, even the destruction of consumption goods can appear to be "economically correct": at the condition, however, of implicitly (and fallaciously) assuming as obvious a series of assumptions (which are adopted more generally than in this extreme case). The *first assumption*, Weber affirms, is that the interest of the individual – in particular, though not exclusively, of the entrepreneur – counts as such, forever and absolutely. *Second*, the "class situation" is ignored, according to which

> under the market rule [. . .] the supply of goods for certain consumers' layers [. . .] [can also worsen] not in spite of, but because of the "optimum" distribution of capital and work in the different branches of production, if that optimum is weighed in view of profitability.
> (Weber, 1968, p. 528).

Then, where the market rule is effective, the *institutional arrangement* is more precisely defined by Weber as that of "the exclusive rule of the organization of goods supply based on private capital, through a free market exchange" (p. 529).

In conclusion, a *strictly* "*economic*" valuation is possible, and correct, only when the economic ends and the social structure are given. In this case, "the problem is only that of choosing among different economic means, which only differ as to certainty, rapidity and efficiency of their effect," but are indifferent as to any other aspect concerning human interests (ibid.). This is in fact, in Weber's view, the proper scope and method of economics, the "limited task" he assigns to it. Economics is concerned with a "purely 'technical' valuation," which belongs to a general type of knowledge, "the 'rational' interpretation through the categories of 'end' and 'means'" (Weber, 1968, pp. 129 and 126). Beyond that economic valuation, there are value judgments, on whose ground it could also be limited or rejected. Those judgments constitute a second degree of valuation, and presuppose a second degree of knowledge "concerning the influence of processes of technical rationalization on the modification of the whole of life conditions" (Weber, 1968, p. 530). The entanglement of the second-level degree of valuation in the first one amounts to a reduction of both knowledge and freedom of choice.

Observing the massive state intervention in the war economy, and writing in the year of the Russian Revolution, Weber says that it is possible to maintain that the state power should be increased "as a technical means to realize different kinds of values" (p. 540). In this connection, he recommends distinguishing the judgments supporting state intervention from economic *science*; he seems very concerned, in fact, about the "typical 'confusion of problems'" economic theories carry out. "Amoral," "individualistic" and "non-state" "pure theory" – which, he says, is "an indispensable methodological instrument" as the *Idealtypus* of rational economic behavior – has been instead erroneously conceived "by the radical free-trade school as representing 'natural' reality" and thereby as a normative ideal, as a value (pp. 536–537).

We could say, in short, that, on the one hand, Weber's theory of economic rationality and of economic science is inspired especially by neoclassical and, in particular, Austrian thought. On the other hand, some pragmatist suggestions, and principally a critical revision of German Historicism and Wilhelm Rickert's Neo-Kantism, which constitute the main aspect of his philosophical formation, lead him, first, to consider societal order and historical processes as the basic object of inquiry, and, second, to assert the irreducible plurality of values. Joseph Schumpeter's concept of "scientific or analytic economics" has a similarity with Weber's conception of economics, and was in fact influenced by it. "Analytic theories," according to Schumpeter, are considered "by the modern economist [. . .] simply as an instrument of research"; they are opposed to "political economy," which includes "views about practical questions" on the basis of a "schema of social values" (Schumpeter, 1963, p. 1141). But there is a decisive difference: Weber's concern with widening the scope of economic knowledge to the institutional setup of the economic activity and his critical attitude towards the *implicit* value judgments and ideological bias of economics are missing in Schumpeter.

2 The economy as a socially instituted system

Weber's methodology, and in particular his conception of "rationality" and "value-freedom," bring him to a definition of economics that, in keeping with its neoclassical developments, privileges its subjective aspect of rational choice and its technical role. The main object of Weber's research is, however, capitalism as a historical social system, its "spirit," its origins and features. Accordingly, both economic reality and economic science become more complex problems. Beyond "technical" analyses concerning the relationship cause/effect and means/end in given conditions, Weber affirms, "the scientific study of the economy has some other tasks": first and foremost that of "inquiring into the totality of social phenomena, insofar as they are conditioned by economic causes," and, reciprocally, "the conditioning of economic forms and processes by social phenomena" (Weber, 1968, p. 538).

The early developments of modern capitalism were marked, Weber writes, by state intervention and "religious drives." The establishing of "the conception of money-making as an end in itself" and thus of "rational economic activity" required a support by political, ethical and religious motives, in a socio-cultural situation where that concept contrasted with moral standards (Weber, 1992 [1905], p. 34). Subsequently, capitalistic attitudes and norms gradually spread and were able to stand by themselves, without their previous "irrational" supports. But irrationality arises again, in a new form, which is inherent in the economic system ruled by the institutions of capitalism and market. It seems "irrational," Weber observes, that economic behavior tends to have in itself its end, instead of being directed toward "personal happiness"; that "a man exists for the sake of his business, instead of the reverse" (p. 32).

Writing at the beginning of the twentieth century, Weber was aware that the utilitarian utopia was definitively on the wane. The assumption of perfect competition and, more generally, utilitarianism had been an ideological shortcut, pretending that the totality of individual rational choices automatically provided the optimal solution of the problem of fulfilling individual wants and social ends. We could say, following Weber's line of reasoning and terminology, that the *Idealtypus* of rational economic behavior was transformed into "'natural' reality" and into a normative ideal, functioning as a pre-established solution to the problem of both the optimal organization of economic activity and social harmony. No room was left for disputes on value principles or for *political* choices.

The above-mentioned "other tasks" of "the scientific study of the economy," and in particular the analysis of capitalism as a historically instituted system, are the basis on which Weber builds his critique, not only of utilitarianism but also of neoclassical economic ideologies. This is clear in *Economy and Society* (1978 [1922]), where Weber turns again to the issue of economic rationality and examines it systematically and in depth. Economic efficiency in terms of purely *technical* economic rationality is here referred to as the "formal" rationality of economic behavior. This rationality characterizes a self-reflexive economy and requires the development of techniques and institutional conditions of calculation. But there is another kind of economic rationality, called "substantive" (*materiale*) by Weber, which is about, he says, the extent to which, on the one hand, economic actions "apply certain criteria of ultimate ends, whether they be ethical, political, utilitarian, hedonistic, feudal (*ständisch*), egalitarian or whatever," and, on the other hand, the results of the economic action are measured "against these scales of *value rationality* or substantive goal rationality" (Weber, 1978 [1922], p. 85).

In the presence of developed "market conditions," "capital calculation" in view of profit achieves the higher degree of formal economic rationality. "Modern capitalism" is characterized, for Weber, by capital calculation and formal rationality as *organizational principles*, as fundamental institutions determining the form of production and cooperation. Thus the economy is no longer "embedded" (as Karl Polanyi says) in society, but follows its autonomous rationality and tends to be an end in itself; this is the reason why *the problem arises* of substantive economic rationality and its relationship with formal economic rationality. Where, by whom and how are needs felt and ends chosen? Is *formal rationality* only the most efficient means of their fulfillment or does it interfere with *substantial choices*? Obviously, production has to satisfy wants, but wants are no longer previously, steadily and culturally determined, as in pre-modern societies. Utilitarianism and free-market doctrines suppose that the organizational principles of capitalism and market allow the optimum or, at least, the best possible fulfillment of freely expressed individual desires. According to these currents of thought, the relationship between formal and substantive economic rationality would again not be a problem, as in pre-modern times: but Weber considers this solution an illusionary belief, suggested by a value judgment taking the place of scientific analysis.

Weber, on the one hand, seems to accept the current formal and "technical" definition of economics as representing a typical trait of modern capitalistic economy; on the other hand, he feels the need to question the economic system in its historically specific social organization and within the wider social system. In the issue he raises there is a resemblance with the foundation of the "critique of political economy" laid by Karl Marx in the first chapter of *Capital* (see in particular Marx, 1977 [1867], pp. 174–175, notes 34 and 35). "What kind of human conduct" and of social organization – Weber asks – constitute the context, indeed the foundation, of phenomena economists analyze in abstract and quantitative terms? Of the price of commodities, for example, or of interest, defined by neoclassical economics "as the marginal utility of future goods relatively to present goods"? (Weber, 1978 [1922], p. 97).

The reply falls to sociologists, whose job is to study the "profit-making" ("acquisitive") organization of economic conduct. This historically specific kind of organization is characterized by the preponderance of "profit-making enterprises with capital accounting" and "oriented to the market," and therefore by "the capitalist economy" (p. 99). The market is the field where autonomous economic subjects, primarily firms, entertain relations of power and struggle, from which price formation depends. The highest degree of formal economic rationality, which "is attained by money accounting when it is applied in the *form* of capital accounting," requires, in short, two principal conditions: free market and such "*power* relation" (*Herrschaftsverhältniss*) within the firm as to warrant discipline (p. 108). Thus it is clear, Weber comments, "that the formal rationality of money calculation is dependent on certain quite specific substantive conditions," which are to be considered "in their sociological importance" (p. 107).

It is on the ground of this "critique" – of the acknowledgment of the historical-institutional reality of social organization – that Weber can also raise, in the following pages, the problem of the "fundamental *limits*" of formal rationality. Limits ensue precisely from its formal character, which renders rationality "indifferent [. . .] as to any substantive postulate" (ibid.). Thus we go back to the above-mentioned question of how substantive rationality is determined and to what extent the economic system actually copes with it. As we have seen, Weber is skeptical as to the free-market and capitalist solution. Formal rationality's "indifference" does not prevent it from determining and exploiting "substantive" wants and their fulfillment: on the contrary. Not only is the market the field of power struggles, Weber maintains, but the very "sociological" organization of the economy determines a systematic asymmetry of power in favor of capitalistic enterprises, since formal rationality and capital calculation, on which their conduct is based, are, at the same time, the general and typical "organizational principles" of the (historically instituted) economic system.

It is difficult to believe, Weber observes, that capital, understood as the subject of production, simply takes into account individual needs and preferences. This problem had been already raised, in its general terms, by Carl Menger and

Friedrich Wieser – the main sources of Weber's economic knowledge – to be dropped by later followers of the Austrian School. Menger and Wieser make a distinction between the "subjective" theory of the economy *in general* and the "objective" situation of the market-capitalist system, in which the formation of prices is *systematically* unable to attain "the highest welfare" through the optimal resource allocation. Prices are systematically distorted, Wieser observes, because, on one hand, demand is biased by differences in purchasing power, and, on the other hand, the private entrepreneur "is not concerned to provide the greatest utility for society generally; his aim is rather to obtain the highest value for himself" (Wieser, 1956 [1889], p. 55). As Polanyi points out, Menger followed a similar path in his unfinished, half-century-long revision of his 1871 *Grundsätze der Volkswirtschaftslehre*, the posthumous edition (1923) of which has never been translated into English (see Polanyi, 1971 and 1977, chap. 2; see also Cangiani, 2010).

"Capital accounting" – Weber writes in his turn – implies that the selection of desires to provide for through production of goods depends on consumers' purchasing power, whose unequal distribution is the result of the functioning of the market as a field of power struggles. Productive choices – those concerning the goods to be produced as well as those concerning technology and the organization of productive processes – depend, in general, "on the profitability of production" of different goods. Naturally, "profitability is indeed a *formally* rational category, but for that very reason it is indifferent with respect to *substantive* postulates unless these can make themselves felt in the market in the form of sufficient purchasing power" (Weber, 1978 [1922], p. 94).

Painfulness of labor and "serviceability for society at large" (to borrow Thorstein Veblen's expression) deserve only a subordinate consideration, if any. Besides, "capitalistic enterprises, through their aggressive advertising policies, exercise an important influence on the demand functions of consumers" (pp. 99–100).

Also the above-mentioned objective necessity of entrepreneurial and managerial "domination," in order to achieve "the *formal* rationality of *capital calculation*," constitutes, in Weber's opinion, "a *substantially* irrational aspect of economic organization" (p. 135). This statement echoes Menger's reflection, that in given social conditions labor is an object of economic activity rather than its subject, to the extent that working does not require choices. Slaves did not perform an economic activity, Menger observes; and modern wage-workers act economically when they sell their work-force on the labor market and when they purchase the necessities of life, but not at all when they are working, because their work does not imply choice (see Menger, 1923, p. 62). The irrationality Weber stresses with regard to labor conditions can be given a wider meaning, as an aspect of the restriction of information and choice concerning the ends and ways of economic activity, a restriction that affects the majority of individuals, and therefore society as a whole.

This second main source of "irrationality" in capitalist society – in its connection with the first one, consisting in the above-mentioned "indifference" (and, actually, priority) of formal economic rationality as to substantive rationality – inspired important sociological reflections in the following decades. It constitutes a central issue, for example, in Karl Mannheim's *Man and Society*, where the vital need is affirmed of the widest diffusion, in our increasingly industrialized and complex mass society, of "'substantial rationality', i.e. the capacity to act intelligently in a given situation on the basis of one's own insight into the interrelations of events" (Mannheim, 1940, p. 58).

Mannheim pleads the cause of a purposeful and democratic social control of the economic process much more clearly and resolutely than Weber. The contribution of the latter, however, has been important for understanding that models of rational action and general equilibrium bring with them a "scientific" fascination, which, combined with the Eden-like vision of the market's virtues, results in an *implicitly normative* design of society. Weber is aware that this is only possible at the condition of concealing the *historical form of social organization*, with its fundamental capitalist character.

Veblen's criticism – inspiring the classical-radical tendency of institutional economics – is similar: conventional economic theories ideologically neutralize, indeed suppress, what should instead be their primary object. "The pecuniary activities of men, efforts directed to acquisition" of wealth, Veblen writes, are relegated "to the background of economic theory"; they are "handled as incidental features of the process of social production and consumption [. . .] instead of being dealt with as the *controlling factor* about which the modern economic process turns" (Veblen, 1919 [1901], p. 286; my italics). Thus crucial problems are excluded, knowledge is made banal, indeed tautological: Veblen's criticism to the neoclassical paradigm could not be more radical. If gains derive from vendibility, he writes, "vendibility need not, even approximately, coincide with serviceability, except serviceability be construed in terms of marginal utility or some related conceptions, in which case the outcome is a tautology" (p. 309).

Weber's conclusion questions a central aspect of neoclassical theories: consumers' calculation, as theorized by marginalism, and producers' calculation, "differ as fundamentally as do the ends of want satisfaction and of profit-making" (Weber, 1978 [1922], p. 92). Consumer's sovereignty is illusionary. More importantly, by observing that *formal* economic rationality has a *substantive* efficacy, he questions the institutional structure of the economic system and its ability to cope with individual needs and to respond to information coming from its social and natural environment. The field of substantial rationality, which should be open to free valuations of individuals, by themselves and through social institutions, is instead constrained by "economic" requirements, basically suggested by "capital calculation" in view of "profitability." To the extent that formal rationality ceases to be the means to realize free individual choices and politically identified ends, economic activity becomes paradoxically an end in itself. We can speak in this sense of a closing of the economic system. Weber helps us to notice that economics tends not only to mirror the phenomena of capitalist economy without explaining them, but also to associate with that kind of economic organization in closing up the scope of knowledge, and consequently the range of possible problems, values, and political choices.

3 After Weber

Weber's epoch is that of the crisis of liberal capitalism, in connection to which economic thought was obliged to question its own concepts and methods. Weber, while drawing his definition of economics from the prevailing neoclassical stream, was on the whole close to the alternative institutional tendency, as the foregoing sections try to show. Not only does he envisage and develop a further level of economic knowledge, that of the social-institutional organization of the economy, but he singles out a source of undue interference of value judgments into scientific inquiry in the entanglement of those two levels. In other words, if capitalist organization of the economy is not acknowledged as such, but tacitly identified with economic efficiency in terms of the relationship means/ends – if, in short, rationality is identified with profitability – this is clearly an instance of value judgment. Such judgment can be, Weber maintains, as legitimate as any other. What should not be allowed is to ignore the second level, where profitability is institutionally determined; this would amount to *implicitly* presupposing that efficiency and profitability are coinciding in general, and not only within "capital calculation." As a result, Weber says, facts and values are confused with each other. In other words, values are immediately inferred from facts that are not (adequately) explained. The consequence is that both rationality and freedom undergo damage. Every non-declared and theoretically non-clarified value presupposition pre-establishes a boundary for both knowledge and free choice.

Lionel Robbins, in his famous essay on "the nature and significance of economic science," refers to the Weberian distinction between formal and substantive economic rationality not only as a source, but also as a support of his theory. The subject matter of economics, he affirms, is the *economic form* of human behavior; not "certain *kinds* of behaviour," but "a particular *aspect* of behaviour, the form imposed by the influence of scarcity" (Robbins, 1962 [1935], pp. 16–17). The problem is that of rational choice, in a situation where both means and ends are supposed as given, means are "scarce" and "have alternative uses" (p. 16).

In that would-be Weberian construction, economics has no concern with ends, which are a moral or political or aesthetical question, a question of substantive, not of formal rationality. The reference to Weber results in avoiding the issues he raises. Robbins, by limiting the scope of economics to the economic form of rational choice as such, excludes the problem of the institutional features of the historically given economic system. Thus he can consider the meaning of his definition of economy to be general. The historical specificity of social arrangements is mentioned by him only as to the greater utility of economic analysis "in the exchange economy," where choice is widespread, indeed unavoidable; "where independent initiative in social relationships is permitted to the individual" (p. 19). This is true concerning the modern condition of society, but it would be hard to maintain that it is all the truth about market society and capitalist economy.

The individualistic method and the Paradise Lost vision, to which Robbins holds, rule out the analysis of those institutional features of the economic system that determine its specifically "formal" character, and therefore its self-reference, resulting in an invasion in the "substantive" field and a constraint on development. Those institutional *facts*, insofar as they are not explained, are confirmed as *values* in everyday life.

Weber conceptually distinguishes between formal and substantive economic rationality precisely to be able to analyze their actual relationship, which remains invisible within the narrow or technical definition of economics, but can be taken into account and explained at the level of the "sociological" analysis of economic processes. Robbins, on the contrary, projects the conceptual distinction onto reality, by supposing that it is *de facto* true, that formal rationality does not interfere with individual and social choices concerning the ends to be pursued. The tacit interpolation of such value judgment into scientific analysis is a consequence of the absence of an institutional analysis of the organization of the economic system as a whole.

"Formalist" theories are an attempt to get over the crisis of economic thought, in the face of the crisis of liberal capitalism. From the last decades of the nineteenth century, state intervention in the economy increases, monopolistic power and trade unionism supersede free competition, free trade is limited and distorted by protectionism and imperialism. The gap between models adopted by economics and actual economic institutions becomes too wide to be ignored. With the First World War, both the institutional crisis and the scientific gap are dramatically accentuated. "The War has destroyed all the achievements of liberal ideology," Antonio Gramsci observes in 1919; "the liberal world disintegrates," and "liberal economic science" outlines "an abstract and mathematical utopia" which is "separate from the general historical process of society" (Gramsci, 1994, pp. 21–22). Theoretical reactions of different sorts, in fact, are not missing; one of them takes the path of formalism.

An early and illuminating example of formalism can be found in a long article Maffeo Pantaleoni wrote during the First World War. Taking for granted that the war is a suitable means for acquiring great material and moral benefits, among which "the satisfaction that is gained by an imperialistic policy," Pantaleoni (1916, p. 166) tries to explain in which way the "economic phenomena of the War" can be tackled by economic theory. According to him, the theory is not concerned with morals or tastes as such, but

> consists only in the study of different choices concerning given tastes and needs; the problem is how to satisfy needs at the minimum cost or with maximum satisfaction. *From this point of view* the theory covers all kinds of actions and this is a problem which does not change.
>
> (p. 164, note)

Thus war, in Pantaleoni's view, can be considered by the economist "as the sudden arrival of a new preference, or need," which has, as any other need, its own scale of intensity and its utility curve "that takes its proper place among the other curves of demand of each individual" (p. 168). The fraction of income available for the war "is determined by the preference for the benefits of war, compared to the other commodities purchasable with our income – we can say more simply, that this fraction depends on patriotism" (pp. 186–187).

In this way, economic analysis is reduced to an abstract skeleton, capable not only of fitting any institutional structure and any value, but also of surreptitiously supporting them with the authority of science. As we have seen, such support results in an implicit value judgment, insofar as the basic institutional features of the economic system and its dynamics are not taken into consideration. Pantaleoni – for whom Schumpeter (1963, p. 857) vouches international reputation and a worthy place in the history of economic analysis – is a good example of the enhanced political adaptability of the liberal *credo*, when it is grounded on formalism. The economist himself seems, in this case, very adaptable. On the one hand, Pantaleoni (1916, pp. 450 and 454) maintains that "rough competition and selection," as opposed to "ties," are beneficial; therefore the laws on "fair treatment of workers" are detrimental. Those laws clash in fact, he says, with the "*scientific truth*" (my italics) that wages are "nothing but a future value, discounted on the day they are paid, of the contribution of the marginal worker to the product" (Pantaleoni, 1917, p. 12). On the other hand, Pantaleoni's faith in free-market laws goes arm in arm with his nationalistic, antidemocratic and racist views, and it does not prevent his support to industrial groups for whom the war was a chance to make huge profits, to achieve vertical integration (from mines to shipbuilding, from weapons production to banking), to carry out important financial operations and to obtain a privileged relationship with the state (Maier, 1975, p. 576). However paradoxical this attitude can appear, it has continued to be widespread among would-be liberal thinkers.

An alternative way out of the crisis of economics has been institutionalism, which also availed itself of the war to raise new problems and widen the debate on the role of economic science. This tendency cannot be dealt with here, with the exception of a rapid reference to Adolf Löwe, whose reflection has also the meaning of a critical reply to Robbins' *Essay*. Löwe characterizes the institutional method as follows: "pure economics" consists in the "theory of choice," but the problem of data of choice, ends included, cannot be avoided; the "occurrence, structural order and evolutionary tendency" of those data are to be included in the scope of analysis: they are, in fact, a result of "the social process as a whole" (Löwe, 1936, pp. 19 and 21). Pure economics *à la* Robbins, according to Löwe, "assumes that the natural, social and technical conditions of production arise exclusively from outside the economic sphere" (Löwe, 1935, p. 105). In reality, on the one hand, "in a system of free exchange the private appropriation of the productive factors cannot but encroach also the order of production"; on the other hand, "in the industrial system the economic process itself produces and changes its data" (pp. 108 and 97).

The exigency is here expressed of widening the scope of economic knowledge to the institutional organization, which has a constraining and leading effect on the dynamics of the economic process and thus constrains individual free choice, especially if that organization remains concealed, outside the boundaries of economic knowledge. This is the case of those liberal neoclassical theories that continue to refer to free-market institutions, without taking advantage of the escape offered by formalism; they were already outdated before the First World War, but never ceased to be proposed. A prominent example of this tendency is Friedrich Hayek's vision of "an effective competitive order." In view of the realization of that order, a suitable "legal framework" should be implemented by the state as the first requirement for "a policy which deliberately adopts competition, the market, and prices as its ordering principles" (Hayek, 1948, p. 110).

The success of neo-liberalism from the late 1970s on has also availed itself of the ideological support of Hayek's theories, in spite of the fact that his "competitive order" appears as a fairy tale if compared with the actual development of contemporary economy. The shining utopia of the competitive order based on "natural" freedom of individual choices has had – and still has – a political influence. Hayek's conception has, in fact, an *implicit* normative content, which depends on its substituting a noble but unreal liberal ideal for the knowledge of the actual features and developments of market society. The final effect of a lack of knowledge is always to limit freedom of choice and the debate on values.

Again, the Weberian and Veblenian point of view is confirmed, that where knowledge of institutional organization of the economic system is lacking, not only do value judgments take its place, but they are masked under a scientific appearance. To the extent that the constraints characterizing that organization fail to be included into the scope of economic science, they can more easily continue to be the "controlling factor" of the economic system, which tends to remain closed within its own "formal rationality." Freedom of choice, and of making and implementing value choices, is correspondingly bounded.

Finally, we can wonder why such old criticisms to economics as Weber's or Veblen's continue to be largely ineffective and even ignored, although evidence accumulated during a century should make them obvious. Moreover, a series of heterodox thinkers have renewed them from time to time. Along with that of Löwe, and Polanyi's radical criticism to the formal definition of economy and the "economistic fallacy" (see in particular Polanyi, 1977, ch. 1 and 2), the example of François Perroux can be cited. Economic models are, in Perroux's opinion, "basically contradictory":

> [O]n the one hand, they consider maximization as a result of supposedly rational and effective individual choices, in the context of competitive markets. On the other hand, they *necessarily* imply a capitalist combination of powers (concerning savings, investment, enterprises), without supplying any means to describe and objectively weigh the economic effects of those powers, [and more in general] without any reference to a given form of society.
> (Perroux, 1970, pp. 2257 and 2260; author's translation)

Those models and concepts are "implicitly normative; they divert the attention of theorists, experts and common people from the critique of *institutions*" (p. 2270). In other words, "the capitalist or market economy is *not* understandable through the concepts and models of orthodox economic 'science'": yet, understanding it as a historical-institutional organization is the "first step towards *explicitly* normative propositions" (p. 2289), while unwarranted value judgments can be avoided.

How can we explain the exceptional resilience of mainstream economics in spite of contrary evidence and age-old and periodically renewed criticisms? Any other science would have been obliged to change its paradigm. The hypothesis can be ventured that the privileged condition of economics is due precisely to its quality of being, as Perroux says, "implicitly normative" and contributing "to divert our attention from facts, whose acknowledgement and analysis would be dangerous for the *ongoing* 'social order'" (p. 2256).

References

Cangiani, M. (2010): From Menger to Polanyi: The Institutional Way. In: H. Hagemann, Y. Ikeda and T. Nishizawa (eds.), *Austrian Economics in Transition*. Houndmills, New York: Palgrave Macmillan, pp. 138–153.

Gramsci, A. (1994): *Scritti di economia politica*, ed. by G. Lunghini. Turin: Bollati Boringhieri.

Hayek, F. A. (1948): *Individualism and Economic Order*. Chicago, IL: University of Chicago Press.

Löwe, A. (1935): *Economics and Sociology*. London: George Allen and Unwin.

Löwe, A. (1936): Economic Analysis and Social Structure. *Manchester School of Economics and Social Studies*, vol. 7, no. 1, pp. 18–37.

Maier, C. S. (1975): *Recasting Bourgeois Europe*. Princeton, NJ: Princeton University Press.

Mannheim, K. (1940): *Man and Society in an Age of Reconstruction*. London: Kegan Paul, Trench, Trubner and Co.

Marx, K. (1977 [1867]): *Capital*, Volume One. New York: Vintage Books.

Menger, C. (1923): *Grundsätze des Volkswirtschaftslehre*, ed. by K. Menger. Wien, Leipzig: Hölde-Pichler-Tempsky und G. Freytag.

Pantaleoni, M. (1916): Fenomeni economici della Guerra. *Giornale degli Economisti*, vol. 52, no. 3, pp. 157–211, no. 5, pp. 381–400, no. 6, pp. 449–470.

Pantaleoni, M. (1917): *Note in margine della Guerra*. Bari: Laterza.

Perroux, F. (1970): Les conceptualisations implicitement normatives et les limites de la modélisation en économie. *Économies et sociétés, Cahiers de l'ISEA*, vol. 4, no. 26, pp. 2255–2307.

Polanyi, K. (1971): Carl Menger's Two Meanings of "Economic." In: G. Dalton (ed.), *Studies in Economic Anthropology*. Washington, DC: American Anthropological Association, pp. 16–24.

Polanyi, K. (1977): *The Livelihood of Man*, ed. by H. W. Pearson. New York: Academic Press.

Robbins, L. (1962 [1935]): *An Essay on the Nature and Significance of Economic Science*, 2nd ed. London: Macmillan/New York: St. Martin's Press.

Samuels, W. J. (1998): The Historical Quest for Principles of Valuation: An Interpretative Essay. In: S. Fayazmanesh and M. R. Tool (eds.), *Institutionalist Method and Value*, vol. 1. Cheltenham and Northampton: Edward Elgar, pp. 112–129.

Schumpeter, J. A. (1963): *History of Economic Analysis*. London: George Allen and Unwin.

Veblen, T. (1919 [1901]): Industrial and Pecuniary Employments. In: *The Place of Science in Modern Civilization and Other Essays*. New York: Huebsch, pp. 279–323.
Weber, M. (1909): Review of: *Die Aufgaben der Volkswirtschaftslehre als Wissenschaft* (by A. Weber; Tübingen: Mohr, 1909). *Archiv für Sozialwissenschaft und Sozialpolitik*, vol. 29, no. 2, pp. 615–620.
Weber, M. (1924): *Gesammelte Aufsätze zur Soziologie und Sozialpolitik*, ed. by M. Weber. Tübingen: Mohr.
Weber, M. (1968): *Gesammelte Aufsätze zur Wissenschaftslehre*. Tübingen: Mohr.
Weber, M. (1978 [1922]): *Economy and Society*, ed. by G. Roth and C. Wittich. Berkeley, CA, and London: University of California Press.
Weber, M. (1992 [1905]): *The Protestant Ethic and the Spirit of Capitalism*. London, New York: Routledge.
Wieser, F. (1956 [1889]): *Natural Value*. New York: Kelley and Millman.

Part II
Theories meet facts

4 Between history and theory
Otto Neurath's economics from 1906 to 1917

Monika Poettinger

1 Introduction[1]

The 1980s witnessed a renewed interest in the *Wiener Kreis* and logical empiricism (Richardson and Uebel, 2007). Historiographical accounts analyzed its adherents while their works were extensively republished. This reevaluation also encompassed one of the most controversial participants to the first Vienna circle: Otto Neurath (1882–1945).[2] Once stigmatized as a volcanic revolutionary, as poor in theory as he was rich in reforming enthusiasm, Neurath has been rediscovered as an astonishingly modern theorist of the philosophy of science, anticipating the much later positions of Kuhn and Feyerabend.

Neurath's role as an economist, though, remains to be fully analyzed, even if his economic writings have been recently republished and partially translated into English (Haller and Höfer, 1998; Uebel and Cohen, 2006). A quite astonishing occurrence, given that Neurath began his scientific and academic career as an economist with an outstanding curriculum. He participated in all debates of his time, discussing in depth questions such as the theory of value, the method of social sciences, the normative content of economics and the possibility of socialist calculation. Due to the vehemence of these debates, contemporaries judged Neurath's accomplishments more with contempt than appreciation. Nonetheless, the silence of historiography is not easily understandable, particularly in the field of economic thought.

The main difficulty in appraising Neurath's economic theory lies in his radical redefinition of the economic science as such, based on his empiricist, or better even "physicalist," approach. The first part of this chapter will briefly introduce Neurath's idea of science and of the role that scientists should have in society. How his epistemology resulted from his early experience in reforming the economic science will also be illustrated.

The second part of the chapter will then relate how Neurath, in the course of the years between the publication of his doctoral dissertation in 1906 and his essay on *Das Begriffsgebäude der Wirtschaftslehre und seine Grundlagen* (Neurath, O., 1917a), completely revolutionized the idea of economics. He did so by refuting both the approach of the historical school represented by Gustav Schmoller, one of his supervisors in Berlin, and the systematic of the school of Vienna which he had already attacked while participating in the seminar held by Eugen von

Böhm-Bawerk in 1906. Neurath redefined economics as the science of wealth, in a holistic effort to reduce to unity all the opposing positions inflaming the economic debates of those troubled years. He envisaged a science that could make space for both abstracting models and empirical verification; a science that applied the same methodology to the study of a market economy and of socialization processes; a science that could comprise List's cosmopolitan economy as a contemporary war economy.

Although quite revolutionary in its outcome, Neurath's definition of economics rested heavily on the past discipline. In his view, no science could or should be rebuilt completely, starting with a *tabula rasa*. From Aristotle to Smith, from Quesnay to Sismondi, all economists still had something useful to contribute to the advancement of science. What had once been cast away could find new validity in some novel form or in a restricted field. History was, thus, an indispensable part of the economist's toolkit.

As described further, many features of Neurath's economics reveal today a striking modernity, justifying the necessity of a new and more complete evaluation of his role in the history of economic thought.

2 Economics as a science

> The fight against today's economic order is a fight against an order of enmity. But it is also a fight against bad economics.
> (O. Neurath, cited in Neurath, M. and Cohen, 1973, p. 260)

At the end of the nineteenth century, political economy attempted to acquire the status of natural science, painstakingly searching for natural laws in human actions. Bent on *erklären* more than *verstehen* (Dilthey, 1997; Droysen, 1977), political economy would claim neutrality toward history and politics as it already had toward religion.

Ironically, economics reached for this goal exactly when Europe's scientists, philosophers and literati questioned, with increasing impetus, the concept of science in itself, degrading and delegitimizing it. The intent was to abandon positivism along with every metaphysical foundation of science, reminiscent of the scholastic past. God was to die[3] while absolute space vanished from physics (Mach, 1883) and grand style disappeared from literature (Magris, 1993).

In *Knowledge and Error*, first published in 1905, Ernst Mach revealed how easily science's natural laws proved to be false because of errors in men's interpretation of facts and data. He further questioned the necessity to discover such natural laws, a result of men's reaction to nature's chaos and a consequence of Europe's specific culture. Men subjectively imposed laws on nature, while nature itself was foreign to such abstraction (Mach, 1992, pp. 447–448).

Otto Neurath collected all the suggestions[4] from Ernst Mach, but also Pierre Duhem (1906) and Gregorius Itelson,[5] and defined science as a logical construction, based on empirical propositions, that justified itself and self-explained itself.

Science thus renounced every external legitimation, be it an ideal and absolute truth,[6] the correspondence to an objective reality or a group of epistemological rules.

Given this definition of science, obviously, every distinction between natural and social sciences became irrelevant and the *Methodenstreit* lost all its significance.[7] The same methodology could and should be used in biology, mechanics, chemistry and sociology. So said Neurath in his scientific legacy in 1946:

> As a sociologist I disliked all this talk about "the national spirit," "mentality of a ruler," etc. Why should we not speak here in the same simple way as in the laboratory? And, as an empiricist I asked myself how we might start from simple observation-statements, on which to base all further scientific discussions. So I developed my suggestions dealing with "protocol statements" (cf. my "Protokolsätze," *Erkentniss*, 1932[8]), frequently discussed since then by various people. I disliked starting from a vague statement of "something red" floating somewhere in the air and therefore I asked for a more exact formulation. Such a formulation always gives the name of the "protocolist" first and then adds his sayings. "Charles told us he had seen a red table in his room on March 4th" seemed to me a fair start, which enabled us to ask the question, "When, where, and how?" which we are accustomed to ask when we make an astronomical or chemical statement. With one stroke, I thought, I could overcome a certain cleavage always felt when scientists want to pass from "sensual elements" to descriptive statements on stars and stones. My suggestion seemed to have the advantage that the "when, where, and how" attitude could be maintained from the bottom to the top. This I call the "physicalist" approach.
> (Neurath, O., 1946, p. 499)

This simple account contains the extraordinary modernity of Neurath's epistemology, refuting idealism and metaphysics, but also the kind of empiricism typical of the Vienna Circle.[9] Only several decades later would epistemologists elaborate what Neurath already affirmed in the first decades of the twentieth century (Haller, 1985, p. 11): science was only one of the methods evolved in history to construe the *Weltanschaaungen* through which societies explained themselves and justified their decisions (Neurath, O., 1913a) and rationality only a belated child of humanity (Neurath, O., 1913b, p. 440). Before science, man had conceived magic and then religion to absolve this function (Neurath, O., 1931a, 1931b).

Neurath's science was, in Weber's terms, a historically determined rationality: the relation between ideas, the ends of human action, and the means to realize them, decisions. While Weber (1944, 2002, p. 185), though, saw in the process of rationalization an armor constraining man's freedom, Neurath (1931b, p. 57) interpreted technology and the scientific method as instruments through which man could finally make his utopias come true and exercise his will on the world. How? Thanks to an enlightening encyclopedic effort to diffuse scientific knowledge. An effort so conceived that the greatest possible number of people could democratically decide which institutional setting would be the best to transform the desired utopia into reality. In his words: "We logical empiricists want to show people that what physicists and astronomers do is only on a grand scale what Charles and Jane are doing every day in the garden and the kitchen" (Neurath, O., 1946, p. 506). The scientist was in no way different from the common man. He only analyzed a greater quantity of data regarding the past (Neurath, O., 1968, p. 106).

In this sense, scientists should and could not take the place of the magicians and priests of the past. The platonic ideal could not become reality[10]:

> People of the totalitarian kind may try to make scientists the leaders of a new society, like the magicians, nobles, or churchmen of former societies. The encyclopedism of logical empiricism does not see why scientists, trained to discover as many alternatives as possible, should be particularly able to select one alternative only (one that never can be based on calculation) by making a decision or performing an action for other people with different desires and attitudes.
>
> (Neurath, O., 1946, p. 505)

Contrary to the rationality of Weber's capitalism, Neurath's scientific method could not be a guide to exit the forest of Cartesio (Neurath, O., 1913a): "In the end we have to reach a 'decision' not based on a calculus. One cannot test the future usefulness of a scientific technique beforehand; unpredictability here plays its part" (Neurath, O., 1946, pp. 501–502). This point marks the substantial difference between Weber and Neurath (Fistetti, 1985, p. 127). While Weber's rationality ventured to become determining, Neurath's science could only propose alternative scenarios to the free decision of man.

If modern science could not definitively solve the problem of decision, what distinguished it, then, from magic, religion or totalitarian ideologies? They all represented solutions to the anguish of doubt, of having to decide in conditions of uncertainty, without the data necessary to act rationally.[11] Neurath, though, considered science to have one major advantage over the other alternatives: it hindered a governing minority from appropriating the decision capacity of individuals as in the case of magical faith, metaphysical ideologies, superstitions or totalitarian institutions. Neurath affirmed:

> The spreading of muddle does not seem to be as simple as the spreading of a successful technique. The frivolity of the race theory developed by the Nazis in many books, on character, physiognomics and heredity, did not even infect the mathematics, astronomy, chemistry, and physics of the Nazis very much.
>
> (Neurath, O., 1946, p. 508)

So "it is possible to sociologically analyze all ideologies one after another, those with a scientific character and those with an unscientific one" but in the end "the unscientific ideologies can be overcome only through a scientific attitude" (Neurath, O., 1981a, p. 350).

Encyclopedism implied cooperation, one of the peculiar characters of modern man, and hence guaranteed personal freedom much more than any other decision-making system of the past. On the eve of WWII, Neurath wrote:

> Without pursuing utopian ideals men capable of judging themselves and their institutions scientifically should also be capable of widening the sphere of peaceful cooperation; for the historical record shows clearly enough that the trend has been in that direction on the whole and that the more co-operative man is, the more "modern" he is.
> (Neurath, O., 1939, p. 132)

In this light, Neurath positively judged the specialization that, from Renaissance onward, had characterized science, making it impossible for one man to comprehend the totality of knowledge (Neurath, O., 1918a, p. 3). Scientists had been constrained to confront themselves continuously with one another, to decide which new protocol or new theory to include, being compatible, in the collective vision of the world, and select which ones to reject, in an unceasing process of redefinition and reconstruction of the *Weltanschauung* or *Weltauffassung*.[12] A definition of scientific activity that he inherited from his father,[13] the economist Wilhelm Neurath,[14] and applied first to the field of economics.

At the beginning of the twentieth century, after the wreckage of classical thought and liberalism, economics needed a new definition, a new vocabulary and a novel defining statute. Neurath's earliest writings, penned between his doctoral thesis in 1906 and his seminal essay on *Das Begriffsgebäude der Wirtschaftslehre und seine Grundlagen* in 1917, all dealt with the economic science and its redefinition, but they did so through the principles that Neurath later articulated in his philosophy of science.

Therefore, the historiography accusing Neurath of having abandoned his own epistemological principles in his economic theorizing, due to his ideological sympathies, utopist visions and sociological naivety (Sebestik, 1999, p. 11), is easily contradicted. A suggestive proof is the well-known metaphor of the ship.

Neurath's style, simple and rich in metaphors, in the wake of Itelson, presented us with suggestive images of scientific activity, diffused and replicated during the whole twentieth century. The metaphor of the ship,[15] loved by Quine[16] is the most famous. In 1921, Neurath wrote:

> We are like seamen having to rebuild their ship at sea, without the opportunity to do it completely. When a beam is taken off, it must immediately be substituted, while the whole ship acts as a supporting structure. The ship will thus be completely renovated, through old and drifting wood, but only in a gradual process.[17]

Neurath's image bore a strong message: no science would ever be complete; no science could be rebuilt from scratch. Scientific innovation resulted from a collective decision-making process through which coalitions of scientists discussed, disregarded or approved changes in the currently prevailing scientific organizing of knowledge. Advancements followed negotiations among the diverse parts of the scientific community: a sociological process that could have erratic outcomes. In 1944 Neurath wrote again:

> Imagine seafarers that in open sea want to change the form of their heavy vessel, transforming its plumpness into a fish's slenderness. To rebuild the ship's supporting structure and the careen, they use timber from the old structure and drifting wood. But they cannot make port to do the renovating work from base up. While they work, they remain in the old structure, amid terrible storms and deafening waves. During the restructuring they have to pay attention not to create some dangerous leak. Step after step a new ship emerges from the old one, but while they work, seafarers already think of a new structure, not always being of one opinion about it. It will be impossible to foresee the exit of such a process. This is our destiny.[18]

The ship's metaphor that so repeatedly showed up in Neurath's work was first articulated, with rhetorical vehemence, while discussing war economics and its role in a new defined economic science as early as 1913, in the essay: *Probleme der Kriegswirtschaftslehre*.[19] In it, Neurath attacked the pretense of scientists to produce perfect and complete systems of thought with no defects or anomalies, allowing no changes or amelioration. Such "systematists" were "born liars" because a perfect system, in economics as in science, could only remain an eternal aim, never attainable (Neurath, O., 1913b, p. 456). Trying to build such a deceitful system was neither a scientific nor a philosophical pursuit:

> In logic, or physics, biology or philosophy we cannot put some undisputable statements on top and then logically derive from them an entire chain of thought. Inadequacies always contaminate the entirety of this ideal world, starting from the premises as from later consequences. No precaution can prevent this outcome, nor can renouncing all previous knowledge, starting from a *tabula rasa*, to achieve a better result.
>
> (Neurath, O., 1913b, p. 456)

A clear accusation toward the systematic turn taken by economics in Vienna.

Neurath's later use of the metaphor of the ship was a consequence of what he himself had experienced in his early redefinition of the economic science in his early writings. In 1917 he summarized such efforts, clearly unveiling the significance of the metaphor itself.

> The reconstruction of the economic science attempted here wishes to maintain as much as possible of the past tradition. Something could be retained only changing its form or being completed, something had to be abandoned. As a result, some explanations, regarding different strata of the underlying problem, competed with one another. Some erroneous statements did not have to

be refuted completely, but found a useful application in more restricted areas. To proceed in the right direction in this process of reconstruction it was also necessary to resort to past arguments.

(Neurath, O., 1917a, p. 485)

Neurath was determined to build a new supporting structure for the economic science, employing concepts and logical constructions still in use – the timber of the old ship – or derived from the past – timber floating on the sea. The role of history in this process was crucial. It was not possible to make port with the ship of science, nor build a new edifice just with new instruments.[20] Parts of old theories had to be maintained, modified or completed, perhaps with a validity in different or more limited fields. Some of the new components, furthermore, innovatively used concepts already known and perhaps once rejected. Along these lines, Neurath construed an economic science based on empirical data, widely collected in in-kind statistics, with the aim of studying the widest possible assortment of organizational structures and classifying them as to their economy, that is, their capability to increment the wealth of humanity.[21]

The economist, then, had to be a sociological technician, with a profound knowledge of the past, who was able to extract from the historical discourse possible organizational models,[22] and who possessed a vivid imagination, necessary to build fictional utopias. The scope of Neurath's economics was to present politicians with the array of alternative organizations that would result from this research activity (Neurath, O., 1931b, p. 17), arranged on the scale of prospective happiness of men. The decision as to which organization would transform into reality could not spring from economics alone. In the modern world, the economist could not be a politician anymore. While Colbert and Turgot had been among the best economists of their time, Bismarck stood in no comparison to Marx. Times had changed: "Those who rule the destiny of states do not possess an extensive knowledge; those who possess extensive knowledge do not govern states" (Neurath, O., 1913a, p. 56). Specialization, as seen, was constrained to cooperation and rationalization to democratic forms of government.

In 1918, Neurath ended his promising academic career in economics by following this ideal down to the chaos of Munich's *Räterepublik*. During the trial for treason that ended the Bavarian Council Republic, Max Weber defended Neurath, citing precisely his political neutrality and his role as an economic technician who only proposed possible economic policies for the decision of politicians.[23] Thanks to this defense line and the influence of many friends, Neurath escaped with his life, but lost the professorship in economics he had just obtained in Heidelberg. From then on, he dedicated his efforts to philosophy and to the democratization of knowledge through museums and his renowned Isotype language. Economics vanished almost completely from his interests and writings, while his achievements in the field were forgotten or even ridiculed. Much of Neurath's later epistemological reflections, though, resulted from these first efforts and, as such, should be revalued.

82 *Monika Poettinger*

3 Otto Neurath, a seafarer on the ship of economics

> We have forsaken the land and gone to sea! We have destroyed the bridge behind us – more so, we have demolished the land behind us! Now little ship, look out! Beside you is the ocean; it is true, it does not always roar, and at times it lies there like silk and gold and dreams of goodness. But there will be hours that you realize that it is infinite and that there is nothing more awesome than infinity. Oh, the poor bird that has felt free and now strikes against the walls of its cage! Woe when homesickness of the land overcomes you, as if there had been more freedom there – and there is no more "land"!
>
> (Nietzsche, 2001, p. 119)

When did Neurath's adventure on board the ship of economics begin? Undoubtedly at an early age, probably in his father's library (Cartwright *et al.*, 2008, pp. 8–10). There he could read many works of economics and science, but also hold lengthy discussions with Wilhelm Neurath himself.[24] On these occasions, Otto absorbed, among many other things,[25] his father's displeasure with the current economic system, and particularly the credit system, cause of economic crises (Neurath, W., 1897).

Seen through the eyes of his father, the ship of economics leaked in many places and was badly in need of reparations; a judgment widely diffused in Vienna in the first decade of the twentieth century. "The classical system of political economy lays in ruins" (Schumpeter, 1908, p. xi) wrote Joseph A. Schumpeter in his own dissertation in 1908, condemning the chaos resulting from the coexistence of manifold paradigms. The "bankruptcy of the science" (Schumpeter, 1908, p. v) seemed a menacing reality, particularly to young scholars of the discipline. Neurath himself, in a youthful essay in 1903, wrote:

> The 20th century takes over longstanding problems. A number of in part very painful experiences lie behind us. Economic atomism has fallen out of favor. What is to take its place is not at all clear [. . .]. That the foundations of the current economic system are faulty is becoming increasingly clear. Everywhere contradictions emerge which are not only of academic import but effect the welfare and suffering of millions.
>
> (Uebel, 2004, p. 16)

Economics, in Vienna as in Berlin, was shaken by a wild storm of change. Innumerable debates opposed in infinite discussions between the best minds of the time. A creative destruction that had had its beginning in the *Methodenstreit*[26] but in time came to involve all fundaments of the youngest of sciences. Neurath's *Problemstellung* derived from this intellectual turmoil and his manifold attempts toward the unity of sciences and holism[27] were a clear response to such fruitless divisions.[28] "Speculation," he would later write, "is of interest only in shaping life and procuring happiness" (Neurath, O., 1928a, p. 134).

In search of a way to prevent a shipwreck, Neurath first considered all timber of the existing ship that could still be of use, and all pieces that, floating on the sea, could be retrieved and similarly be adapted to new use. He eagerly began studying economic history and history of economic thought. Following the advice of Ferdinand Tönnies, after publishing a short essay on interest in antiquity in 1904 (Neurath, O., 1904), he left Vienna for Berlin, where he completed his studies under the supervision of the renowned economic historian Eduard Meyer.[29]

Neurath himself recalled, in a letter to his son, how his rare competences, comprising economics as classical culture, could find highest appraisal among the followers of the German historical school, motivating his transfer (Neurath, P., 1982, p. 230). In Berlin Neurath attended the economics seminar of Gustav Schmoller and studied statistics with Ladislaus Bortkiewicz, becoming involved in the *Methodenstreit* and in the debate on Marx's theory of value.[30]

His time in Berlin resulted in two dissertations: a study on economics in antiquity (Neurath, O., 1908, 1909) and a history of social classes based on Cicero's *De Officiis* (Cicero, 1994). Meyer selected this last one to grant Neurath the title of Doctor. The thesis also received the honor of publication of its first part (Neurath, O., 1906a), and was subsequently published in its entirety in Schmoller's *Jahrbücher für Nationalökonomie und Statistik* in 1906 and 1907 (Neurath, O., 1906b, 1907).

Neurath's thesis, although being a juvenile work, already showed his attitude toward history and economics. *Zur Anschauung der Antike über Handel, Gewerbe und Landwirtschaft* was dedicated to a sketched representation of the historical evolution of social classes based on different evaluations of Cicero's work, from antiquity to the eighteenth century. Through a complex study of all translations made of *De Officiis* and their reception and diffusion, Neurath exemplified the stance toward diverse professions and crafts and the cultural use of historical past made at different times in different countries. As he would later vindicate, sometimes the analysis of literary texts could explain much more about the social and economic situation of a time than many useless statistics, based on erroneous or partial theories.

After obtaining his doctoral title, Otto Neurath returned to Vienna where he participated, between 1905 and 1906, in the seminar in economics held by Eugen von Böhm-Bawerk. The seminar is justly famous, given the participation, next to Neurath, of Otto Bauer, Rudolf Hilferding, Emil Lederer, Joseph Schumpeter and Ludwig von Mises (Hagemann, 2015). The seminar concentrated on the theory of value and the criticism of Marx, but the liberal direction of Böhm-Bawerk granted participants the freedom to express their ideas and theories, so that often harsh and heated debates erupted. Von Mises, in his memoirs, recalled Neurath's intent on defending with fanaticism theses devoid, in von Mises' view, of any sense.[31] That Neurath's intended reconstruction plan for economics was unheard of and innovative can easily be deduced from such vehement judgment.

Given that no further details have been preserved on Neurath's participation in Vienna's seminar, how much of his renovating scheme derived from forgotten theories, how much from existing concepts and statements, and how much from the empirical observation of reality, must be deduced from his later writings on economics, up to 1917.

In 1911, Otto Neurath published on the *Zeitschrift für Volkswirtschaft, Sozialpolitik und Verwaltung* an article on *Nationalökonomie und Wertlehre, eine systematische Untersuchung*. The essay was his answer to the lively debate on the theory of value he had witnessed at Böhm-Bawerk's seminar (Neurath, O., 1911). Von Mises' disconcert is understandable, reading a text in which the problem is confronted, never issuing once the term "capital," while chastising the excessive use of price theory and the widespread belief in the efficiency of the market economy. Outside Neurath's vision of science and scientific endeavor, his fellow seamen could not easily understand his renovation plan. In fact, the essay represents a perfect exercise of Neurath's methodology, comprising a holistic effort to include the greatest possible number of past and present theories while at the same time deepening the hermeneutical value of concepts. Vienna's systematists (Neurath, O., 1913b, p. 456) could surely not approve.

The first step in Neurath's plan consisted in seeking a definition of the economic science that nullified the debate on the theory of value, a definition that, at the same time, could salvage and include both equilibrium theory and Marxian economics. As the main girder sustaining the careen of the rebuilt ship, Neurath chose wealth, retrieving a piece of wood that had been drifting in the sea of science for a long time. He so affirmed: "We meet an old tradition selecting wealth as the object of political economy" (Neurath, O., 1911, p. 53). Such tradition, born out of Aristotle's *Nicomachean Ethics*, considered economics as the science that aimed at maximizing social wealth and had been relevant up to Adam Smith, falling into discredit only with the rise of liberalism. Its historical development can be followed through the reader of economic texts, compiled in 1910 by Otto Neurath and his wife Anne Schapire for his courses at the *Neuer Wiener Handelsakademie* (Neurath, O. and Schapire-Neurath, 1910).

A definition of wealth exactly like his own, though, Neurath found only in Isaak Iselin (2011),[32] whose works he undoubtedly had encountered while attending the seminar of political economy at the University of Bern. In 1784, Iselin, a Swiss illuminist, affirmed that the highest law in economics should be to

> do everything possible so that the greatest quantity of earth's and culture's products should be made available to the enjoyment of the greatest possible number of men, while avoiding everything that could cause a diminution of the quantity of goods or enjoyments.
>
> (Neurath, O., 1911, pp. 82–84)

In his holistic intent of using as many theories and concepts as possible, determined not to create perilous leakages by throwing away precious timbers, Neurath intended to unite Smith's definition of wealth (*Volkswohlstand* – welfare of people – as translated in German in Neurath's anthology; Neurath, O. and Schapire-Neurath, 1910, vol. 1, pp. 125–127) as wealth of the nation with individual well-being. In doing so, he again retrieved a piece of drifting wood, adapting it to a new use. He defined the individual basis of wealth as *Lebenstimmung* (life mood[33]), a balance of pleasure and pain of Epicurean origin.[34] Such *Lebenstimmung* was directly linked with all kinds of human experiences, "eating, drinking, reading, perceptions of art, religious sights, moral reflections, love, hate, brave and cowardly behavior" (Neurath, O., 1917a, p. 485). Substituting *Lebenstimmung* to utility, Neurath denied that wealth had a particular role in the construction of the world or that men acted only in consideration of utilitarian motives, rationally pursuing their happiness and pleasure.[35] Neurath's man operated according to rationality, but also following primary driving forces and traditional behavior.

> If someone doesn't want to act overvaluing his own wisdom or the wisdom of others he will be obliged, in many cases, to resort to tradition or to his own impulses to decide his course of action, without being able to correctly evaluate the consequences of it, if not even feeling constrained to appeal to fate.
> (Neurath, O., 1913b, p. 441)

Neurath's felicitology (Neurath, O., 1917a, p. 487) did not presume a *Homo felix*, a simplistic reduction of the modern man as was *Homo oeconomicus*,[36] and so was not limited to that "little island on the sea of unknown" (Neurath, O., 1913b, p. 441) that represented the world of rationality. Neurath preserved to men the possibility to err also in theory. He ventured to say:

> Rightly many empiricist economists reproach theorists for eliminating mistakes and errors from their conceptions. This is even more preoccupying considering that in the thought of many economists it is exactly the error, the incapacity to evaluate the consequences of single actions, which characterizes our social order and particularly the market, causing its most typical damages.
> (Neurath, O., 1911, p. 63)

Neurath maintained a theory of value based on utility as an analytical instrument, but through his more precise definition of utility as *Lebenstimmung* granted it a much greater hermeneutical value. This way he also aimed at reconciling "men of action," usually diffident toward economics, to the discipline, offering an alternative to theories based on rational behavior that appeared to statesmen limited and diverting, incapable of grasping the problems of reality (Neurath, O., 1917b, p. 8).

Having increased the hermeneutical validity of his individual theory of happiness, though, did not particularly help Neurath out of all problems involved in the further necessity to measure and compare individual *Lebenstimmungen* or even sum them up to groups' or nations' wealth: in this sense he was well aware of all difficulties later encountered by welfare economics. In the essay on "Die Kriegswirtschaftsrechnung und ihre Grenzen," published in 1917 in *Weltwirtschaftliches Archiv* (Neurath, O., 1917b), he clearly faced the impossibility of measuring individual sensations, but also of comparing them among different persons and groups.[37] The comparison of different *Lebenstimmungen* for a precise set of people proved feasible only assuming the existence of a political leader always driven by the consideration of general welfare. From such a statesman,

> in reality it is expected that in such indecisive cases as the ones described, he so vividly puts himself in the shoes of all persons involved, at the same time, that he can compare the resulting sensation with the one resulting from another state of happiness of the same group.
> (Neurath, O., 1917b, p. 4)

A benevolent dictator would thus be needed to act upon the evaluation of different *Lebenstimmungen* among his people.

Alternatively, a measurable proxy could substitute the comparison of individual or group happiness. "Given that the statistical elaboration of sensations is impeded by great difficulties, it is necessary to substitute it with the statistic of sensations' causes" (Neurath, O., 1913b, p. 458). Nonetheless, it was practically impossible to determine single causes of sensations either. The best course would thus be to analyze entire sets of causes of *Lebenstimmungen*, such as good air, a clean environment, a good state administration, the availability of food, housing and education, etc. (p. 459). In 1917, to these stimuli of sensations, Neurath added also the capacity of people to perceive pleasure and pain (Neurath, O., 1917b, p. 6), a set of variables that changed in time and space. Similarities between Neurath's theory and recent contributions of Amartya Sen to welfare economics,[38] as well as with statistical instruments such as the human development index, are unmistakable and should at least be mentioned.

Neurath further developed his theory, defining as *Lebenslagen* those life conditions that influenced individual happiness. Life conditions included primarily goods and services available for consumption and, consequently, the productive forces and impediments of a country, but also "its state organization, the diffusion of innovative capability, the organizational know-how, stupidity and laziness and so forth" (Neurath, O., 1917b, p. 8). All available data on those quantities should have been collected in statistical tables as had already been done, under absolutist rule, by a class of clerks and civil servants of the likes of Wenzel Anton von Kaunitz-Rietberg (ibid.). Neurath, in his later statistical book *Modern Man in the Making*, published in 1939, realized this earlier intent and vividly represented statistics regarding *Lebenslagen* with Isotypes comparing the availability of food and drinks, raw materials and sources of power in the United States and Canada, Europe and the Soviet Union (Neurath, O., 1939, pp. 66–68). Out of these collected data, Neurath further construed silhouettes for many countries in the world, depicting the average length of life of female population, suicide rates, literacy and the possession of radio sets. The resulting Isotype allowed an intuitive comparison of the wealth, in Neurath's definition, of the respective nations. Compared, for example, with simple data on income per capita, the suicide rate cast a shadow on the otherwise brilliant performance of the US and Great Britain, while giving merit to countries traditionally considered poor, such as India, Spain and Italy.

All the cited magnitudes regarded in-kind measures, not monetary measures. Neurath was convinced that useful statistical data had to refer to quantities and not prices, and that the quoted indexes could better represent *Lebenslagen* than monetary income. The difference between the two types of measures of wealth, in-kind and monetary, had something to do with economic theories, but also with their originating *Weltanschauungen*. In-kind calculations had been typical of absolutism's tradition of universal statistics and economic planning, while income statistics and price indexes had spread along with liberalism during the nineteenth century.[39] Both represented sources of information useful to measure happiness, but the first, in Neurath's opinion, could be collected and evaluated also in absence of a market economy and so had a wider use along with a wider hermeneutical value.

At the beginning of time, Neurath considered *Lebenslagen* as fully determined by the natural and physical conditions of the world, in form of fields, minerals, forests, water supply, etc. He consequently defined such a situation of the world at a precise time as *Lebensboden* (life base) (Neurath, O., 1917a, p. 487). With the evolution of society, though, an order of society had emerged that could counter the effect that such primary conditions had on *Lebenslagen*: the *Lebensordnung*. This slow emergence of a *Gesellschaft* out of the originary *Gemeinschaft* had also led to the appearance of theories studying the dependence of individual sensations (pleasure and pain) from the newly established institutions (Neurath, O., 1913b, p. 442). A calculation of happiness had arisen, as can be found in Aristippus and Epicurus, that through mercantilism had developed all the way down to modern economics. On this point, Neurath particularly quoted James Steuart, also including excerpts of his *An Inquiry into the Principles of Political Oeconomy* in his anthology of economic thought (Neurath, O. and Schapire-Neurath, 1910, pp. 96–124). Steuart had defined the task of the political leader to conceive many possible organizations of the state and then select the one that suited best his people. Steuart had moreover underlined the necessity to link the new organization to existing traditions and base it on the fact that people would choose the common good in their own interest (Neurath, O., 1913b, p. 443). Neurath's own definition of the economy derived from this tradition of thought.

Denominations were, as always in Neurath, full of significance: *Lebensboden* is the base of life, *Lebenslage* is the condition of life, and *Lebensordnung* is the order of life. *Lebensboden* is historically determined, while *Lebensordnung*, as the institutional construction of the *Weltanschauung*, is determined by men and given only in a delimited time-span. Comparing the *Lebenstimmung* caused by a *Lebensboden* with the *Lebenstimmung* of another, gave as a result a judgment of relative happiness. Given the same *Lebensboden* to start with, instead, comparing the *Lebenstimmungen* related to diverse *Lebensordnungen* resulted in a judgment of relative economy (Neurath, O., 1917a, p. 490).

The renewed use of old concepts on the part of Neurath led to a definition of economies as the collected set of actions, prescriptions and attitudes – *Lebensordnungen* – having in any way influence on the happiness/wealth of men.

In his words: "The scientific study of these economies, the Lebensordnungen determining the Lebenstimmungen, will be named economic theory, so to remain sufficiently near the linguistic habit to make it unnecessary to look for a new denomination."[40]

Neurath's spasmodic attention toward the lexical value of his definitions in the reconstruction of economic theory is apparent. Far away from any polemic or ideological intent, this attention for the language of economics stemmed from the influence of Friedrich Nietzsche and French linguistics, transmitted via Hofmannsthal (Hofmannsthal, 2007) to the German-speaking world. As Mach had unveiled the historicity and cultural dependence of natural laws and scientific paradigms, so Anatole France had uncovered the primitive and sensual origin of Europe's metaphysical language, reducing most of its philosophical reflection to white mythology (France, 1894). Neurath, himself, brought into economics this rejection of metaphysical jargon that had slowly matured during the second half of the nineteenth century. Famous, or perhaps infamous, in contemporaries' remembrance, was Neurath's loud interjection "Metaphysics!" cried out during the discussions on Wittgenstein's *Tractatus*, every time someone spoke out words with no empirical correspondence (Vaccaro, 2005, p. 53). The word "capital" was one of the first victims of Neurath's empiricist purge.

This effort of linguistic purification, culminating in the later attempt to create a universal scientific jargon, began during Neurath's university studies when he had analyzed Smith's *Wealth of Nations* from a linguistic point of view.[41] In this case, also, economics proved to be the sector in which Neurath first experimented what he later systematized in his methodological approach to science in general. Between his writings of 1911 and 1917, in effect, the terminological evolution clearly reflected the intent to create an empiricist language for economics. As Anatole France put it: "Metaphysically, either the world is the whole thing, or it is nothing"[42] (France, 1894). Empiricism as methodology needed an empiricist vocabulary.

Hence, Neurath in 1917: "I did not create all these concepts as an artificial intellectual game, but following the stringent necessity to adequately analyse every day's experiences and in particular important present events through the observation of their singular components" (Neurath, O., 1917a, pp. 516–517). Undoubtedly Neurath's was an empiricist research program, but even in a linguistics redefinition process the tool kit could not be completely replenished with new instruments.

> The reconstruction of the conceptual and linguistic framework here attempted must be limited to the essential. It is futile trying to create an entire new conceptual world with the related denominations. In fields of research as ours, unclearly defined, it is much too easy to end up in the wrong direction by adapting names and concepts, with terrible results. Every change imposed to an important concept, alters the entire conceptual structure, causing a chain reaction of redenomination.
>
> (Neurath, O., 1917a, pp. 516–517)

Neurath shows here that he had a very clear view of the relative value of words' significance, particularly in science. "We must try to capture the world in a net of concepts and thoughts with multiple connections. Object of the whole science is to structure the net's connections so that every part of it can be used in a similar way." Therefore, *"from the old conceptual framework we inherited we won't be able to escape at once.* Its reconstruction always happens with the aid of the concepts of the past" (ibid.).

As seen, Neurath exactly followed this research program and, uniting tradition and innovation in his definition of economics, extended the hermeneutic capacity of the science, at the same time recovering long lost knowledge. Neurath's economics, depending on the group of people whose happiness/wealth was the object of study, could include families' economy, political economy and even cosmopolitan economy, all subdivisions that, taken from Aristotle to Friedrich List, were now granted validity in new fields. Not only past economies, but also present and future *Lebensordnungen* possessed the right to be studied and classified as to their effects on people's sensations. Economics thus became a comparative science based on empirical data statistically collected, but consisting of an infinite number of models, many of which bore no relation whatsoever to reality.

In this sense, Neurath excluded any kind of ethical prejudice from restricting economic analysis. In his view, acquiring methods such as war and smuggling should have been studied exactly as market exchange and production, being evaluated, by economists, only in their effect on people's *Lebenstimmungen*.[43] Economic analysis should also comprehend planned and war economies.

In the early years of his scientific activity, Neurath gave particular attention to war economics as the study of all changes in the *Lebensordnung* brought about by war and their effects on *Lebenstimmungen*. Far away from any interventionist stance, Neurath considered the Balkan wars and WWI as extraordinary occasions to gather information (Neurath, O., 1913b, p. 23) about the emerging of barter trade, even at international level (Neurath, O., 1918b), the centralized administration of production, the controlled distribution of consumption goods and the destabilizing or even vanishing of financial systems. His extraordinary efforts in this field were acknowledged not only with a Carnegie Endowment for International Peace and an official commendation from the Austrian government, but also with the appointment as director of the Museum of War Economy in Leipzig in 1916 (Cartwright et al., 2008, pp. 19–21).

Above all, studying a war economy in its development meant, for Neurath, the possibility to demonstrate that a certain grade of administrative control over the economy, based on a general system of in-kind calculations, could prevent what he considered the worst trait of a *Lebensordnung* based on the market economy: economic crises.

Neurath had identified many cases under which, in a market economy, the results of exchange were sub-optimal. For example when consumers had to choose among two identical products with identical prices, or when limited rationality claimed the scene as with differentials in stock prices (Neurath, O., 1917a).

The major distortion to an economy, in terms of *Lebenstimmungen*, though, was consequent to the widespread adoption throughout the market economy of a calculation based on prices. Such calculations, along with the institution of credit, constrained the production to maximize profits, so causing recurrent crises of overproduction. Were the economy to be ruled by the maximization of productivity instead of profitability, crises, for Neurath, would no longer plague the world. An Isotype in particular, from his volume of 1939, bears testimony of such stance (Neurath, O., 1939, p. 87). The image illustrates a statistic on coal production in the United States between 1914 and 1936, underlining how in 1917, a year of war, production steadily remained at its maximum capacity, showing no sign of seasonal or cyclical fluctuation.

To the naive arguments of pacifists, then, Neurath countered that the origin of present wars, wars between social classes like wars between nations, had to be found in the lack of economic efficiency of the present *Lebensordnung*. He wrote:

> The present underemployment of existing forces, that is typical of our *Ordnung*, incites to war: it is necessary, for example, to defend oneself from foreign wares and foreign laborers or oblige others to buy our wares or accept our workers, and all of this because it is not spontaneous to enter in cooperative relations between states; furthermore it is easy to alleviate the costs of war thanks to reparations; and lastly because at times war frees productive forces that would otherwise be bound. The uneconomic construction of our *Lebensordnung* is the cause why at present war causes lesser evils than would be the case in a more economical *Lebensordnung*.
>
> (Neurath, O., 1913b, p. 500)

To eliminate war, humanity had only two alternatives. The first would have been to render it uneconomical, by constituting coalitions possessing the same amount of productive forces. Given this balance of power, such coalitions would only stand to lose from starting a conflict (Neurath, O., 1913b, pp. 465–466). As to this end, in 1939 Neurath represented in a couple of Isotypes the relative economic power between three different coalitions in a prospective world war (Neurath, O., 1939, pp. 84–85). Incidentally, it might be noted that results were clearly negative for the coalition headed by Germany in all the possible alliances.

A second opportunity to foster peace, obviously, would have been to abandon the present inefficient *Lebensordnung* for a more effective one. To decide, though, which *Lebensordnung* to implement in reality was not the task of an economist but of democratic decision-making. After abandoning theoretical economics in the wake of the disastrous experience in Munich's *Räterepublik*, Neurath continued to collect statistical data and transform it into easily understandable Isotypes, in order to enable the largest possible section of the population to decide actively and scientifically about their future.

4 Conclusions

The ship of science, in Neurath's metaphor, has no captain. Seafarers continuously create plans for its renewal but then must win supporters to realize them. Scientific progress is thus the result of a sociological process that involves not only individuals and their ideas but also scientific communities, schools of thought and institutions of education such as universities and schools. It is from the interaction among these groups that new ideas emerge and a clear route is set for the ship. Surely, the "spreading of mud" is not so easy any more, but there is no guarantee that the plan chosen will prove to be better in respect to the past or the present of a discipline.

Otto Neurath's economic theory could not find enough support to become the new paradigm, nor did his epistemology become the methodological tool for twentieth-century research. His concepts, linguistically refined and hermeneutically profound, have remained vastly ignored, drifting wood abandoned to the sea. Many aspects of his theory, though, anticipated what would become, in the course of the century, common tools for economists. For example, his continued research for an objective measure of individual and social wealth, made out of non-monetary measures; his insistence on a precise statistical collection of macroeconomic data at country level; his perseverance in guiding research towards economic organizations different from the market; the hints he scattered about his writings, on the existence of market failures, of areas of limited rationality, of the perverse effects of self-fulfilling prophecies. Many more could be added.

The richness of Neurath's legacy in the field of economics is undeniable. It is his methodological attitude, though, that represents today his most fruitful bequest, a timber worth fishing out of the sea. Neurath's spasmodic attention to linguistics, for example, hints at manifold research fields for historians of economic thought. Many concepts in economics changed their significance in time, acquired symbolic or metaphysical content, lost empirical relevance, and were used for political and propagandistic purposes. Studying such developments in time could bear many fruits. The diffusion of economic thought, then, could be followed by researching the frequency of certain words and concepts in journals, newspapers and literary works; across national borders, the same could be done watching attentively for translations of economic texts. Science being a complex net of interdependent significances, studying how just the changing of one knot altered the entire complex, through all subsequent variations of the interrelated concepts, could also be significant.

The use Neurath made of the historical past in reinventing the discipline is another inheritance that economists and historians of economic thought could rediscover with profit. Particularly in times of heavy storms, when uncertainty befalls economics as to its object, its methodology and its hermeneutical value, looking back in search of useful material to repair the ship could avoid perilous leakages and possible shipwreck. History of economic thought would thus no longer be a mere "chronological sequence of discoveries and authors' biographies"

(Neurath, O., 1915, p. 371), nor would it only "try to clarify the psychology of a researcher" (ibid.) or "logically subdivide theories to obtain from their structure the development possibilities subsequently realized by this or that scholar" (ibid.). It would instead primarily aim, as Neurath intended, to unveil the theoretical structure of *Lebensordnungen*, the *Weltanschauungen* that had succeeded in time. In this sense, studying the ship's own supporting structure in its historical changes and retracing the plans that in time had guided its unceasing renovation effort, rediscovering which ones succeeded, which ones failed and why, retrieving all useful drifting wood, would not be a mere academic exercise but a necessary step to establish the future structure of economics as a science and even the form of the economic organization of the world in general.

The lesson of Otto Neurath has, in conclusion, not lost every significance to today's researchers, also, and particularly, in the field of economics, and merits a careful reappraisal. His cautious and precise use of language, his appreciation of history along with theoretical logic, his preference for an inclusive science in contraposition to exclusive systems should undoubtedly find their place in the instrument case of economists who wish to build the future of the discipline.

Notes

1 All translations in the text, if not otherwise attributed, are by the author.
2 For a complete biography of Otto Neurath, see Sandner (2014), Vaccaro (2005) and Cartwright *et al.* (2008).
3 Francesco Fistetti remarks on the striking similarities between Neurath's stance and Nietzsche's position expressed in *The Gay Science*, *Human, All Too Human* and *Daybreak* (Fistetti, 1985, p. 118).
4 "I shall therefore try to describe how I myself, as a logical empiricist, developed my attitude toward the sciences and their unity. Many of us, beside myself, have been brought up in a Machian tradition, e.g., Franck, Hahn, von Mises. Because of this, we tried to pass from chemistry to biology, from mechanics to sociology without altering the language applied to them. We, as many others all over the world, were also influenced by scientists such as Poincarè, Duhem, Abel Rey, William James, Bertrand Russell, and I, in particular, by Gregorius Itelson. I think that Poincarè and Duhem made me realize that wherever one hypothesis can be elaborated, it is possible to elaborate any number (cf. my 'Prinzipielles zur Geschichte der Optik', *Archiv für Geschichte der Naturwissenschaften*, 1915)" (Neurath, O., 1946, p. 497).
5 On Itelson and his influence on Neurath, see Freudenthal and Karachentsev (2011).
6 Neurath could not be clearer: "We have no possibility of discussing the 'truth' of anything, since there is no imagined arbitrator in the chair. Therefore I suggested that we drop the term 'truth' with the whole of its large family. Everything will then be based on the comparison of statements with protocol statements, leaving open the many ways in which such a comparison can be made. It is essential that all statements should be 'connectible', as von Mises happily puts it" (Neurath, O., 1946, p. 501). Neurath excluded the existence of an absolute truth. Truth was a concept that in time had assumed different metaphysical connotations and semantic significances. See Fistetti (1985, p. 132).
7 On Neurath's stance in the *Methodenstreit* involving, at the beginning of the century, Weber, Menger and Meyer see Cartwright *et al.* (2008, pp. 213–224).

8 Neurath published this article (Neurath, O., 1932) as part of the controversy with Rudolf Carnap (Carnap, 1932a) that originated the famous debate on protocols (Carnap, 1932b). While Carnap supported an empiricist position, Neurath considered even protocols to be subject to revision. See Uebel (1993, 2009).
9 Francesco Fistetti reasonably defines Neurath as the "Nietzsche of the Vienna Circle" (Fistetti, 1985, p. 127).
10 On the harsh criticism expressed by Neurath toward the use made of Plato's *Republic* on part of supporters of Nazism, see Soulez (1999).
11 This view can also be found in Ernst Mach (1992, pp. 448–449).
12 The stance of Neurath in the debate on protocols has been the object or recent reappraisal with contrasting results (Uebel, 1993, 2007, 2009; Nottelmann, 2006).
13 Neurath remembered: "My father, an economist, used to ask: 'What would happen if someone were to force scientists to follow up consistently all the declarations they make. Fortunately', he would add, 'they compare their deductions again and again with their experiential material.' So it is; our scientific practice is based on local systematizations only, not on overstraining the bow of deduction [. . .]. I thought it in accord with the historically given situation to acknowledge these 'localized' contradictions, and to think of an 'encyclopedia as a model' (cf. my 'L'Encyclopédie comme "modèle",' Octobre, 1936, Revue de Synthèse) as intentionally opposed to the 'system as a model'. Let me call this approach 'encyclopedism'" (Neurath, O., 1946, p. 498). The article quoted refers to Neurath, O. (1936).
14 On the influence of Wilhelm Neurath on the ideas of his son, see Uebel (1995).
15 On the origin of the seafarers' metaphor, see Cartwright *et al.* (2008, pp. 89–95).
16 On the extensive use that Quine made of Neurath's metaphor, see Rabossi (2003).
17 "Wie Schiffer sind wir, die auf offenem Meer ihr Schiff umbauen müssen, ohne je von unten auf frisch anfangen zu können. Wo ein Balken weggenommen wird, muss gleich ein neuer an die Stelle kommen, und dabei wird das übrige Schiff als Stützte verwendet. So kann das Schiff mit Hilfe der alten Balken und angetriebenen Holzstücke vollständig neu gestaltet werden – aber nur durch allmählichen Umbau" (Neurath, O., 1981b, p. 184).
18 "Stellen wir uns Seefahrer vor, die auf hoher See die Form ihres schwerfälligen Schiffes von einer mehr runden zu einer mehr fischähnlichen verändern wollen. Neben dem Holz des alten Baus verwenden sie Treibholz, um Skelett und Rumpf ihres Schiffes neu zu gestalten. Aber sie können das Schiff nicht ins Dock bringen, um ganz von vorne zu beginnen. Während sie arbeiten, bleiben sie auf dem alten Bau und trotzen wilden Stürmen und donnernden Wogen. Beim Umbau des Schiffes tragen sie Sorge dass kein gefährliches Leck auftritt. Ein neues Schiff erwächst aus dem alten, Schritt für Schritt, und während sie noch bauen, mögen die Seefahrer bereits an den neuen Bau denken, und sie werden nicht immer einer Meinung sein. Die ganze Sache wird in einer Weise vorangehen, die wir heutzutage nicht einmal erahnen können. Das ist unser Schicksal" (Neurath, O., 1981d, p. 978).
19 "Wir sind wie Seefahrer, die auf offenem Meere sich genötigt sehen, mit Balken, die sie mitführen, oder die herantreiben, ihr Schiff völlig umzugestalten, indem sie Balken für Balken ersetzen und die Form des Ganzen ändern. Da sie nicht landen können, wird es ihnen nie möglich sein, das schiff ganz zu beseitigen, um es neu zu bauen. Das neue schiff geht durch ununterbrochene Umgestaltung aus dem alten hervor" (Neurath, O., 1913b, p. 457).
20 As suggestive as the metaphor of the ship, is Neurath's metaphor of craftsmen: "Imagine craftsmen who are building a settlement, with a chest of drawers full of instruments,

94 *Monika Poettinger*

only part of which are well arranged and the usage of which is only partly known by them; imagine that, from behind, new instruments are continually put in the drawers, that some instruments are modified by unknown people, and that the craftsmen learn to use some of the old instruments in a way hitherto unknown, and now imagine further that the plans of our craftsmen dealing with the building of the settlement are changing too. This resembles to some extent the situation of our scientists" (Neurath, O., 1983, p. 217).

21 He wrote: "Scientific progress in economics is achieved when systems of empirical observations build abstractions and from these abstractions, then, new combinations are derived, the reality or feasibility of which is the object of study [. . .]. In our research, so, only the elements and the relations among elements are strictly empirical, the complex organizations that can be derived from them, instead, are only partially to be met in reality" (Neurath, O., 1911, p. 82).

22 On Neurath's theory of historiography and his earliest writings in economic history, see Poettinger (2012, pp. 12–30).

23 Weber's testimony has not been preserved in official archives, but has been reconstructed from articles published by the *Münchner Neuesten Nachrichten* (Baier, 1988).

24 Only some obituaries give clues on the life and works of Wilhelm Neurath (Schullen, 1902; Oncken, 1903). Curiously, works of Wilhelm Neurath were reviewed by the Italian *Rivista Internazionale di Scienze Sociali e Discipline Ausiliarie* (Böhmert, 1902; Rivista Internazionale di Scienze Sociali e Discipline Ausiliarie, 1902).

25 A recent study on the intellectual relationship between father and son is Uebel (1995).

26 For a recent appraisal, see Köster (2011).

27 On Neurath's definition of holism, in derivation from Quine, see Sebestik (2011, pp. 41–57).

28 On the influence that participating in the debate had on Neurath's later idea of the unity of science, see Cartwright *et al.* (2008, p. 167). A critical appraisal of the *Methodenstreit*, instead, is to be found in Hands (2001, pp. 72–94).

29 On Eduard Meyer and his work, see Demandt (1990) and Bertolini (1991).

30 On this debate, see Kurz and Salvadori (1997, pp. 384–385).

31 "Especially disruptive was the nonsense that Otto Neurath asserted with fanatical force" (Mises, 2009, p. 32). On this see also Kurz (1995, p. 13).

32 On this renowned Swiss illuminist, see Follmann (2001).

33 This is the English translation of *Lebensstimmung* to be found in Cartwright *et al.* (2008, p. 30).

34 On the relation of economics with Epicurean philosophy, see Neurath, O. (1928b).

35 "Damit daß man das Glück zum Gegenstande besonderer Untersuchungen macht, soll weder zum Ausdruck gebracht werden, daß die Menschen ausschließlich im Hinblick auf das Glück handeln, noch auch, daß sie dies tun sollen, es soll damit auch nicht zum Ausdruck gebracht werden, daß das Glück im Weltgebäude eine besonders wichtige Rolle spielt" (Neurath O., 1917a, p. 488).

36 On the critic of Neurath to the concept of *Homo oeconomicus* particularly in the version of von Wieser, see Neurath O. (1911, p. 64, and 1981c, p. 32).

37 An even lenghtier discussion of the matter is to be found in Neurath, O. (1917a, pp. 504–511).

38 On similarities between Neurath and Sen, see Leßmann (2007).

39 "Die Nationalökonomen interessierten sich seit jeher dafür, wie Menschen arm oder reich werden. Soweit dies durch Bebauung der Felder, durch Betrieb von Fabriken geschehen konnte, waren es technische Fragen, aber bald merkte man, daß das Vertragssystem, das System der Steuern und Zölle von entscheidender Bedeutung

sei, die Organisationssysteme wurden so Gegenstand der Untersuchung. Was die klassische Schule der Volkswirtschaftslehre untersuchte, war eine einzelne Form solcher Organisationssysteme, das der freien Konkurrenz; sie hat dasselbe ebenso angepriesen wie die Merkantilisten das ihrige. Bei der Untersuchung dieses Systems als Ursache der Volksvermehrung mußte man dessen Struktur im einzelnen prüfen. Dabei kam man auf Probleme, die nichts mehr direkt mit dem Reichtum zu tun hatten, man beobachtete z.B. das Fallen und Steigen der Preise ganz unabhängig davon, ob damit eine Vermehrung oder eine Verringerung des Reichtums verbunden sei. Da hier, sowie bei Ernteerträgen usw., meßbare Größen auftauchten, die leicht eindeutig feststellbar waren, wurde die Preislehre bald eine besonders eifrig betriebene Doktrin. Die Erwägung, ob das untersuchte Organisationssystem den Reichtum fördere oder nicht, wurde stark zurückgedrängt oder überhaupt nicht mehr behandelt. Zum Teil hing das mit der Anschauung zusammen, daß die Geldrechnung die Reichtumsverhältnisse ohnehin richtig widerspiegele" (Neurath, O., 1981c, p. 30).

40 "Die wissenschaftliche Behandlung der Wirtschaften, das ist der Lebensordnungen als Bedienungen von Lebensstimmungen soll Wirtschaftslehre heißen, wodurch wir soweit mit den Sprachgebrauch im Einklang bleiben, daß eine neue Namenbildung nicht erforderlich ist" (Neurath, O., 1917a, p. 492).

41 "Particularly I was busy with reading Adam Smith's *The Wealth of Nations* along the lines of an analysis of language. I found out that such butchering criticism lacks constructive power and that a long self-education has to be the first step. I altered successively my own terms in all my articles and books in accordance with my increasing Index by eliminating 'emotional', 'concealing' and 'confusing' terms" (Neurath, O., 1983, p. 217).

42 "Métaphysiquement, ou le mot est toute la chose, ou il ne sait rien de la chose."

43 "That pillage is prohibited by law, should not impede economists from studying it. Why should the consequences of trade and domestic manufacture be worthy to be analyzed, while the effects of smuggling are ignored? In consequence of such considerations war has been vastly ignored by economists as a form of acquisition" (Neurath, O., 1917a, p. 493).

References

Baier, H. (ed.) (1988): *Max Weber Gesamtausgabe*. Tubingen: Mohr.
Bertolini, F. (1991): Eduard Meyer: uno storico universale. *Quaderni di Storia*, vol. 34, no. 1, pp. 165–182.
Böhmert, V. (1902): Der Arbeiterfreund. Anno XL, Der österreichische Volkswirt Wilhelm Neurath und seine neue Lehre über die Lösung socialer Probleme. (L'economista austriaco Guglielmo Neurath e la sua nuova dottrina intorno alla soluzione dei problemi sociali). *Rivista Internazionale di Scienze Sociali e Discipline Ausiliarie*, vol. 29, no. 114, pp. 267–269.
Carnap, R. (1932a): Die physikalische Sprache als Universalsprache der Wissenschaft. *Erkenntnis*, n. 2, pp. 432–465.
Carnap, R. (1932b): Über Protokollsätze. *Erkenntnis*, vol. 3, no. 1, pp. 215–228.
Cartwright, N., Cat, J., Fleck, L. and Uebel, T. E. (2008): *Otto Neurath: Philosophy Between Science and Politics*. Cambridge: Cambridge University Press.
Cicero, M. T. (1994): *De officiis*, ed. by M. Winterbottom. Oxford, New York: Clarendoniano.
Demandt, A. (ed.) (1990): *Eduard Meyer. Leben und Leistung eines Universalhistorikers*, Leiden, New York: Brill.

Dilthey, W. (1997): Abgrenzung der Geisteswissenschaften von den Naturwissenschaften. In: V. Spierling (ed.), *Die Philosophie des 20. Jahrhunderts: ein Lesebuch*. Munich: Piper, pp. 33–40.

Droysen, J. G. (1977): Grundrisse der Historik. In: *Historik*. Stuttgart, Bad Cannstatt: Frommann Holzboog.

Duhem, P. M. M. (1906): *La théorie physique: son objet, et sa structure*. Paris: Chevalier et Riviere.

Fistetti, F. (1985): *Neurath contro Popper. Otto Neurath riscoperto*. Bari: Dedalo.

Follmann, S.-U. (2001): *Gesellschaftsbild, Bildung und Geschlechterordnung bei Isaak Iselin in der Spätaufklärung*. Münster: LIT.

France, A. (1894): *A Monsieur Horace de Landau, Ariste et Polyphile ou le Langage Métaphysique*. In: *Le Jardin d'Épicure*. Paris: Calmann-Lévy.

Freudenthal, G. and Karachentsev, T. (2011): G. Itelson: A Socratic Philosopher. In: J. Symons, O. Pombo and J. M. Torres (eds.), *Otto Neurath and the Unity of Science*. Dordrecht: Springer, pp. 109–128.

Hagemann, H. (2015): Capitalist Development, Innovations, Business Cycles and Unemployment: Joseph Alois Schumpeter and Emil Hans Lederer. *Journal of Evolutionary Economics*, vol. 25, no. 1, pp. 117–131.

Haller, R. (1985): Prefazione. In: F. Fistetti, *Neurath contro Popper. Otto Neurath riscoperto*. Bari: Dedalo, pp. 7–13.

Haller, R. and Höfer, U. (eds.) (1998): *Otto Neurath. Gesammelte ökonomische, soziologische und sozialpolitische Schriften*. Wien: Hölder, Pichler, Tempsky.

Hands, D. W. (2001): *Reflection Without Rules: Economic Methodology and Contemporary Science Theory*. Cambridge: Cambridge University Press.

Hofmannsthal, H. (2007): *Lettera di Lord Chandos*. Milan: Mimesis.

Iselin, I. (2011): *Filosofische und Patriotische Träume Eines Menschenfreundes*. Charleston: BiblioBazaar.

Köster, R. (2011): *Die Wissenschaft der Außenseiter: Die Krise der Nationalökonomie in der Weimarer Republik*. Göttingen: Vandenhoeck und Ruprecht.

Kurz, H. D. (1995): Marginalism, Classicism and Socialism in German Speaking Countries 1871–1932. In: I. Steedman (ed.), *Socialism and Marginalism in Economics 1870–1930*. London: Routledge, pp. 7–86.

Kurz, H. D. and Salvadori, N. (1997): *Theory of Production: A Long-Period Analysis*. Cambridge: Cambridge University Press.

Leßmann, O. (2007): A Similar Line of Thought in Neurath and Sen: Interpersonal Comparability. In: E. Nemeth, S. W. Schmitz and T. E. Uebel (eds.), *Otto Neurath's Economics in Context*. Wien: Springer, pp. 119–125.

Mach, E. (1883): *Die Mechanik und ihre Entwickelung*. Leipzig: F. A. Brockhaus.

Mach, E. (1992): *Conoscenza ed errore*. Turin: Einaudi.

Magris, C. (1993): Grande Stile e Totalità. In: *Il ventesimo secolo*, Milan: Electa, pp. 219–236.

Mises, L. von (2009): *Memoirs*. Auburn: Ludwig von Mises Institute.

Neurath, M. and Cohen, R. S. (eds.) (1973): *Empiricism and Sociology*. Dordrecht: Springer.

Neurath, O. (1904): Geldzins im Altertum. *Plutus*, vol. 1, pp. 569–573.

Neurath, O. (1906a): *Zur Anschauung der Antike über Handel, Gewerbe und Landwirtschaft*. Inaugural-Dissertation zur Erlangung der Doktorwurde genehmigt von der Philosophischen Fakultät der Friedrich-Wilhelms-Universität zu Berlin. Jena: Gustav Fischer.

Neurath, O. (1906b): Zur Anschauung der Antike über Handel, Gewerbe und Landwirtschaft. *Jahrbücher für Nationalökonomie und Statistik*, vol. 32, no. 5, pp. 577–606.
Neurath, O. (1907): Zur Anschauung der Antike über Handel, Gewerbe und Landwirtschaft, *Jahrbücher für Nationalökonomie und Statistik*, vol. 34, no. 2, pp. 145–205.
Neurath, O. (1908): Die Entwickelung der antiken Wirtschaftsgeschichte. *Jahrbücher für Nationalökonomie und Statistik*, vol. 36, no. 4, pp. 502–510.
Neurath, O. (1909): *Antike Wirtschaftsgeschichte*. Teubner: Leipzig.
Neurath, O. (1911): Nationalökonomie und Wertlehre, eine systematische Untersuchung. *Zeitschrift für Volkswirtschaft, Sozialpolitik und Verwaltung*, vol. 20, pp. 52–114.
Neurath, O. (1913a): Die Verirrten des Cartesius und das Auxiliärmotiv (Zur Psychologie des Entschlusses). Vortrag gehalten am 27 Januar 1913 von Otto Neurath Wien. *Jahrbuch der Philosophischen Gesellschaft zu Wien*, 1913, pp. 43–60.
Neurath, O. (1913b): Probleme der Kriegswirtschaftslehre. *Zeitschrift für die gesamte Staatswirtschaft*, vol. 1, no. 3, pp. 433–501.
Neurath, O. (1915): Prinzipielles zur Geschichte der Optik. *Archiv für die Geschichte der Naturwissenschaften und der Technik*, vol. 5, no. 27, pp. 371–389.
Neurath, O. (1917a): Das Begriffsgebäude der Wirtschaftslehre und seine Grundlagen. *Zeitschrift für die gesamte Staatswissenschaft*, vol. 73, no. 4, pp. 484–520.
Neurath, O. (1917b): Die Kriegswirtschaftsrechnung und ihre Grenzen. *Weltwirtschaftliches Archiv*, vol. 10, no. 2, pp. 1–15.
Neurath, O. (1918a): *Antike Wirtschaftsgeschichte*, 2nd ed. Leipzig, Berlin: Teubner.
Neurath, O. (1918b): Grundsätzliches über den Kompensationsverkehr im internationalen Warenhandel. *Weltwirtschaftliches Archiv*, vol. 13, no. 2, pp. 23–35.
Neurath, O. (1928a): *Lebensgestaltung und Klassenkampf*. Berlin: Laub.
Neurath, O. (1928b): Marx und Epikur. *Der Freidenker*, vol. 32, no. 12.
Neurath, O. (1931a): Magie und Technik. *Erkenntnis*, no. 2, pp. 529–531.
Neurath, O. (1931b): *Empirische Soziologie*. Wien: Julius Springer.
Neurath, O. (1932): Protokollsätze. *Erkenntnis*, no. 3, pp. 204–214.
Neurath, O. (1936): L'Encyclopédie comme modèle. *Revue de Synthèse*, vol. 12, no. 2, pp. 187–201.
Neurath, O. (1939): *Modern Man in the Making*. London: Secker and Warburg.
Neurath, O. (1946): The Orchestration of the Sciences by the Encyclopedism of Logical Empiricism. *Philosophy and Phenomenological Society*, vol. 6, no. 4, pp. 496–508.
Neurath, O. (1968): Fondazione delle scienze sociali. In: *Sociologia e Neopositivismo*. Rome: Ubaldini.
Neurath, O. (1981a): Bürgerlicher Marxismus. In: R. Haller and H. Rutte (eds.), *Gesammelte philosophische und methodologische Schriften*. Wien: Hölder, Pichler, Tempsky, vol. 1, pp. 349–356.
Neurath, O. (1981b): Anti-Spengler. In: R. Haller and H. Rutte (eds.), *Gesammelte philosophische und methodologische Schriften*. Wien: Hölder, Pichler, Tempsky, vol. 1, pp. 139–196.
Neurath, O. (1981c): Zur Theorie der Sozialwissenschaften. In: R. Haller and H. Rutte (eds.), *Gesammelte philosophische und methodologische Schriften*. Wien: Hölder, Pichler, Tempsky, vol. 1, pp. 23–46.
Neurath, O. (1981d): Grundlagen der Sozialwissenschaften. In: R. Haller and H. Rutte (eds.), *Gesammelte philosophische und methodologische Schriften*. Wien: Hölder, Pichler, Tempsky, vol. 2, pp. 925–978.
Neurath, O. (1983): Universal Jargon and Terminology. In: R. Cohen and M. Neurath (eds.), *Otto Neurath Philosophical Papers 1913–1946*. Dordrecht: Springer, pp. 213–229.

Neurath, O. and Schapire-Neurath, A. (1910): *Lesebuch der Volkswirtschaftslehre*. Leipzig: Werner Klinkhardt.

Neurath, P. (1982): Otto Neurath und die Soziologie. In: R. Haller (ed.), *Schlick und Neurath. Ein Symposion*. Amsterdam: Rodopi, pp. 223–240.

Neurath, W. (1897): *Die Wirthschaftskrisen und das Cartellwesen*. Wien, Leipzig: Gloeckner.

Nietzsche, F. (2001): *The Gay Science*. Cambridge: Cambridge University Press.

Nottelmann, N. (2006): Otto Neurath on the Structure of Protocol Sentences; A New Approach to an Interpretative Puzzle. *Journal for General Philosophy of Science*, vol. 37, no. 1, pp. 165–186.

Oncken, A. (1903): Neurath als volkswirtschaftlicher Theoretiker. *Schweizerische Blätter für Wirtschafts- und Sozialpolitik*, vol. 11, pp. 617–27.

Poettinger, M. (2012): *Mercante e società: riflessioni di storia comparata*. Lugano: Casagrande.

Rabossi, E. (2003): Some Notes on Neurath's Ship and Quine's Sailors. *Principia*, vol. 7, no. 1–2, pp. 171–184.

Richardson, A. and Uebel, T. (eds.) (2007): *The Cambridge Companion to Logical Empiricism*. Cambridge: Cambridge University Press.

Rivista Internazionale di Scienze Sociali e Discipline Ausiliarie (1902): Gemeinverständliche Nationalökonomische Vorträge. Geschichtliche und letzte eigene Forschungen by Wilhelm Neurath. *Rivista Internazionale di Scienze Sociali e Discipline Ausiliarie*, vol. 30, no. 120, pp. 647–648.

Sandner, G. (2014): *Otto Neurath: Eine politische Biographie*. Wien: Paul Zsolnay.

Schullern zu Schrattenhofen, H. R. (1902): Wilhelm Neurath. *Jahrbücher für Nationalökonomie*, vol. 79, pp. 166–169.

Schumpeter, J. A. (1908): *Das Wesen und der Hauptinhalt der theoretischen Nationalökonomie*. Leipzig: Duncker und Humblot.

Sebestik, J. (1999): Vorwort. Der Wiener Kreis und die Geschichte-Erkenntnistheorie und Wissenschaftstheorie im Werk Otto Neuraths. In: E. Nemeth and R. Heinrich (eds.), *Otto Neurath: Rationalität, Planung, Vielfalt*. Wien: Oldenbourg, pp. 7–13.

Sebestik, J. (2011): Otto Neurath's Epistemology and Its Paradoxes. In: O. Pombo, J. Symons and J. M. Torres (eds.), *Otto Neurath and the Unity of Science*. Dordrecht: Springer, pp. 41–57.

Soulez, A. (1999): Does Understanding Mean Forgiveness? Otto Neurath and Plato's "Republic" 1944–45. In: E. Nemeth and R. Heinrich (eds.), *Otto Neurath: Rationalität, Planung, Vielfalt*. Wien: Oldenbourg, pp. 167–183.

Uebel, T. E. (1993): Neurath's Protocol Statements: A Naturalistic Theory of Data and Pragmatic Theory of Theory Acceptance. *Philosophy of Science*, vol. 60, no. 4, pp. 587–607.

Uebel, T. E. (1995): Otto Neurath's Idealist Inheritance: "The Social and Economic Thought of Wilhelm Neurath." *Synthese*, vol. 103, no. 1, pp. 87–121.

Uebel, T. E. (2004): Introduction: Neurath's Economics in Critical Context. In: T. E. Uebel and R. S. Cohen (eds.), *Otto Neurath Economic Writings: Selections, 1904–1945*. Dordrecht: Springer, pp. 1–108.

Uebel, T. E. (2007): Interpreting Neurath's Protocols. Reply to Nottelmann. *Journal for General Philosophy of Science*, vol. 38, no. 2, pp. 383–391.

Uebel, T. E. (2009): Neurath's Protocol Statements Revisited: Sketch of a Theory of Scientific Testimony. *Studies in History and Philosophy of Science*, vol. 40, no. 1, pp. 4–13.

Uebel, T. E. and Cohen, R. S. (eds.) (2006): *Otto Neurath. Economic Writings: Selections 1904–1945*. Dordrect: Springer.
Vaccaro, E. L. (2005): *Vite da naufraghi. Otto Neurath nel suo contesto*, Tesi di Dottorato in metodologia delle scienze sociali, ciclo XV, Università La Sapienza, Rome.
Weber, M. (2002): *Protestantesimo e spirito del capitalismo*. Turin: Edizioni di Comunità.
Weber, M. (1944): Lecture to the Verein für Sozialpolitik in 1909. In: J. P. Mayer, *Max Weber and German Politics*. London: Faber and Faber, pp. 125–131.

5 The Freiburg scholars and interwar Germany

Anita Pelle

1 Introduction

The German school, perhaps iniquitously underrepresented in contemporary economic literature, started in the 1930s and can be related to (though not exclusively) Walter Eucken, whose impact on today's Germany is considerable (Mátyás, 2003).[1] This impact, however, was at its strongest and most direct in the development of the post-Second World War social market economy as Eucken himself took an active part in it until his sudden and unexpected death in 1950.[2] Nevertheless, his thoughts have filtered into the whole of post-war German economic policy, into the 1957 competition regulation, but also served as a basis for the anti-inflation monetary policy of the Bundesbank. And, if we take into consideration that German ideas have influenced the monetary policy, economic policy coordination and competition policy of today's European Union, Eucken and his fellow scholars are not at all just a historic curiosity.

Ostrom, for example, in his study on Buchanan and constitutional economics says nothing less than the following:

> Those who would take economics seriously need to read Walter Eucken's *The Foundations of Economics* (1940–1951) to avoid the pitfalls of using simple theoretical models when the relevant experience is one of artifactual construction embedded in multiple levels reflecting the three worlds of constitutional consideration, collective choice, and operational choice.
> (Ostrom, 1999, p. 131)

Turning back to mid-twentieth-century Germany, we can say that the Freiburg School laid down the foundations of German neoliberalism, a school of thought led by Alfred Müller-Armack, Wilhelm Röpke and Alexander Rüstow, also considered as the fathers of social market economy. However, the above-mentioned scholars and the Freiburg School did not think fully the same way: Müller-Armack represents a more result-oriented and interventionist approach than the Freiburgians, Röpke and Rüstow are characterised by more procedure- and regulation-orientation (Vanberg, 2004). While the Freiburg School thought that the market had an ethical order, Müller-Armack was convinced that it should be created by social policy. Without going into details, we can state that the original (theoretical) model of social market economy heavily eroded in the second half of the twentieth century, quite likely due to the social benefits. Many people in today's Germany express their desire for a 'Neue Soziale Marktwirtschaft' (new social market economy) (Siebert, 2005), which revives the thoughts of the Freiburg School.

2 State, market and competition as the core concepts of the Freiburg School

The Freiburg School started in 1932–33. In that time, Walter Eucken, Franz Böhm and Hans Grossmann-Doerth jointly started to study the question of what power an individual has in a free society. The three scholars quickly started to work in cooperation. Böhm habilitated in 1933 with his dissertation titled *Wettbewerb und Monopolkampf* (Competition and Monopoly Battle). This work inspired the theory of 'the interdependency of orders'. Franz Böhm then took an active part also in the post-war construction of the German social market economy; we can say that he was the intellectual father of the 1957 competition regulation as he saw through the whole regulatory process. Regarding his official positions, he became a minister in Hessen after 1945, was a member of the Bundesrat (Federal Council) between 1953 and 1965, and then a consultant to the Bundeswirtschaftsministerium (Federal Ministry of Economy) from 1948.

In the 1930s, the three Freiburg scholars were very keen on discovering the relations between law and economics as well. They thought competition regulation to be the strongest link between the two areas of science besides the principle that the right to private property is the backbone of a market economy. This research led to the analysis of the relation between state and economy and of the tasks the state has. They claimed already at this early time that state intervention has a number of negative impacts on the operation of the economy. We call them ordoliberals as they believed free market and order to be the fundaments of society and economy. Their first joint publication dates to 1937 and has the title *Ordnung der Wirtschaft* (Order of the Economy). Ordoliberalism then grew into an individual school of thought after the Second World War. The journal edited by them also had the title *Ordnung der Wirtschaft*. Besides the three founding fathers, the most prominent members of the school were Constantin von Dietze (1891–1973), K. Paul Hensel (1907–1975), Adolf Lampe (1897–1948), Friedrich A. Lutz (1901–1975), Karl Friedrich Maier (1905–1993), Fritz W. Meyer (1907–1980) and Leonhard Miksch (1901–1950).

Why *Ordnung*? The word in the German language has two meanings: in the positivist sense it refers to the form of economic coordination, while in the normativist sense it means the putting together of diversity into unity. So order is some kind of a(n economic) constitution, the system of the rules of the game. It has nothing to do with the connotation of order as 'dictate'; it can rather be deduced from the word '*ordo*' by which the order of nature was described in Latin. To create order, economic analysis based on human intuition and factual evidence, is needed. There should be an order which is not only economically effective but which also gives way to a responsible and free human life.

Eventually, order is the fundament (*Rahmenordnung*) that mankind has an inherent need for. The primary order covers the formal legal and institutional framework. Several other relations, organisations and spontaneous interactions are linked to this primary order. So, theoretically, primary order has to be distinguished by the order describing how actors behave (that is, how they select within the framework of the primary order).

Accordingly, the major task formulated by the Freiburg scholars was to find the constitutional framework of a free economy and society (Albert, 2005). Their liberal principle was that market itself is a constitutional-institutional order. Eucken systematically elaborated the systems of *Ordnunstheorie* and *Ordnungspolitik*. The founding fathers emphasised that the way to economic development is through the development of the institutional framework of (economic and legal) order. Within this order, law is one of the tools. Generally speaking, the Freiburgians worked on the establishment of a feasible and humane socio-economic and political order.[3] However, they not only intended to answer their own questions at the theoretical level, but they also aimed at providing inputs to practical economic policy: how a favourable economic constitution can be introduced and operated (*Wirtschaftsverfassungspolitik*).

The main idea behind their economic policy recommendations was that intervention is indirect: it aims to shape the primary order and influences real economy that way. The development of the primary order must work so that the representation of individual interests eventually serves the common interest. Primary order has to be improved in this direction. To phrase it in another way, they believed that *Wirtschaftsverfassungspolitik* should create an order in which Adam Smith's invisible hand (Smith, 1992) can do its good work.

Eucken and Böhm emphasised especially after the Second World War that the economic order in which we operate is the outcome of a political choice. On the other hand they admitted that markets evolved in an evolutionary process of several thousands of years and not by some chosen deliberate action. However, they were convinced that economic order could be designed and formed by human intentions. This approach is obviously deductible in the construction of the social market economy.

The Freiburg scholars, though they considered themselves liberals, highlighted that liberalism in their interpretation did not mean that there was no state, but neither did they regard state to be a natural phenomenon. In their view, the state operates according to the authorisation granted to it by the constitutional order. The findings of the Freiburg School are relevant to us also because they go further than formulating economic objectives when providing political recommendations which result in economic efficiency, but guarantee the freedom of citizens at the same time (Gerken and Renner, 2000). Eucken wrote in a late letter of his: 'I am not giving recommendation to the solution of every-day problems but bring up thoughts for longer terms. I am satisfied if my thoughts serve as a starting point to further research' (Eucken, 1952, p. 9).

It is not by accident that we mentioned both economic theory and economic policy above, as the positive and normative ideas of the Freiburg School are clearly distinguishable. In order to make the distinction unambiguous, they used two separate names for the two areas: *Ordnungstheorie* lays down the theoretical basis and gives the framework to *Ordnungspolitik* which formulates recommendations for practical economic policy. In their opinion, an effective national economy has to meet two requirements: it has to rely on theory but, at the same time, has to prove to be feasible in practice. So, theory and practice have to address the solution of the same problems (Gerken and Renner, 2000). The applicability – and application – of theory was especially important to Eucken (Schlecht, 1989).

Competition is the basis of the market order but competition is not an objective in itself but a tool which could and should (*'kann und sollte'*, Eucken, 1949, p. 57) be used to serve mankind. Eucken's description of desired competition is *'funktionsfähig und menschenwürdig'* (workable and humane) (mimeo, p. 56). Workable competition calls forth efficiency while humane competition guarantees a free life based on individual responsibility, as taking responsibility brings freedom with itself! Eucken thought that nobody had solved mankind's problem of restricting freedom since the industrial revolution, moreover, socio-economic systems introduced since then have only strengthened the power of a few, at the expense of the others. So, the freedom of the individual has to be protected twofold: from the restrictive power of other individuals and from the state itself. The policy of *Wettbewerbsordnung* aims at fulfilling these two objectives in parallel as shown below.

Eucken summarises the theoretical fundaments in his work *Die Grundlagen der Nationalökonomie* (Fundaments of the National Economy) published in 1940 (Eucken, 1989).[4] The relevance of this comprehensive work is given by the intention to fill the gap sensed between theory and practice. He saw that the school of Historicism, dominating German economic research of that time, lacked strong economic fundaments. Eucken strived for examining economic reality and, to this end, he was convinced that economics had to be freed from the historical approach. He was also inspired by Edmund Husserl[5] who was his personal friend. Eucken's criticism of Historicism was that people should feel that they were not passively assisting to the historic development happening around them. We note here that Historicism had an idea acknowledged by the Freiburgians also, namely that the existing socio-economic order is the result of a multi-century development and that market was not established in a planned way but 'developed'. On the other hand, they saw that historic development could be influenced and that 'order' could and should be actively shaped. Eucken went further by saying that social science consists of facts, just as a house consists of bricks, but just as a pile of bricks will not develop into a house by itself, a pile of facts will not constitute science. It is theory that gives the structure to it.

At the same time Eucken also criticised Neoclassicists by pointing out that products and competitors are not homogeneous, as presumed by the neoclassical model. In his theory, five factors determine the economy: needs, nature, labour as a factor of production, technological knowledge and the stock of consumer products. He supplemented these with the environment: the way of life of the people, state organisation, and social structure with its own habits and laws. The legal-social order, in which economic interactions are undertaken, includes the monetary system and monetary policy, as well as the real de facto existing market structures (*Marktformen*). The analysis of market structures led him to the recognition that economic formulae vary by market forms (Mátyás, 2003). In this respect, we may regard Eucken as a forerunner of the I/O (Industrial Organization) methodology.

Based on pricing methods, Eucken classified market structures into five categories: competition, partial oligopoly, oligopoly, partial monopoly, monopoly. Nevertheless, he did not go into details regarding these categories; he only stated that real economy was determined by these market structures.[6] To him the relationship between theory and practice was that practice provided the actual data for the theoretical framework. He found that, due to the constantly changing nature of reality, theory continually faces new challenges so economics can never be 'ready'.

He also dwells on the task of economic science. He defines it as the following: the clearance of the individual (scientific) intuition regarding the complexity of modern society and the clear explanation of these to others. However, he warns that economic theory often contradicts the 'voice' of those with a controlling economic power. This resistance has to be borne.[7] Many persons who are not professionals express their views on the economy. Eucken was convinced that the economic scientist has to enter the stage of publicity and has to take part in this battle. In the meanwhile, he has to save his intellectual independency and must not lean to the actually dominant opinions. He must do so even if he appears radical, nevertheless, the scientist is distinguishable by the radicalism of his questions.

Eucken analyses his own political-ideological environment as well. In 1932 he speaks about the need for structural changes in the functioning of the state, and about the crisis of capitalism. He said that, in the nineteenth century, the state politicised economy. An 'economic state' (*Wirtschaftsstaat*) emerged. In the Bismarckian times the state's dominance in the economy grew further. In this way the state became strong enough to force its ideology on the society. This system is apt for certain interest groups to show their own interests as if they were the interests of the society. Practically all ideologies in the history of mankind have, in the background, served the economic interests of certain groups. In this way, eventually, economic policy ideologies themselves become powerful and, as a consequence, become dangerous.

At the same time we must accept that political influence goes together with economic power. Economic policy ideology becomes a weapon in the economic battle. In order to solve the problem, we must return to the roots: policy has to aim at confining economic interest groups.

In Eucken's view, economic history is a history of failures. The nineteenth century failed to solve the social problem: the worker's income was hardly enough to live on. In time of the Weimar Republic mass unemployment was the manifestation of failure. According to him, pre-economic policy was that of 'laissez-faire' while the post-First World War economic policy can be called the policy of experiments

(Tuchtfeld, 1989). Eucken thought that neither of these was appropriate for solving the problems of the modern, industrialised society as neither of them guarantees the sustainability of national economic performance.

The starting point of Eucken's critique on the policy of laissez-faire is that the expression is already a field for misunderstanding as it does not mean that politics does not intervene in the economy. In his view, the greatest failure of the policy is that actors, in fact, find competition inconvenient and try to eliminate it by forming cartels, by merging and by restricting the positions of competitors in order to monopolise markets. As a result, competition left on its own ends up in such monopole situations. This has two negative effects, namely that monopoly undermines the workability of the market economy and, by the increase of the power of a few, the freedom of the others is violated.

On the other hand, Eucken also criticised the policy of experiments. He identifies two types of these: one is the so-called middle-course policy which washes away the borderlines between economy and state; the other is the socialist and national socialist experiment to centralise the direction of economic procedures (Gerken and Renner, 2000). Middle-course policy, a characteristic of the Weimar Republic, for example, brings up two problems. First, the state, by its own power, hands economic power over to powerful groups. Second, eventually it results in a weakened state as the state merely appears to be powerful; in fact, it is dependent itself. So it is a vicious circle. As an ultimate consequence, the individual loses his or her own freedom as both state and private power deprives him or her of it. State intervention and subventions increase the dependency of the individual. In this logical deduction, Eucken phrases an open critique of Keynes, which can be regarded as radical in the 1930s.

Eucken's view of centralised systems, such as Nazi Germany, came to light in 1942 when he published a book with the title *Wettbewerb als Grundprinzip der Wirtschaftsverfassung* (Competition as the principle of economic constitution). Here he explained that economy cannot be directed centrally as there are numerous actors. The problem of power was not solved either; dependency remains and results in the lack of security. In 1940 the German citizen was in the hands of 'the office'. On the whole, the Weimar system was a direct way to centralisation (Ptak, 2004).

Eucken dealt quite a lot with the problem of power (this aspect of his work is introduced by Lenel, 2000). In his writings, Eucken points out a number of times that economic power (*Macht*) is not new; it has always existed. However, many people choose not to notice that economy is a battle of powers. In his view, anyone who does not understand this does not understand the economy. This battle requires strength. However, the frequent manifestation of abuse of power and economic theory are closely related. Capitalism is eventually the manifestation of private power. Eucken discovered quite early that economic power is not only determined by market share but also by company size. For this reason, he chose not to use the expression '*Marktstellung*' but, rather, '*Machtstellung*' as only those who have enough strength (power) have enough time to wait in the market. Eucken also discovered that, when markets close up, a dominant position is more likely to occur![8] Dominance is determined by the level of independence.

What can be done against economic dominance? Experience shows that 'laissez-faire' does not stop the evolution of dominant/dependent positions. This leads us back to the basic problem: the solution is the construction and sustainment of an order (*Ordnung*). The best tool to limit economic power is competition. The legal system has to ensure that competition works. Böhm claims that competition is the superb and most genial '*Entmachtungsinstrument*' (power-depriving tool) (Böhm, 1980). He was the one who repeatedly emphasised that competition is the only instrument that can effectively restrict power (Herrmann-Pillath, 1991). At the same time, we must not forget that the acquisition of a dominant position is strongly related to the restriction of competition. For this reason, the dominant position has to be limited. Ordoliberals have always stressed that the degree and objective of complete competition is when there is no dominance. It is impossible to set the limits of a dominant position: it changes by case and also in time.

We must see that *Ordnungspolitik* is economic and social policy at the same time. The major strength of the theory lies in its logically deduced arguments; democratic openness (transparency) being its focal point; the specific economic policy recommendations and the method of placing economy within the society. *Ordnungspolitik* approaches political problems in a scientific way; it aims at meeting scientific standards. Incidentally, Eucken and Hayek show similarity in this respect: the two scholars talk about the fundaments but, instead of asking 'whether', they ask 'how'. Instead of asking 'to what extent', they ask 'in what way' policy can be improved to be the most result-oriented possible (Madarász, 2005; Pies, 2001). However, the core problem remains of an ideological nature.

The unsuccessfulness of economic policy before 1918, and then between 1918 and 1945, inspired Eucken to question the role of the state. He thought that the problem was not merely of quantity but also of quality. The solution is the distinction between *Ordnung* as a status and as an objective. The state should be the *Ordnung* as a form but should not intervene in economic procedures. *Wettbewerbsordnung* is what ensures efficiency and individual freedom at the same time. Limiting economic freedom is not allowed by the state, while state power is limited by its self-restrictive competition policy, which aims at sustaining competition.

According to the Freiburg School, market order has to fulfil the following requirements: it has to be fully free, indiscriminative and privilege-free. Market order is based on ethical fundaments (this thought originates in German Protestantism – von Dietze, 1946; Brakelmann and Jähnichen, 1994); the market gives the 'primary order'. The rules of the game ensure that actors are equal and the market is distortionless. As for the market, the Freiburg scholars criticised the Neoclassicists and agreed with the Historicists that the market did not exist by itself but was a result of an evolutionary process, in the course of which political decisions were made. In a free market there is free competition where all actors are legally equivalent (everybody is an equipollent subject of civil law), exchange and contracts are executed voluntarily and economy is operated by these voluntary agreements. The Freiburgians also saw that reality was often far from theory, especially regarding equality and voluntariness. So, in their view, the practical use of theory is that reality could be evaluated according to its divergence from theory.

In Böhm's interpretation, free market means that all actors are legally equivalent and that exchange and contract are voluntary. These serve as the reference to the development of the constitutional order of a functioning market economy (Vanberg, 2004). The first step in this direction occurred in the eighteenth–nineteenth centuries, with the shift from feudalism towards a society of civil rights. The greatest change was the abolition of privileges and the declaration of equality before law. However, a functioning market economy means more than this shift: competition has to be sustained by all means, against the anticompetitive forces. In Böhm's view, constitutional order has to be developed in such a way that, on the sub-constitutional levels, contracts restricting competition could not be agreed on. That is: the freedom of contract cannot be abused for by-passing constitutional order. And the Freiburgians regarded cartel as a contract of this kind. They said that rules developed by business actors themselves should not be expected to serve public interest (it was Grossmann-Doerth and Eucken who emphasised this). At this point, the Freiburg School came into conflict with von Mises' theory of the unhampered market as, according to the Freiburgians, the business sector is incapable of constructing acceptable rules. The strictest follower of von Mises in the US was Murray Rothbard who, on the contrary, was convinced that agreements between market actors should not be intervened in in any way, even if the cartel was restricting competition (Kirzner, 2001; Rothbard, 2004).

Although freedom of contract is a basic principle in the free market, no contract may aim at restricting the freedom of contract or at evading the primary order. Courts are entitled to guard the fulfilment of these criteria. The most difficult question regarding the freedom of contract is generated by cartels themselves: in light of the principle, are cartels voluntary and free agreements?[9] Or are they agreements that restrict the freedom of others, thus being contradictory to the primary order? (Salin, 1996).[10] As we can see, the Freiburgians shared the latter view.[11] So, *Wettbewerbsordnung* is a realistic alternative both to laissez-faire and to interventionism. It appears as a third way (*dritter Weg*); Eucken himself called it so. However, it does not equate to middle-course policy as the latter is a victim of interest groups and is thus pointless and unaccountable. The orientation of *Wettbewerbsordnung* is clear: the policy aims to put competition in service of consumers and to rule out all behaviours which impair consumers and restrict their decision-making. The Freiburgians say that there should be performance competition (*Leistungswettbewerb*). At the same time, they warn that *Wettbewerbsordnung* does not develop by itself; moreover, companies will always look for ways to eliminate it. This is, however, not a new phenomenon as craftsmen of the same profession in Germanic territories formed alliances as early as the thirteenth century in order to escape competition.

During his work, Eucken considered the following problems relevant in relation to the *Wettbewerbsordnung* (Volkert, 1991):

- *Monopoly situations arising from efficiency* (*effizienzbedingte Monopolstellungen*): even if fulfilling the above principles, there may be monopolies organised on the basis of efficiency, so an outcome of the principles is not competition. For such cases Eucken recommends the establishment of a cartel office which is entitled to control whether these monopolies abuse their power. Eucken decisively opposed the nationalising of monopolies as a state monopoly is just as problematic as a private one or, it is even more problematic as the state is able to provide further protection to its monopolies by adopting regulations and, in this way, it is fully capable of impeding the entry of a competitor into the market.[12]
- *Income redistribution* should be based on competition. This is better than state redistribution even if it is not perfect because state redistribution is, eventually, the enforcement of the power of individuals over other individuals. But, based on the primary order, some correction system can be introduced. A core element of this can be, for example, progressive income tax.
- *Social policy problems* have to be examined in a broader scheme than that in which they occur. The social problem has become more and more severe with industrialisation. The tools applied are counter-productive as they support the citizen but deprive him of his freedom (and, of course, of responsibility); they create 'state slavery'. And the restriction of freedom (the dissolution of individual responsibility) is the fordoing of the essence of human life. We should accept that social tensions have always existed. The state's role is to provide possibilities to all its citizens to care for themselves.[13] However, the initiative lies at the individual; the social order can be effective only in this way.
- Regarding *labour markets*, Eucken sees two problems. One is the sinking of wages below the cost of living, the other is unemployment. But he missed to look for solutions in this field.

Franz Böhm dedicated a greater role to competition than Eucken. According to him competition is the moral backbone of a profit-based economy. It is not a mere incentive; it is a power-depriving mechanism. Therefore, no other competition is desirable but *Leistungswettbewerb* when an actor realises an advantageous market position by offering something better to the consumers. The opposite to it, with Böhm's expression, is *Behinderungswettbewerb* (setting back competition) when an actor achieves its goals by setting back others (Böhm, 1980). Eucken described economic policy fostering *Leistungswettbewerb* as a gardener who does not create anything himself but ensures the ideal environment for natural growth. Böhm developed the metaphor even further by saying that a highly cultivated park needs constant gardening. In this way the Freiburg School gave legitimacy to active competition policy.

Ordnungspolitik, in the Freiburgian term, means competition policy in the first place: to continuously ensure competitive processes serving consumers. However, their specific competition policy recommendations are not consistent. The output-oriented concept of complete competition (*vollständige Konkurrenz*), for example, does not fit into their theories. This, on the other hand, does not weaken the truth of their statement on competition: that it is not a natural state of things but something that always has to be fought for and cared for (gardener metaphor).

Although they saw private power as the greatest threat restricting competition, they also thought the state embodied similar threats as the state is able to create monopoly by its policies (protection of intellectual property rights, trade policy, tax policy, etc.). The state first creates these then becomes dependent on them. They called this phenomenon 'refeudalisation', contemporary American literature calls it rent-seeking. As for them a criterion for effective competition was the full exemption of privileges, they denied that the state provided such privileges. This situation is guaranteed by civil law.

All in all, we can say that, according to the Freiburg scholars, a strong state is needed that does not incline to interest groups but remains independent of these. On the other hand, the state should be 'weak' in the sense that it should not intervene in economic processes; the *Wettbewerbsordnung* should prevail over the political system. In our critical view, this thought is somewhat elitist: it reminds us of Plato's state where a philosopher king leads the republic (Plato, 1943). Eucken does not think that way but he definitely presumes a moral-ethical standard, on behalf of all actors, and it remains a question whether he was right.

3 Robert Liefmann's ideas on why cartels are 'good'

Before turning to Robert Liefmann's ideas, let us have a quick look at the economic situation in the Germany of the times when he published most of his work; that is, post-First World War Germany.

As is widely known, the First World War was originally planned by the Germans to be a '*Blitzkrieg*' (lightning war) but, despite their success in the beginning, they lost: on 4 October, 1918, they requested the cessation of arms from US President Thomas Wilson[14] (Fulbrook, 1990). After a series of conciliation talks, Wilson announced his Fourteen Points. In this speech he promised that, after the peace treaties were negotiated openly, there would not be any more secret international agreement. Contrary to the promises, the Germans were handed over the completed peace treaty on 7 May in Versailles (Németh, 2007).[15] On 28 June, having no other choice, the Germans signed the treaty. The Versailles Treaty changed economic space substantially. Germany was forced to disclaim territories of large size and strategic importance, exceeding the most pessimistic scenarios (Winkler, 2005). Keynes, who, on behalf of the British ministry of finance, was present at the negotiations, was devastated by what was happening there (Keynes, 2000). In his work, originally published in 1919, he strongly criticised the whole system of reparations. He claimed that the vast sums of money imposed on beaten Germany would not only destroy the German economy but weaken the whole of Europe. Germany losing the war obviously resulted in a great economic fall-back (Tokody, 1972). Golo Mann, the brother of Thomas Mann also wrote: 'peace was war-laden' (Mann, 1997, p. 11).

As a response to the non-fulfilment of the peace decree, after several warnings by the French, to which no acceptable answer was received, French armed troops occupied the Ruhr region in January 1923, to which the Germans reacted with passive resistance (Ádám, 1998).[16] The treaty on reparation was eventually signed on 10 October 1924. This finally put an end to the delicate issue spanning several years, among other things by elevating it to the international level. As a consequence, capital flow into Germany (mainly from the US) started to rise after 1924. The German currency was finally stabilised after the hyperinflation of 1923–24 and a general economic upswing followed. The adoption of the Dawes Plan resulted in the gradual withdrawal of armed troops, which gave an impetus to German industrial production (Kaposi, 1998).

Already in 1890, Germany counted the largest number of national industrial cartels. At that time there existed 122 registered cartels in the country, besides the ten international and 52 American cartels present in the German economy (Beck and Peschka, 1989). While in the US the Sherman Act was adopted in 1890, cartels were not regulated in Germany in any way, moreover, such cooperation among companies was not at all intended to be limited. It was thought that ruthless competition and price wars in certain markets can be successfully fought this way. For these reasons, and because at that time the freedom of contract was one of the principles of (competition) law, price-fixing was not only allowed but it could be enforced by law. Investigations against cartels were launched very rarely, for example if a cartel fully monopolised a market or over-exploited consumers. No wonder that in such an environment the number of cartels grew considerably around the turn of the century. In 1905 their number reached 385 and an overall 12,000 companies were affiliated with these cartels (Motta, 2004).

German economic history has long witnessed that those pursuing similar occupations cooperate with each other: guilds had been working like that for centuries and modern industrial cartels developed from these types of cooperation (Liefmann, 1930). So, industrial cooperation had historical roots in Germany. As for the cartels of the nineteenth century, they were mainly formed to prevent the increasing competition in industries with large capital needs but in the twentieth century, so-called modern cartels were formed. Modern cartels were evoked by the modern economy, that is, large company size and mass production. Companies recognised in the new circumstances that, if they cooperated, they would be able to improve their positions (Pelle, 2006).

Until 1923 cartels were not regulated in Germany in any way. For this reason their number had exceeded 1,500 by then. However, this year brought about a turning point by the adoption of cartel regulation as one of the responses to hyperinflation. The reasoning behind this was that price agreements would lead to the increase in the price of products. In the meanwhile, economic circumstances changed again and it was no longer necessary to break the power of cartels. Moreover, contrary intentions appeared: following the bankruptcies of 1929 caused by the crisis, it became compulsory in 1930 to form cartels in the sensitive industries.[17] According to national statistics, around 3,000 cartels existed in the middle of 1925, of which 2,500 operated in industry, 400 in wholesale and 150 in retail. However, according to wholesaler organisations, only 30–35 cartels operated in this field (Liefmann, 1930).

The Freiburg scholars and interwar Germany 111

After 1924, concentration is not to be interpreted like in the times of the hyperinflation when private assets were vertically interlinked in order to maximise them but should be looked at as sectoral concentration (Mann, 1997): cartels regulated prices and fixed production norms but also carried out considerable innovation in production planning. Due to such interlinks, industry manifested a power against the state to an extent never seen before. These advantages were discovered by the employees as well and, in order to counterweigh the cartels, they gathered in trade unions that operated as sort of labour-selling cartels.

Robert Liefmann was the person to call German trade unions 'labour-selling cartels', and the conflicts between employers and employees 'healthy rivalry' (Liefmann, 1930). He thought that the relevance of trade unions was that they formed an organised gathering, in the framework of which those pursuing similar activities could cooperate.

Robert Liefmann spent most of his professional life in Freiburg. He was born in Hamburg on 4 February 1874, the son of Jewish merchant Semmy Liefmann and his wife, Auguste Juliane. He executed his studies in economics and law in the cities of Freiburg, Berlin, Munich and Brussels. Upon the inspiration received from Max Weber, he started to deal with corporations' alliances and cartels; he based his doctorate and habilitation on these topics, the latter in 1900. From 1904 on he was professor of economics at the University of Freiburg. In 1907 he made a study visit to the US. In his research, he continued to focus on forms of entrepreneurship, with special regard to cartels and trusts.

Due to his myasthenia he was confined to a wheelchair for some time in the 1920s. Despite converting to Christianity, the family was categorised as '*Volljude*' (fully Jewish) in 1933 so from this time on Liefmann lived under house arrest and could not continue his work at the university. Facing the derogatory circumstances, the family did not leave Freiburg. In 1940, at the age of 64, together with his two sisters and all the Jews of Baden and Pfalz, Liefmann was deported to the lager at Gurs, Southern France, where he lived until his death which occurred on 20 March 1941 at the nearby Morlaás. He was rather unlucky not to survive to fulfil an invitation from the New York University but at least his sister could be freed from the concentration camp. The Liefmann house was confiscated by the national socialist regime following the deportation. The building was used by the Gestapo until the end of the Second World War. Then, after the war, the French army took possession of it, until handing it over to the region of Baden-Württemberg. Until 2000 the Liefmann house served as police headquarters. Today it is owned by the University of Freiburg and operates as a guest house.[18]

Liefmann wrote about competition policy in one of his large synthesising works called *Kartelle, Konzerne und Trusts*, first published in Germany in 1924, then several times in the 1920s. Its first appearance in English was an Oxford publication (its invariable reprint is in Liefmann, 2001).[19]

Liefmann, as a German professor of economics, was situated (both geographically and intellectually) in the buffer zone of two large theoretical systems, namely the Anglo-Saxon free-market capitalism and the socialist views on state and economy. In his book mentioned above he continuously criticises both systems and 'sends messages' to the German representatives of both of these, in the form of sharp critical remarks. He thought that the theoretical system of free-market capitalism was not realistic as, if we take its statements seriously, in a free-market capitalism eventually everybody is the full monopolist of their own product and every contract aims at restricting competition. Moreover, in his view, no market is ever stable. Theoretically it continuously oscillates between the two ends of competition and monopoly, even reaching the extreme points sometimes. Additionally, Liefmann was also influenced by the public mood in 1920s' Germany, in which a general suspicion accompanied the ideological pressure on behalf of the winning Allies: politically they saw strong power interests hidden behind the key word of democracy, and the general opinion was the same on free-market capitalism in economic terms. In this period, anti-liberalism in Germany (meaning the disapproval of Anglo-Saxon free-market capitalism) was linked with the fight against the 'English spirit' (Karácsony, 2005, p. 72).

On the other hand, Liefmann considered socialism unfeasible. He claimed that the state should not act as proprietor as it cannot act as a successful 'landlord'. Its participation in industry leads to unnecessary over-investments and a loss in efficiency. Liefmann thought that the exalted objectives of socialism are no more than mere exaggerations and empty phrases. He saw the major role of the state as a regulator but by no means through active participation in the market. In this respect he can be regarded as a forerunner of the Freiburg School, as we will see later.

We are convinced to call Liefmann an original figure of economic history who was not afraid of being critical in his uncertain political, economic and social, nevertheless theoretical environment, and was brave enough to stand up with a completely new set of arguments, even compared to the mainstream in Germany at that time (Historicism). When reading his works, outside the individual, easy-to-read style enjoyable even today, we may be surprised by some expressions which he in fact uses with great consistency. Below, we give an overview of the most relevant of the expressions used by him and will use them between quotation marks. When providing the Liefmannian interpretation of the concepts, we will see the obvious impact of his environment and of his critical responses to these, based on which we consider him an independent thinker.

- *'Ruthless competition'*: the synonym of free-market capitalism. It is ruthless as in this competition 'everybody is against everybody'. In 'ruthless competition' the consumer is 'the laughing third party'. Moreover, in the post-war[20] German production structure examined by him, selling 'at the lowest price possible' often meant great losses in capital and was thus not favoured.
- *'Extreme individualism'*: the other synonym of free-market capitalism. It implies that all forms of cooperation restrict competition, including every contract.
- *'Healthy rivalry'*: an alternative to 'extreme individualism'. Its main content is that those 'pursuing similar professions' are cooperating with one

another and thus rivalry is not realised at the individual level but between industries, between industrialists and merchants and between industrialists and their suppliers. This, thanks to the guilds, has been so in Germany for centuries.
- Trade unions as cartels: trade unions' operation is, in many aspects, similar to that of cartels as they eventually are *'labour-selling cartels'*. Therefore, the analysis of their operation can be executed with the methodology applied for any cartel.
- *'Old capital'* vs. *'new capital'*: 'old capital' refers to capital invested in previous technologies and capacities while 'new capital' is capital invested in new technologies and capacities. Distinguishing between the two is relevant in respect of capital risks.
- *'Fresh competition'*: in cartelised or monopolised industries, if economically rational, new or outside actors may appear. They incorporate 'fresh competition' which is healthy and incites the cartel or the (earlier) monopoly to improve their efficiency or, if that is necessary, to split.
- *'Acceptable price'*: in the terminology of free-market capitalism the concept is continuously used though it is a fully useless theoretical expression that has no practical relevance. Nobody knows in a given market what would be the price if the market structure was different. Nobody can tell what price is 'acceptable'. However, the concept that can be captured is the stability of prices.
- *'Supply'* = *'demand'*: in the examined economic situation (1920s' Germany) supply and demand are eventually commutable concepts. The demand of the consumers' society of our days was at that time fully unknown.

Liefmann, in his quoted work, examined the major organisations restricting competition, namely cartels, concerns and trusts. The interpretation of the concept of cartel varies by country and by culture. His starting point was that industrial cooperation has long traditions in Germany. He gave the following definition to modern cartels: 'voluntary agreement among similar but independent corporations to assure monopoly in the market'. This says nothing new as parties in selling and buying have always strived for monopoly. However, modern cartels had been evoked by modern economy, namely large company size and mass production. Mass production requires large-scale fixed capital investments which increases risks. This way, cartels are eventually the result of the divergence of capital risk and profit. The forming of cartels is directly implied by the 'ruthless competition' experienced in industries requiring large capital investments. Firms recognised that, by cooperating, they could eliminate unfavourable factors. Therefore, cartels may be formed in industries where:

- there is mass production;
- there is little difference in the quality of products; and
- the proportion of fixed capital in the price of the product is high.

Consequently, agriculture is not likely to cartelise and commerce is difficult to organise in cartels as most of the invested capital is turnover capital.

Liefmann carried out investigations on industrial cooperation in other countries as well and came to the conclusion that in other Central European countries cartels similar to those in Germany are found, many of which are cooperating with the German ones and were generated by these. England is the country that differs most from Germany. In his view, this difference can be explained by the individualist culture which implies that any form of cooperation is equal to the restriction of competition. Other reasons why cartelisation tendencies are low in England are the low level of customs, greater exposure to world market impacts, greater openness. On the whole, England is characterised more by mergers rather than cartels which, according to Liefmann, are much more damaging than cartelisation as 'healthy rivalry' is no longer granted. Regarding the United States, cartelisation started in the market of railway freighting but was opposed by law. Therefore, American companies, similarly to the English ones, moved towards concentrating into trusts. A result of these processes was the development of giant corporations with too much power.

In the spirit of free-market capitalism 'everybody's fight against everybody' is an inherent part of life. Liefmann states that this may cause more damage to the national economy than benefits so cooperation within industries may be desirable. In this way Liefmann takes a stand: economic policy aspects are at least as important as competition policy aspects. With this commitment, Liefmann provides a theoretical basis for the cartel regulation of the European Community (Török, 2001). If so, competition is moved from the arena of producer–producer to the two sides of the market – producer–consumer. However, 'healthy rivalry' remains the organising principle. Moreover, it should not be forgotten that the people are not merely consumers but they are, at the same time, employees and, through the spreading of public corporations and employees' share programmes, they are also shareholders and thus proprietors, so the situation is not as simple as that.

Liefmann summarises the advantages of cartels which are mostly of a stabilising nature, which makes them crucially important in post-war Germany. These advantages are, for example, decreasing capital risks, more stable employment, a more stable solution to economic downturn and to the devaluation of the currency. The smaller volatility of prices is a further advantage which, in Liefmann's view, is much more 'valuable' in the given socio-economic environment than prices higher than the 'acceptable price', this latter often mentioned as the greatest disadvantage of cartels. Liefmann considers the frozen market structures, the impediment of technological development and the proliferation of bureaucracy as the realistic disadvantages of cartelisation.

Liefmann uses a rather interesting reasoning in connection with the employees of cartels and the companies distributing the products produced by the cartels. Regarding the employees, he lists a number of advantages, of which the most relevant is that cartels are preferable to concerns and trusts as the latter make the employer much more powerful than the trade union. On the other hand, the rivalry within the cartel makes the 'labour-selling cartel' (that is, the trade union) stronger. A further consequence is that, due to the stabilisation effects, wages and employment itself is much more stable than in the case of companies under 'ruthless competition'. Liefmann comes up with a rather particular idea, namely that cartels had helped the development of 'healthy' socialist thoughts: he states that cartelisation in Germany had contributed to the acknowledgement of workers' rights and to the improvement of the social status of workers. Regarding the merchants, Liefmann experienced that, in free-market capitalism, merchants make industrialists compete with one another. However, cartels are capable of limiting the 'power' of the merchants. As a response, merchants may also start organising themselves into cartels, as a consequence of which the distribution chain becomes shorter, thus moderating the price of the consumer product. Liefmann had the courage to say that production and commercial cartels in 1920s' Germany had eventually led to the stabilisation of the German mark.

We should dedicate some thoughts to the dilemma of whether cartels definitely and necessarily hold back technological development. Liefmann, based on his 30 years' observation, states that it is not always so due to the rivalry within the cartel: companies, in the hope of larger quotas, are interested in reducing their costs by developing their technologies. Moreover, larger companies cooperating with one another can realise developments needing large capital, and lower capital risks can foster technological development. Liefmann thought that, if markets/sectors were cartelised, firms would not take up so much risk with investing 'new capital' into new technologies because they were not forced to do so (as there is less competition). As a result, technological development might indeed be slowed down by cartelisation. On the other hand, it also implies that, this way, less firms go bankrupt (as they avoid risks related to 'new capital'), which Liefmann thought was favourable. This logic might appear strange today.

How do cartels affect consumers? It is important to remember that the consumer equals 'the supplied', or rather the 'to-be-supplied' in this environment. Liefmann claims that, while in 'ruthless competition', price adjusts to demand, in case of a cartelised market it is the production that adjusts. This way production, that is, supply, is guaranteed also in times of crisis. The higher prices of the cartel do not bring up problems and most of consumption (supply) is assured by agriculture and commerce, which are not affected by the industrial cartels. Moreover, industrial products are much less fulfilling of basic needs so the price flexibility of their demand is much higher than that of food products.

At the end of his book, Liefmann invites his readers to a rather unconventional thought. He thinks that the major dilemma evoked by the post-war German economy and the world economic crisis is whether stable or volatile prices are more favourable to the national economy. Whether companies' ability to survive or their constant appearance–disappearance is more costly to the society. And, eventually, if cartels are able to smooth out economic cycles in respect of employment, prices and production (supply), why is that a problem?

When we make an attempt to outline Robert Liefmann's impact on contemporary economic thinking, we can say the following:

1 Partly by being a Freiburg economist, partly by emphasising the mere regulatory role of the state and by opposing the state's intervention in the market, he can be regarded as a forerunner to *Ordnungspolitik* and post-Second World War West-German economic policy.
2 He was early and precise in describing the processes which, contrary to other countries, led to the strengthening of industrial trade unions in Germany.[21]
3 Although not widely accepted, Liefmann highlighted very early the bad efficiency of the US antitrust regulation, namely that it is incapable of impeding the formation of giant trusts abusing their power.
4 Liefmann foresaw the significance of barriers to entry in light of market structures already in the 1920s although economic theory only identified these in the 1950s and 60s (Török, 2003).
5 By saying that 'in free-market capitalism, eventually everybody is the monopolist of their own product', Liefmann laid down the model of monopolistic competition a few years ahead of Robinson (1933) and Chamberlin (1933) (Kopányi, 1993) even if he did not call it that way.

On the whole, Liefmann's main idea is that cartels are 'good' because employees will not revolt, because continuous supply is guaranteed and because this way concerns and trusts are not formed, of which the disadvantages at the level of the national economy are much greater than those of the cartels.

4 Conclusions

The Freiburg School approached the necessity of regulating restrictions on competition in a new manner. Their starting point was to ensure competition; they saw the greatest threat in power, be it private or of the state. Therefore, they did not propose an absolute, per se type prohibition on restrictive behaviours but, by examining the objective or, much rather, the effect of such behaviours, emphasised that regulation should aim to ensure competition, to control power (dominant position), and to impede the development of disproportionate market positions. A further relevant observation of the Freiburg scholars was that (competition) regulation has to guarantee that regulation is not abused in service of individual interests. Walter Eucken was very early in discovering a deficiency of neoclassical theory by pointing out that product and competitors are not homogeneous, as presumed by the neoclassical model.

Liefmann was the one who emphasised that economic efficiency can be achieved not only through competition and that the legal regulation of the economy serves other objectives outside ensuring competition.[22] This statement is usually referred to as the most significant 'European thought' in competition regulation. Liefmann is significant also in the sense that he was the one who, as early as in the 1920s, revealed the failure of the Sherman Act; namely that it was unable to prevent the creation of powerful trusts which abused their power, thus implying that absolute prohibition is not a realistic form of competition regulation. Outside revealing the failure of such regulation, Liefmann has, in some way, foreseen the significance of barriers to entry regarding the formation of market structures, although the theory of barriers to entry was first laid down explicitly as late as in the 1950s and 1960s. By claiming that, eventually, in free-market capitalism everybody is the monopolist of their own product, he foresaw the model of monopolistic competition a few years ahead of Robinson (1933) and Chamberlin (1933), even if he did not call it that way. Last but not least, in connection with Liefmann, it is necessary to note that he made an early but rather precise attempt to project the strengthening of German trade unions; which he called 'labour-selling cartels'.

Notes

1. The University of Freiburg encompasses the Walter Eucken Institut which is the publisher of the journal called *ORDO*. The main objective of the institution is to further develop the thoughts of the Freiburg School in the actual socio-economic environment.
2. He suffered a heart attack the night before a lecture in London.
3. Social sciences of that time were not characterised by the sharp distinction experienced in our days anyway.
4. We draw the attention to the fact that Walter Eucken and the Freiburg School were active in the national socialist regime and also during the Second World War. Soon after Hitler came to power, Eucken became the leader of the opposition at the University of Freiburg: in his lectures he openly criticised the system, several of his publications were banned. Böhm condemned anti-Semitism and hence he lost his university job in 1940 and regained it only in 1946. In the course of the war, the opposition organised itself into the so-called Freburgian Clubs (*Freiburger Kreise*) which covered professional and church communities. Their principle was that individuals have free right to opposition; they decisively rejected the war. As they took part in the 1944 attempt to assassinate Hitler, several of them were called to account. Eucken himself was interrogated. Others were freed by the Allies. Hans Grossmann-Doerth was killed on the Russian front-line in 1944 (Blümle and Goldschmidt, 1993).
5. Edmund Husserl (1859–1938), German philosopher, the founder of phenomenology.
6. His work is generally characterised by the complete lack of mathematisation which so much characterises Anglo-Saxon theories. He uses logical deductions instead, embedded in linguistically sophisticated texts.
7. In the 1930s this was partly a political message.
8. By saying this, Eucken, similarly to Robert Liefmann, was rather early in understanding the significance of barriers to entry, even if he did not use the expression either.
9. Liefmann, then later Rothbard, thought so.
10. The dilemma is discussed in chapter 3.2.
11. This is the greatest difference between the viewpoints of Liefmann and the Freiburg School.
12. I/O drew attention to the problem of abusing private power through the abuse of state power only in the 1980s.
13. See the slogan '*Hilfe zur Selbsthilfe*' of social market economy.
14. His achievements were rewarded with the Nobel Peace Prize in 1919.
15. This is the reason why the Germans considered it a peace decree.
16. Passive resistance was one of the factors resulting in hyperinflation in 1923.

17 This obligation was extended to further areas in the national socialist regime as this was the way to bring industry under state control and to strengthen sectors serving military purposes. It was thought that, if companies cooperated, the German economy would be stronger.
18 http://www.io.uni-freiburg.de/downloads/gaestehaeuser/liefmann.pdf. *Downloaded 28 February 2010.*
19 As we had access to the 1930 Stuttgart edition (Liefmann, 1930), we used that in our work. Henceforth we do not refer to it any more.
20 The 1924 edition implies that this refers to the First World War.
21 This phenomenon has become one of the most significant political obstacles to the reform of the German welfare state (Gedeon, 2001).
22 This was especially so in the Germany of the 1920s when Liefmann published his views.

References

Ádám, M. (1998): *Az elszalasztott lehetőség. A Rajna-vidék megszállása.* Budapest: Kossuth.
Albert, H. (2005): Wirtschaft, Politik und Freiheit. Das Freiburger Erbe. In: N. Goldschmidt (ed.), *Wirtschaft, Politik und Freiheit. Freiburger Wirtschaftswissenschaftler und der Widerstand. Untersuchungen zur Ordnungstheorie und Ordnungspolitik.* Walter Eucken Institut. Tübingen: Mohr, pp. 405–419.
Beck, M. and Peschka, V. (eds.) (1989): *Akadémiai Kislexikon.* Budapest: Akadémiai Kiadó.
Blümle, G. and Goldschmidt, N. (2003): Walter Eucken – Vordenker einer freiheitlichen Ordnung. In: T. Hartman-Wendels et al. (eds.), *Das Wirtschaftsstudium,* vol. 32, pp. 1027–1030.
Böhm, F. (1980): *Freiheit und Ordnung in der Marktwirtschaft.* Baden-Baden: Nomos Verlagsgesellschaft.
Brakelmann, G. and Jähnichen, T. (1994): Die Protestantische Wurzeln der Sozialen Marktwirtschaft. In: G. Brakelmann and T. Jähnichen (eds.), *Die Protestantische Wurzeln der Sozialen Marktwirtschaft.* Gütersloh: Gütersloher Verlagshaus, pp. 13–38.
Chamberlin, E. (1933): *Theory of Monopolistic Competition.* Cambridge, MA: Harvard University Press.
Eucken, W. (1949): Die Wettbewerbsordnung und ihre Verwirklichung. *Ordo. Jahrbuch für die Ordnung von Wirtschaft und Gesellschaft,* vol. 1, pp. 56–90.
Eucken, W. (1952): *Grundsätze der Wirtschaftspolitik.* Tübingen: Mohr.
Eucken, W. (1989): *Die Grundlagen der Nationalökonomie.* Berlin: Springer.
Fulbrook, M. (1990): *A Concise History of Germany.* Cambridge: Cambridge University Press.
Gedeon, P. (2001): Merre tart a német jóléti állam? *Közgazdasági Szemle,* vol. 48, pp. 130–149.
Gerken, L. and Renner, A. (2000): Die ordnungspolitische Konzeption Walter Euckens. In: L. Gerken (ed.), *Walter Eucken un sein Werk. Rückblick auf den Vordenker der sozialen Marktwirtschaft.* Tübingen: Mohr, pp. 1–48.
Herrmann-Pillath, C. (1991): Der Vergleich von Wirtschafts- und Gesellschaftssystemen. Wissenschaftsphilosophische und methodologische Betrachtungen zur Zukunft eines ordnungstheoretischen Forschungsprogramms. *Ordo. Jahrbuch für die Ordnung von Wirtschaft und Gesellschaft,* vol. 42, pp. 15–68.
Kaposi, Z. (1998): *A XX. század gazdaságtörténete I. 1918–1945.* Budapest, Pécs: Dialóg Campus.

Karácsony, A. (2005): A konzervatív forradalom utópiája a két háború közötti Németországban. *Századvég*, no. 1, pp. 69–104.
Keynes, J. M. (2000): *A békeszerződés gazdasági következményei*. Budapest: Európa.
Kirzner, I. M. (2001): *Ludwig von Mises. The Man and His Economics*. Wilmington: ISI Books.
Kopányi, M. (ed.) (1993): *Mikroökonómia*. Budapest: Műszaki Könyvkiadó.
Lenel, H. O. (2000): Über private wirtschaftliche Macht. In: B. Külp and V. Vanberg (eds.), *Freiheit und wettbewerbliche Ornung. Gedenkband zur Erinnerung an Walter Eucken*. Freiburg, Berlin, Munich: Haufe Verlagsgruppe, pp. 303–320.
Liefmann, R. (1930): *Kartelle, Konzerne und Trusts*. Stuttgart: Ernst Heinrich Moritz.
Liefmann, R. (2001): *Cartels, Concerns, and Trusts*. Kitchener: Batoche Books.
Madarász, A. (2005): Friedrich August von Hayek. In: Z. Bekker (ed.), *Közgazdasági Nobel-díjasok 1969–2004*. Budapest: KJK-Kerszöv, pp. 151–168.
Mann, G. (1997): *Németország története 1919–1945*. Budapest: Balassi.
Mátyás, A. (2003): *A modern közgazdaságtan története*. Budapest: Aula.
Motta, M. (2004): *Competition Policy. Theory and Practice*. New York: Cambridge University Press.
Németh, I. (2007): *Demokrácia és diktatúra Németországban 1918–1945. Az 1918 novemberi forradalom és a weimari köztársaság*. Budapest: L'Harmattan.
Ostrom, V. (1999): Taking Constitutions Seriously. Buchanan's Challenge to Twentieth-Century Political Science. In: J. E. Alt, M. Levi and E. Ostrom (eds.), *Competition and Cooperation. Conversations with Nobelists about Economics and Political Science*. New York: Russell Sage Foundation, pp. 123–136.
Pelle, A. (2006): Az 'európai gondolat' egyik korai megjelenés. Robert Liefmann elképzelései a versenyszabályozásról az 1920-as évek Németországában. In: K. Gazdasági (ed.), *Gazdaságtudományi Tanulmányok*. Veszprém: Veszprémi Egyetem, pp. 273–278.
Pies, I. (2001): *Eucken und von Hayek im Vergleich*. Tübingen: Mohr.
Plato (1943): *Plato's Collected Works. Vol. 1*. Budapest: Hungarian Association of Philosophers.
Ptak, R. (2004): *Vom Ordoliberalismus zur Sozialen Marktwirtschaft. Stationen des Neoliberalismus in Deutschland*. Opladen: Leske, Budrich.
Robinson, J. (1933): *The Economics of Imperfect Competition*. London: Macmillan.
Rothbard, M. M. (2004): *Man, Economy, and the State with Power and Market*. Auburn, AL: Ludwig von Mises Institute.
Salin, P. (1996): Cartels as Efficient Productive Structures. *The Review of Austrian Economics*, vol. 9, no. 2, pp. 29–42.
Schlecht, O. (1989): Macht und Ohnmacht der Ordnungspolitik. Eine Bilanz nach 40 Jahren Sozialer Marktwirtschaft. *Ordo. Jahrbuch für die Ordnung von Wirtschaft und Gesellschaft*, vol. 40, pp. 303–320.
Siebert, H. (2005): *The German Economy. Beyond the Social Market*. Princeton, NJ: Princeton University Press.
Smith, A. (1992): *Nemzetek gazdagsága. E gazdaság természetének és okainak vizsgálata*. Budapest: Közgazdasági és Jogi Könyvkiadó.
Tokody, G. (1972): *Németország története*. Budapest: Akadémiai Kiadó.
Török, Á. (2001): Piacgazdasági érettség többféleképpen? Néhány alapfogalom értelmezése és alkalmazása a világgazdaság három nagy régiójában. *Közgazdasági Szemle*, vol. XLVIII, no. 9, pp. 707–725.

Török, Á. (2003): A piacra lépési korlátok átalakulása és a világgazdaság kibontakozása. *Közgazdasági Szemle*, vol. L., no. 3, pp. 195–208.

Tuchtfeld, E. (1989): Das 20. Jahrhundert als Zeitalter der Experimente. *Ordo. Jahrbuch für die Ordnung von Wirtschaft und Gesellschaft*, vol. 40. pp. 283–301.

Vanberg, V. (2004): *The Freiburg School. Walter Eucken and Ordoliberalism*. Freiburg Discussion Papers on Constitutional Economics, Walter Eucken Institut, vol. 11.

Volkert, J. (1991): Sozialpolitik und Wettbewerbsordnung. Die Bedeutung der wirtschafts- und sozialpolitischen Konzeption Walter Euckens für ein geordnetes sozialpolitisches System der Gegenwart. *Ordo. Jahrbuch für die Ordnung von Wirtschaft und Gesellschaft*, vol. 42, pp. 91–116.

Von Dietze, C. (1946): Aussagen evangelischer Christen in Deutschland zur Wirtschafts- und Sozialordnung. In: G. Brakelmann and T. Jähnichen (eds.), *Die Protestantische Wurzeln der Sozialen Marktwirtschaft*. Gütersloh: Gütersloher Verlagshaus, pp. 363–368.

Winkler, H. A. (2005): *Németország története a modern korban I.* Budapest: Osiris.

6 When a generally accepted theory fails to meet the facts
The case of Real Business Cycles Theory

Jorge Turmo Arnal, Ángel Rodríguez García-Brazales and Oscar Vara Crespo

1 Introduction

The history of economic thought has evolved through a twofold process. On one hand, there has been an increase in its internal consistency due to the continuous efforts to improve theories and models whose foundations had been settled before. On the other hand, the challenge of the facts has led economic thought to deep changes that sometimes have implied large modifications of the accepted wisdom. Both processes coexist and co-evolve and are difficult to disentangle. The drift of events may erode the adequacy of a theory to explain the facts unless we make a very serious effort of improving it. This is not to say that economic theories have to be set afresh every ten or twenty years, but some minor changes are always necessary and sometimes changes have to be large.

This is the case of Real Business Cycles Theory (RBC). It has been one of the more successful economic theories over the last thirty years and it has driven a lot of changes in our discipline. Furthermore, it has allowed us to establish a link with growth theory and it has formed the backbone of a handful of models widely used by theorists. However, the current crisis casts many doubts about its usefulness and its future is at stake.

In this chapter we first study the evolution of RBC and we explain why it has been so successful and why it is now under severe scrutiny. In the second part we explain the starting point of RBC and point out that it was a bold conjecture because it challenged the established wisdom on economic cycles. Before RBC, the economic cycles had been shown as a disequilibrium phenomenon; a kind of oscillation between a high peak and a deep hole. RBC theorists stated that the evolution of GDP over time was the joint outcome of an economic equilibrium and an external impulse, namely a technological shock.

In the third part we show the evolution of the theory following its own internal logic.

RBC was very well acknowledged among theorists who engaged on a process of refining its ideas, measuring the required data, testing the predictions of the theory and in some cases introducing minor changes to fit the data, and applying the approach to the analysis of the cyclical behavior of the main economies. Since the theory had some flaws, the second phase helped to reduce these and to gain internal coherence as well. The theory spread out in many fields and gained a lot of support.

One of the reasons for the success of RBC was that from 1985 onwards, the figures of the world's largest economies fitted very well with the main features of the theory. Developed countries grew following a fairly smooth trend, and the scope and size of the economic crisis in these countries did not challenge the backbone of RBC. We address this point in the fourth part of the chapter. Then, we show that RBC has focused mainly in the transmission process and has paid less attention to the impulse process. Besides, it has stressed that the impulses came from outside the economy, or that they could be considered that way. The fifth section of the chapter addresses the improvements made in the analysis of the impulse process.

The current crisis has shaken RBC theory. In part six we use the Spanish case to show that impulse mechanisms do not fit the evidence. The shocks that RBC theory proposes as candidates to explain the crisis do not hold in the Spanish case. Furthermore, it is hard to believe that the impulse has been exogenous.

Now RBC theory is facing its largest threat because it was unable to predict the current crisis. For many years it has explained a large amount of facts and data, but it now seems useless. In the final part we examine the future of RBC theory and the role it can play.

2 Real Business Cycles Theory

"That wine is not made in a day has long been recognized by economists" (Kydland and Prescott, 1982, p. 1345). This is the first phrase of the seminal article that launched the first version of the RBC model. The authors stressed the fact that the right characterization of the investment function in the economy had to take into account the "time to build." There is a lag between the moment in which an investment decision is taken and the availability of the investment good. They believed that this feature has been underscored in previous investment models so they could not explain accurately the medium-term cycles of the economy. "A thesis of this essay is that the assumption of multiple-period construction is crucial for explaining aggregate fluctuations" (Kydland and Prescott, 1982, p. 1345).

Then, they proceeded to explain the advantages of this approach over the single capital good adjustment cost technology. Setting aside the technical details, Kydland and Prescott's RBC theory introduces many novelties beyond the characterization of investment. RBC is a paradigm-switch approach to the analysis of the medium-term economic cycles. Although they state that this approach had been developed prior to Keynes, such a statement is hard to maintain.

The departure point of RBC theory is Solow's growth theory. In his main papers Solow (1956, 1957) developed a dynamic equilibrium model in which all the variables grow at the same rate, so per capita variables reach a steady-state level. Endogenous forces, mainly saving rate and population growth, drive the evolution of the variables to their steady-state level. If the values of the variables are out of their steady-state level, these forces drive them back to the dynamic equilibrium. When these forces change, for instance a higher saving to GDP ratio, the economy has to reach a new steady-state level, which means a different per capita GDP.

The main feature of Solow's model is that in every economy there is a steady-state level of the variables that will be reached sooner or later because of the values of the subjacent variables, saving rate, depreciation rate and population growth rate. There is something like an automatic mechanism at work here. If we look at the economy from outside, only changes in internal factors can affect its performance and the final outcome can be easily predicted by knowing the values of some relevant variables.

This is the approach that RBC theorists, and particularly Kydland and Prescott, have borrowed from growth theory and they have applied to medium-term fluctuations. For them, economic cycles are not a continuous trip from slumps to peaks and back. There are slumps and peaks, but they are not as large as it was believed. They are not continuous either; GDP and other variables can grow for some periods without experiencing a decrease. Instead of drawing business cycles as movement of perpetual ups and downs, they draw a straight line that shows minor disturbances.

The peaks and slumps approach implies that the economy is seldom close to equilibrium, and that disequilibrium prevails. The approach chosen by RBC theory implies that the economy is almost always in equilibrium or near the equilibrium.

Before them, Sargent (1979) pointed out that the co-movement among variables was the point that had to be addressed, while peaks and slumps, although meaningful, were not. Sargent believed that the general rule was equilibrium because it was more frequent, so we have to pay attention to the behavior of the variables and the co-movements among them. The co-movements are the structure of the economy and they allow us to explain and predict its evolution. Peaks and slumps are the consequence of external changes, external shocks. If they do not affect the co-movements among variables, it is not worthwhile to study them, because there are just changes of level, not structural changes. RBC theorists agree on it and this is one of the most important features of the model.

Lucas (1977) had defined business cycles as the fluctuations of output about trend and the co-movements among output and other aggregates. He was also focusing on trend (a dynamical equilibrium concept) instead of fluctuations. He was interested in the variables that explained the trend, the general evolution of an economy, and he believed that fluctuations were local phenomena whose interest was small.

These approaches were just the opposite of Keynesian ideas. The Keynesian economy is always out of equilibrium, so it is necessary to devote a lot of effort to analyze the causes of the disequilibrium and how to avoid it. Besides, the Keynesian approach focused on internal sources of disequilibrium, endogenous factors, which could be corrected by the appropriate set of economic policies. As we explain, RBC theorists do not share this point of view.

Kydland and Prescott explain that fluctuations are deviations from the path. They state that the path increases monotonically over time at a very slow rate, the trend. The meaning of the trend is not based on the mean of a stochastic process.

It is defined by the computational procedure used to fit the curve through the data, provided that the data is smooth. In doing that they are using the growth trend of the absolute variables *à la* Solow and they take for granted that the trend is always growing. If that is right, fluctuations around the trend are less important and we have to focus on the co-movements among variables.

Thus, trend definition becomes very relevant. The method is to take the logarithm of the variable and to select a trend path that has two properties: to minimize the sum of the squared deviations from a given series and to be as smooth as possible. The first condition means that the trend has to follow as closely as possible the values of the variable. The second means that the squared second differences are as small as possible. Provided that both requirements are contradictory, the final outcome is a trade-off between the value of the series and the smoothness of the trend. The trend, once defined, is used to calculate the deviations of each series, which are the raw data to be compared with another series.

In Lucas' model (1977) deviations from the trend arise due to holding wrong expectations, caused by government economic policies. As a consequence, economic agents act correctly and rationally for the wrong reasons, so the economy deviates from the trend. When new and better information allows agents to correct their expectations, their behavior changes and the economy comes back to the trend. Kydland and Prescott do not follow Lucas. They believe that agents form their expectations correctly, they are not misleading in anyway. But there are technological shocks, which cannot be forecasted, that lead them to change their choices. That way, the variables also change and deviate from the trend.

The economy is populated by a representative infinitely lived household. Households value consumption and leisure so they have to decide how to share their time between them. The time-to-build assumption implies that multiple periods are needed to build new capital goods, and only finished capital goods are included in the capital stock despite all of them requiring resources. Household preferences exhibit non-time-separable utility, because the representative household takes into account present and future leisure. This crucial feature implies a greater intertemporal substitution of leisure. That way, the household can react to technological changes by increasing the ratio of present leisure to future leisure or vice versa. Their behavior adapts to the new environment by choosing to work more or less today or in the future. This hypothesis is necessary to explain the aggregate changes in employment over time in an equilibrium model.

There is large cross-sectional evidence of this behavior. For instance, some household members go into and out of the labor market for some months and there are vacations as well. Besides, it has been shown that the number of hours worked varies a lot in different seasons. Furthermore, jobs with more variable employment patterns do not earn better salaries, so we can discard that seasonal variation is driven by different payment schedules. Thus, intertemporal substitution of leisure is an optimal answer to the changes driven by technological shocks.

To test the theory, Kydland and Prescott compare the behavior of the selected US series and the behavior of the series generated by the model. They do not focus on the level of the variables, but on its trend and the deviations from the trend. They are only interested in the co-movements of the smoothed series and the deviations from the trend. Again, they believe that shocks are external and unforeseeable, so we can only check the structural reaction of the economy to them. They find that the figures of the theory fit quite well with US post-war figures:

> "Economic theory implies that, given the nature of the shocks to technology and people's willingness and ability to intertemporally and intratemporally substitute, the economy will display fluctuations like those the US economy displays" (Prescott, 1986, p. 21).

Additional but important predictions are that fluctuations in output of 5 percent from trend are accounted for by variations in employment and the rest depend on changes in the technology parameter. Investment is three or more times as volatile as output while consumption is less volatile than output. The RBC theory predicts that deviations from the trend will display high serial correlations. Summing up, theory predicts what is observed and this is the main reason to trust it. The only shortcoming of the model is labor elasticity of output is clearly lower than observed and more research had to be devoted to improve the performance of the model.

One outstanding consequence of the theory concerns the effectiveness of economic policy.

"Economic fluctuations are optimal responses to uncertainty in the rate of technological change" (Prescott, 1986, p. 22). Before RBC, economic fluctuations had been considered a matter of disequilibrium, implying that there were some weaknesses in the economy that generate the slumps. RBC theorists believe that there are two different issues at stake. On the one hand, the impulse, the shock, that is supposed to be external to the economy; on the other hand, the transmission mechanism, the way in which rational agents react and take into account in their consumption/leisure decisions the effects of the shocks. If reactions are optimal, as RBC theorists claim, agents are choosing the best option, so economic policy cannot outperform it. In many cases economic policy will hinder agents by impeding them to react correctly. That way, economic policy should not focus on stabilizing the economy because the stabilization process is automatic. It should focus on the determinants of the technical advance and how to foster it. In so doing, economic policy would improve the well-being of every individual and the whole society as well. This approach is closely linked with the role technology plays in economic growth in augmented Solow's models. Provided that technology can help the economy to escape from the steady-state, and that it was the only engine of growth when the first RBC models were launched, economic policy has to foster this process by a careful study of the measures required to assure the technological advance.

3 Extensions of the theory

RBC was a success from the very beginning. There were critics, such as Summers (1986), who showed their discomfort with an equilibrium approach to business cycles and the kind of procedures used to calibrate the model, but the great majority of theorists welcomed the theory. There were several points that explained this reaction. First, it was a macroeconomic model based on micro foundations. The Keynesian approach had been criticized a lot because it was unclear about the processes that drove changes and about which were the reactions of agents to these changes. This is the reason why new classical economics stressed that every model had to be solidly grounded on microeconomic foundations. RBC theory fulfills this requirement. The representative agent is the cornerstone of the model and their optimal responses to economic shocks drive the economy.

Second, RBC is an equilibrium model with links with General Equilibrium Theory that allows economists to study the effects of changes in the whole economy without going out from the common framework. General Equilibrium Theory was incompatible with Keynesian macroeconomics, but RBC theory is not. The third reason is that RBC theory is devised to mimic the data, more precisely postwar US data, so the model can be used to explain the evolution of the US economy. More generally, the model can be used to explain the evolution of other developed economies because Kydland and Prescott claim that the general features of its model can be found in other countries. The data of countries other than the US have been compared with the theoretical results of the model. That implies the opening of a very wide research field in every country and comparing different countries among them. It is easy to understand why RBC was so welcomed.

The next stage was to address the more difficult or controversial points of RBC theory or to correct the discrepancies between the theory and the data. Kydland and Prescott were aware that there was a lot of work ahead. Once the theory was adopted as a useful tool by many theorists, the improvement process started. In this way, the theory evolved following its own internal logic and the challenges that new data were generating. Thus, we are going to explain now the main extensions of the model that can be considered as an improvement process. As we will explain later, the improvement was large, but not enough to overcome the effects on the theory of our current crisis.

The larger discrepancies between the model and the data were located in the labor market. Hours worked fluctuated much more than productivity and the correlation between hours worked and productivity was close to zero. Hansen and Wright (1992) addressed the first issue. Provided that there are only technological shocks in the economy depicted by RBC theory, it is difficult to explain why small changes in productivity drive large fluctuations in the hours worked. It is necessary to assume that short-run labor supply elasticity is large and the initial model could not explain this feature.

To address this issue Hansen and Wright consider that utility depends not only on present leisure but on past leisure as well, so that households exhibit non-separable preferences. In this model, they show that non-separable preferences lead agents to increase the number of hours worked when there are small productivity increases. Agents want to profit from every productivity improvement, however small, and their intertemporal leisure choice changes a lot. But agents' behavior is different depending on whether they believe that the shock is temporary or permanent. The above-mentioned reaction only happens if the shock is temporary.

If agents believe that productivity changes are permanent, they do not change their hours-worked pattern. That way, they reconcile the short-term evidence with the long-run tendency, a reduction in hours worked as productivity increases.

A second extension related to the same topic is described in Hansen (1985). Variation in the labor input comes about by changes in hours per worker or in the number of employed workers. The first is the standard approach, but Hansen focuses on the second. He states that all changes in labor input are because of the changing number of workers. He builds an indivisible labor model in which workers can only work a defined number of hours per day or not work at all, so changes in hours worked do not play any role. In equilibrium, a random process allocates individuals to jobs. That way, individual labor supply elasticity is very small because employed people value leisure as well and they do not want to increase the hours worked. But aggregate labor supply elasticity is large enough to explain that small productivity changes can drive larger hours worked figures.

Both extensions solve one of the shortcomings of the models, but are unable to cope with the other: the model predicts that there is large positive correlation between hours worked and productivity while data do not confirm it. The technological shocks shift the labor demand schedule to the right while labor supply does not change and the number of hours worked increases a lot. There are two additional extensions that have been built to bridge the gap. One of them is Christiano and Eichenbaum's model (1992). They add to the model government spending shocks. Although they are not supply-side shocks, they have similar effects provided that economic agents cannot forecast them. If public consumption and private consumption are not perfect substitutes, an increase in government spending will reduce individual wealth. As a consequence, agents decide to work more because leisure is a normal good. This can be interpreted as labor supply schedule moving to the right, like demand, and the model can generate a pattern of hours versus productivity more similar to the data.

A different approach was developed by Benhabib, Rogerson and Wright in 1991. They state that agents derive utility not only from market-produced goods, but from home-produced goods as well. As a consequence the time spent at home only adds utility to the agent if they devote it to leisure, but the time spent producing consumption goods at home generates disutility as well as in the market. There are two consequences of this kind of behavior. First, agents can increase hours worked in the market by reducing the hours worked at home without reducing its utility. Second, if shocks to household production are not perfectly correlated with shocks to market production, substitution between home and market activity is very easy. When there is a negative shock to market production, agents substitute hours worked in the market by hours worked at home, and vice versa. Both effects can be represented as a shift in the labor supply schedule. That way, the extended model does not exhibit a strong positive correlation between productivity and hours worked. Both extensions have improved the adequacy of the model to real data and are very good examples of the evolution of RBC theory.

Cooley and Hansen (1989) develop another extension of the model. They remind us that one of the roots of RBC theory were Friedman's articles and books on monetary issues. Despite this, RBC had refused to include money as a relevant variable. On the contrary, Kydland and Prescott (1982) had stated that the effects of money on the cycle were a myth. Cooley and Hansen, based on Hansen (1985), built a RBC model with indivisible labor where money plays a role in generating fluctuations.

Money is introduced in the model using a cash-in-advance constraint. Provided that in this simple model leisure cannot be bought using money, it only affects consumption. Investment is not affected either. Following the monetarist tradition, if money is supplied in a regular manner, for instance according to a monetary rule that is generally known, it does not disturb the economy, provided that the amount of money supplied meets the requirements of the economy. But if money supply is irregular without taking into account its effects on the real side of the economy, cyclical fluctuations can arise. In the first case the cash-in-advance constraint is not binding but in the second case it has effects: consumption becomes more variable relative to income and the price level is quite volatile. Besides, the correlations between these variables and GDP become smaller in absolute value. That way the introduction of an erratic money supply in the model helps explain better the co-movements among variables.

4 The success of Real Business Cycles Theory

RBC has been, and still is, the dominant paradigm in medium-term economic dynamics. Nearly all experts in this field are working using concepts, variables, relationships and measurement tools defined by RBC theorists. Besides, the model as such has been used by scholars of other fields as a common framework of analysis to develop their own models and to compare its performance.

Several reasons lie behind the influence of the theory. The first one is linked with microeconomic foundations. Many economists felt uncomfortable with Keynesian economics because of the radical separation between microeconomics and macroeconomics that it implied. Despite the well-known "fallacy of composition" explained by Samuelson, the lack of links that might bridge the gap between micro and macroeconomics was perceived as a serious failure of Keynesian models. RBC theory gave a clear-cut answer to these concerns: macroeconomics must be based upon a careful study of agents' microeconomic behavior. Once it has been determined what the agent's decisions are, we can aggregate them to explain the evolution of macroeconomic variables. In this way, we can be sure that we actually understand what is going on in the economy.

This is the reason why micro foundations have reassured many experts that they were on the right track and has led them to use this kind of model as the departure point of macroeconomic analysis. Besides, RBC theory claims to be a general equilibrium one in which good markets, money market and bonds market, clear because all prices are flexible and all agents are rational. General equilibrium is the ideal point of the economy, because efficiency attains its maximum. RBC theory states that, given agents' preferences and the state of the technology, the economy is in equilibrium. Only external shocks, whatever the origin, can drive the economy out of equilibrium, but prices flexibility and agent's reaction to the new environment drive the economy back to the equilibrium. If this approach can be taken for granted, difficult issues about the existence of multiple equilibria, the policy measures that should be taken to reestablish the equilibrium or the time lag that it implies, need not be addressed.

There was some criticism about one main feature of the model: the representative agent. The only way to reduce the highly complex system of a large number of agents is to consider that there is a representative agent, a kind of "average of behavior" whose preferences and choices can be used as a common pattern to compute the equilibrium along with flexible prices and the state of technology. The representative agent is an abstraction, a device to ease the analysis, in the same way as the only good in Solow's growth model. The critical issue is whether the use of the representative agent distorts the analysis or not. If agents' behavior variance is very large, the representative agent, an average, might be useless. In spite of recognizing that such shortcomings exist, RBC theory adherents believe that the advantages exceed them. Thus, the representative agent is one of the key elements of the analysis.

Another reason to understand the success of RBC theory during the 1980s and 90s is that figures did not challenge the theory. RBC theory implies that variables evolve along a definite trend and only external shocks drive them out of it. The deviations from the trend are the aggregate fluctuations that we study. A very important objective of RBC theory was to show that variables fluctuated around the trend, but showed just minor deviations. Prior to RBC theory it was supposed that cycles were a roundabout of peaks and slumps; Kydland and Prescott showed that the roundabout was a myth. Using the Hodrick and Prescott filter, or any other de-trending procedure, figures and graphs show that actual deviation, the cycle compound, is small. There is a cycle, of course, but large aggregate fluctuations are not pervasive. The theory was applied to developed economies, whose data was long and robust enough to be analyzed, and one of the salient features of the data, and more precisely GDP, in several countries, is its increasing trend during two decades. As an example, in Figure 6.1 we show GDP figures for Germany, Japan, the US and the UK from 1986 and 2006. Figures are in billions of national currency, except in Japan where they are in trillions of yen.

The data show that GDP increased in the UK, the US and Germany. Japanese GDP increased less than other countries. Since variables are at current prices and not in logarithms, the slope of each one does not show the actual rate of growth. More important still is to realize that GDP growth, no matter if it is large or small, is very smooth. This smoothness is the proof that RBC theory performs well. RBC theory predicts that the trend of a variable might change, but the deviations from the trend will not be large because agents adapt to external shocks easily and quickly. Large deviations from the GDP trend would imply that agents do not adapt to external shocks, allowing a roundabout of peaks and slumps. These data are strongly backing the model: deviations exist, but are not large. As a consequence, data give experts more confidence in the model and its usefulness.

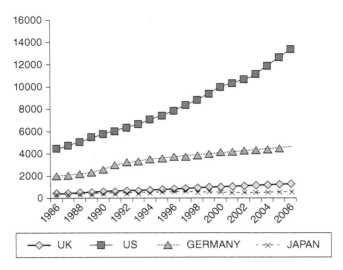

Figure 6.1 GDP of the UK, the US, Germany and Japan from 1986 to 2006

The second consequence of the smoothness of GDP data in developed countries is that experts have focused mainly in co-movements among variables. Following Frisch, the analysis of aggregate fluctuations must distinguish between impulse mechanisms and transmission mechanisms. Each one has to be studied in itself. A glance at the data makes it evident that impulse mechanisms are less important than transmission mechanisms since the evolution of the variable through time is very smooth. This is the reason why RBC theorists have focused mainly on transmission mechanisms and the impulse mechanism has deserved less attention. The co-movements among variables have been carefully studied in many countries using different samples. The outcome has been a generalized agreement on the "stylized facts" of economic cycles. Since these stylized facts have proved to perform very well in nearly all the economies, they are now a proof of RBC theory success. The remaining issue was the impulse mechanism.

5 Improving the impulse mechanism

RBC is based on the statement that unanticipated technological shocks generate aggregate fluctuations. In one article Prescott says: "The finding that when uncertainty in the rate of technological change is incorporated into the growth model it displays the business cycle phenomena was both dramatic and unanticipated" (Prescott, 1986, p. 12).

Technological change is measured by Prescott, following Solow (1957), as the difference between changes in output less changes in the number of production factors, weighted by share of every factor in the production function, which is Total Factors Productivity. TFP measures the production growth that does not depend on the number of factors employed. The estimate of TFP for the US economy between 1955 and 1984 was 1.2. Starting from Solow and refining his analysis, Prescott states that the standard deviation of technological shocks is 0.763 (Prescott, 1986, p. 18).

The size of the technological shocks are very large and it casts some doubts on it. Some experts stressed that the TFP is a measure of our ignorance and it was wrong to explain it by exogenous factors only. Some endogenous factors may contribute alongside the exogenous ones. Besides, and more important still, positive technological shocks can certainly explain GDP increases, but output decreases should be driven by negative technological shocks, a technological regression that is very unlikely. These reasons lead some authors to take into account the behavior of endogenous variables alongside technological shocks.

Galí (1999) criticizes the role of technological shocks on aggregate fluctuations. He addresses the above-mentioned problem of the zero correlation between hours worked and productivity. Instead of improving RBC theory, as we have explained before, Galí builds a different model, which contains monopolistic competition, sticky prices and more elements. Galí studies the effects on this model of a non-technological shock. Money supply grows according to the technological growth of the economy. If there is a technological shock, the amount of money changes as well. He discovers that the monetary shock generates a positive co-movement between hours worked and productivity, according to the data, but the technological shock displays a negative co-movement. In the aggregate, there is no correlation between productivity and hours worked, as the data show. And Galí says:

> Whether the technology shocks in *actual* economies are responsible for the pattern of GDP and labour-input fluctuations associated with business cycles remains an open question, and one which should provide a critical test of the relevance of a research program that aims to interpret the bulk of aggregate fluctuations as resulting from those shocks.
>
> (Galí, 1999, p. 265)

A different approach is to maintain that TFP changes are the cause of fluctuations but other factors amplify them. That way, small TFP changes can generate the observed fluctuations. Burnside, Eichenbaum and Rebelo analyzed the effect the amount of work carried out had on economic cycles behavior. Production depends on workers' effort, not only on hours worked. Firms hire workers depending on technology and demand. If there is a technological shock, firms demand from their workers an effort increase that is compensated because work disutility increases as well (Burnside *et al.*, 1993, p. 249). Work effort is pro-cyclical and it helps to partly explain output growth. Thus, a small technological shock drives an upward change in labor effort and a larger output increase. Following the same pattern, in one article in 1996, they stress that capital use is more important and more significant than the amount of capital. When there is a positive technological shock, capital utilization grows and the effect of a small technological shock is amplified by this element. Their estimates show that the effect of productivity shocks decreases up to 70 percent. Thus TFP changes much smaller than previously supposed can produce the same output fluctuation.

RBC has evolved and it has become a general framework to analyze economic dynamics. Thus, its focus has widened, from economic cycles to different issues. For these reasons the origin and nature of shocks has changed as well. Kydland and Prescott stated that shocks were only technological and that the real side of the economy matters while the monetary side does not. The evolution of RBC theory has allowed monetary shocks to be taken into account. The influence of monetary mechanisms has a clear Keynesian flavor that leads us to consider sticky prices and salaries. There are monetary shocks that influence the economic cycle in different ways, not only directly. However, these shocks are not an endogenous mechanism that may drive cycles once and again; they are just single events, like technological shocks, that push the economy away from its trend.

Galí, López-Salido and Vallés (2003) analyzed the systematic reactions of the FED to technological shocks that hit the US economy from 1954 to 1998. They studied whether the monetary policy modified, amplified or reduced their effects on the economy or not and the evolution of this monetary policy. They show that while Paul Volcker and Allan Greenspan were FED chairmen they focused on stabilizing prices following an optimal behavior rule. In so doing their aim was that the monetary policy did not amplify shock effects.

Another approach was proposed by Bernanke, Gertler and Gilchrist (1999). The authors pointed out that market credit frictions widen the effects of the shocks in output fluctuations. The reason is the existence of agency costs in the process of intermediation between lenders and borrowers. These costs are based on asymmetric information and depend on the net wealth of the borrower. If the borrower is "rich," he invests partly his own money and borrows the rest. That way, his incentives are better aligned with the lender's incentives. If the borrower's net wealth is reduced and agency costs are high, the amount of credit is smaller. If we take for granted that the agent's net wealth is pro-cyclical, when the economy grows agency costs are smaller and the credit flow eases. This generates a financial accelerator that amplifies the positive effect of shocks. Conversely, if the economy does not grow, the borrower's net wealth is more reduced and credit access worsens. In this way, the financial accelerator can transform a small negative shock into a larger output decrease. Bernanke *et al.* show that an unexpected reduction of 25 base points of federal funds interest rate increase the output by 0.8 percent after three quarters.

6 The crisis

The crisis has shaken the economies and has shaken the economic theory as well. It has been the first deep crisis in developed countries since the Second World War. The GDP of developed countries had been growing more or less steadily since then, although some countries have grown more than others. For several decades economic growth has been the rule and stagnation the exception. Suddenly in many countries growth has become an objective that is out of reach.

One of the most salient features of the current crisis is that their effects are pervasive in developed economies, while developing and emerging countries are not suffering from it. In the past, we watched economic crisis in Latin American countries, such as Argentina and Mexico, and in Southern Asian countries, such as Indonesia, the Philippines and others, as a distant event that could not affect us. Currently, the crisis is very severe in the European Union, mainly in eurozone countries, it has been tough in the US as well and Japan is not free from contagion. Features common in many developed countries are recession, massive layoffs, financial sudden stops, and a strong preference for liquidity. The amount of public and private debt is threatening large countries such as Italy and Spain. Capital flies away from Spain to look for a safe harbor in Brazil, for instance. Chinese politicians and financial experts travel to Europe to decide whether to invest in European firms and European public debt or not. IMF experts land in the Southern European airports to perform the same kind of careful analysis that they have been doing routinely in Africa and Asia for decades. China is pulling up middle-range Southern Asian economies, while Germany is not pulling up the economies of the eurozone. The middle class is growing in Brazil, China and India while wealth inequality increases in the US and Europe.

Additionally, the crisis is long lasting. Nearly all European countries and the US experienced a deep recession in 2009. After a slight economic recovery in 2010, 2011 was worse and 2012 finished without any sign of economic recovery in Europe, although US growth rates are better. Southern European countries plunged into a recession in 2009 and they have not escaped from it yet. Economic perspectives are not good either, and some experts fear the contagion of the crisis to emergent economies. The growing interconnectedness among economies transforms regional problems into global difficulties. Americans, Chinese, Russians, all of them urge Europe to solve their internal problems to avoid the spillover effects. Strong growth is not predicted yet.

To explain why the crisis is so deep and so long we have to point to financial issues. The departure point has been the dissemination of toxic assets, mainly created in the US, across countries' financial systems, firms and households. When Lehman Brothers fell in September of 2008, the expansive wave reached virtually all countries that belonged to the financial circuit. A combination of low interest rates for years, a decrease of risk perception among agents, the financial engineering that allowed sharing, distributing and even postponing risks and new investment conduits whose drawbacks were not evident, led to a financial turmoil the consequences of which we are still suffering.

The financial crisis destroyed, first and above all, the confidence among economic agents. We have to bear in mind that the economy works with small amounts of money and large amounts of confidence. If confidence diminishes or even vanishes, the small amount of money required for the daily routine operations disappears as well. Feasible transactions are not carried out, profitable firms file for bankruptcy because of liquidity problems, bank runs are more likely to happen, private debts become public debt and economic problems pile up.

RBC has been shaken as well. RBC implies that shocks are external and unanticipated, so it cannot be blamed for not having predicted it. Besides, it must be clearly stated that the co-movements among variables in the countries hit by the crisis are those explained by the model. But the model struggles to fit the facts in two ways: the impulse mechanism and the economic policy.

We address first the economic policy. Since RBC is an equilibrium theory, it is supposed that an agent's adjustment to the new environment is optimal. Thus, economic policy either is useless or it could worsen the final outcome. The two economic areas that have been affected the most by the turmoil are the US and the eurozone.

Because of many factors we are not going to explain here, eurozone response to overcome the crisis has been austerity. The hypothesis is that our indebtedness level is too high and it must be reduced by any means to rebound from the bottom and to grow again. Austerity is a process of reaching a new equilibrium without any economic policy at work. Thus, it fits well the RBC approach to the crisis, because it implies that the economy can recover without any external, say public, support. But our economies actually are not recovering. We suffered a deep recession in 2009 and after a slight and weak recovery in some countries in 2010 and 2011 the GDP of the eurozone is very close to negative figures. Four years after the beginning of the crisis, our economies have not recovered, and they seem to be very far from the equilibrium.

Conversely, the US has adopted, for many reasons, a proactive attitude. From the very beginning the FED and the US government have launched recovery programs. They have used both fiscal and monetary policy to stimulate growth and to avoid the worst consequences of the crisis. Although the US economy plunged into recession in 2009, it has exhibited continuous growth since. Growth rates have not been brilliant, but the US economy has fared far better that the eurozone from 2010 on. We may discuss to what extent the economic policy of the FED and the US government is the only factor responsible for the performance of the US economy, but the difference between the US and the eurozone economies is undeniable. Economic policy has succeeded while the absence of it has not.

To analyze the failure of the impulse mechanism of RBC theory we apply it to the Spanish case. The first mechanism is a technological shock which can be measured using TFP. The figures are shown in Table 6.1.

A technological shock implies a TFP change. If the technological change was the cause of the crisis the data would show a downward movement on the eve of the crisis, 2007. But data show that from the base year, 2000, TFP has been changing slightly while the Spanish economy was growing 3 percent yearly. If we suppose that TFP describes the trend of the Spanish economy we would expect a sudden decrease in 2007 to show a dramatic change in trend and to announce the beginning of the crisis. But such change does not exist and we have to conclude that no technological shock has shaken the Spanish economy.

Table 6.1 TFP in Spain (2003–2007)

Year	2003	2004	2005	2006	2007
TFP	99.5	99.3	99.3	99.3	99.1

Another possible shock is the increase of European Central Bank (ECB) interest rate. Econometric studies show that a 1 percent increase of interest rates reduces output by 0.3 percent the first year and 0.7 percent in the second. From January to July of 2007 the interest rate increased by 0.75 percent. If the monetary shock had been the impulse mechanism of the crisis, Spanish GDP would have decreased by 0.3 percent in 2008 and 0.7 percent in 2009. Figures show that GDP growth fell from 4.0 percent to 2.9 percent in 2008 and there was a 4.0 percent negative growth in 2009. Thus, we cannot single out the interest rate increase as the impulse of our crisis. Besides, ECB interest rates decreased markedly afterwards, reducing the theoretical effects of the first change.

The approach of Bernanke, Gertler and Gilchrist explained above points to the relationship between the unexpected increased of interest rate and the reduction of GDP growth. We cannot apply this approach to our case because ECB interest rates were not unanticipated. Before the upward change, the ECB had sent a clear message about what it was intending to do.

Summing up, we do not find any impulse mechanism in RBC literature that may explain the cause of the crisis in the Spanish case, and we take for granted that the same applies to many other countries. Despite the improvements made by RBC on impulse mechanisms, the roots of negative shocks are not well grounded. RBC has focused on co-movements among variables because external shocks could not be forecasted in any way. They are right if shocks are external, but they have failed to recognize that endogenous shocks may appear as well. Exogenous shocks or shocks that can be approached "as if" they were exogenous can explain small and medium-size changes in the economy. But the main forces driving them are only partially exogenous. RBC theory cannot cope with endogenous shocks because they entail a feedback loop that cannot be isolated. The clear-cut separation between impulse mechanism and transmission mechanism becomes more complex and difficult to handle. But we must handle it, no matter whether models may accommodate it or not. If models do not perform well, we must change them.

7 The future of Real Business Cycles Theory

The economic crisis has raised several concerns about the usefulness of RBC. Criticism of RBC is not new but the evidence of the difficulties to explain the crisis has taken it to the forefront. Many experts pointed out many years ago that the micro foundations of the model were wrong because the use of the representative agent involved a tautology. Others have stressed that the equilibrium approach of the model is useful to obtain mathematical results, but is less useful to describe the main features of actual economies.

From another point of view, the simplicity of the model, alongside its mathematical tractability has led to its use as a tool to analyze the business cycle worldwide, allowing economists to compare the results in different countries and in different time spans. The addition of some neo-Keynesian elements has transformed the model into a standard that is used not only to explain medium-term aggregate fluctuations, its initial objective, but to analyze the evolution of an economy from different perspectives. It has become a generalized tool whose usefulness is undeniable, although with some serious drawbacks. Also, calibration methods, a radical novelty in itself, have spread throughout the economic analysis as an alternative or additional approach to estimate, quantify and measure the relationships among variables.

One possible answer about the future of RBC theory would be that the crisis has falsified the theory and it would not be used anymore because all the conclusions obtained from a radically wrong theory are false. We do not agree. The crisis has shown that the impulse mechanism of RBC theory is defective or wrong, but the transmission mechanism still performs well. The crisis has also shown that economic policies have been effective while spontaneous re-equilibrium has failed to run as RBC theory predicts.

Thus, our first conclusion is that RBC theory is a very useful tool to analyze the relationship among variables' trends and deviations. We should not discard the theory, because it can greatly help us to deal with these issues. Besides, the comparison between the same relationships in different countries and economies may substantially increase our knowledge. The tools that have been developed are useful and we have to refine them as much as possible.

The second conclusion is that we must rethink the impulse mechanism in two different ways. First, technological shocks are not the only factor that explains aggregate fluctuations because the technological regress that would underline a negative shock has little, if any, empirical support. We have to engage in further research in all areas to find new elements that can generate a shock. One of the toughest lessons of the crisis is that monetary and financial issues are very important, not just a veil. We must take into account seriously the monetary and financial side of the economy, not constrain ourselves to the real side of it.

Third, and closely linked with the previous point, some shocks that hit the economy might be endogenous. It is a prejudgment to state that all shocks are exogenous. The economy is too complex to be described like an equilibrium system that is pushed away from it due to external shocks. We are aware that endogenous shocks are more difficult to handle because they may imply feedback loops, but we have to bear them in mind. Sometimes we can deal with endogenous shocks as if they were exogenous, but in other cases we simply cannot and we should not. An open-minded research on the causes of aggregated fluctuations has to be carried out.

The fourth issue is to distinguish between small and large aggregate fluctuations. The de-trending procedures we are using calculate the trend by smoothing the series. That way a large aggregate fluctuation is partly hidden and decomposed into two parts: a change in trend and a deviation from the trend. Since we focus on deviations from the trend, the actual size of fluctuations is underscored. Besides, large fluctuations may imply a structural change that cannot be addressed by using tools that have been devised to analyze small fluctuations without structural change. Additionally we must clearly distinguish middle-term aggregate fluctuations, the economic cycle, from structural change that belongs to the long-term side of the economy and has to be analyzed by growth theory.

One of the main tenets of RBC theory was its close relationship with Solow's model and growth theory. Although it has been criticized, we believe that a better interplay between cycle theory and growth theory is desirable. Growth theory gives room to structural changes in the underlying elements of an economy that explain why growth rates might change. In medium-term aggregate fluctuations a structural change entails a large trend modification. We might treat this not as a cycle phenomenon, but as part of the long-run tendency of the economy. The problem is that establishing whether a change in trend belongs to the middle-term or to the long-term is not straightforward.

As a general conclusion, we state that RBC theory will be helpful in the future. We should not discard it, although some elements have not been endorsed by the facts and figures of the crisis. We have to preserve the parts that have fared well, mainly the co-movements among variables in every country and the relationship among different countries, but we can no longer accept the impulse mechanism of the theory. This is not to say that we should eliminate it; we want to improve its performance by adding more suitable explications of the aggregate fluctuations, regardless of whether they imply large modifications in the theory. Also, once we have established that shocks can be both exogenous and endogenous, and taking into account the experience of the current crisis, we may not take for granted that after a shock the economy bounces back and reaches a new equilibrium quickly and easily. That is wrong. Economic policies have a role to play in stabilizing the economy.

RBC theory is not condemned to disappear from the tool box of macroeconomic analysis, but it is obliged to undergo large changes to improve its performance. If RBC theorists refuse to make the necessary changes, the theory will become irrelevant and it will not be used anymore.

References

Benhabib, J., Rogerson, R. and Wright, R. (1991): Homework in Macroeconomics: Household Production and Aggregate Fluctuations. *Journal of Political Economy*, vol. 99, no. 6, pp. 1166–1187.

Bernanke, B., Gertler, M. and Gilchrist, S. (1999): The Financial Accelerator in a Quantitative Business Cycle Framework. In: J. Taylor and M. Woodford (eds.), *Handbook of Macroeconomics*. Amsterdam: North Holland, vol. 1, pp. 1341–1393.

Burnside, C., Eichenbaum, M. and Rebelo, S. (1993): Labor Hoarding and the Business Cycle. *Journal of Political Economy*, vol. 5, no. 101, pp. 245–273.

Christiano, L. J. and Eichenbaum, M. (1992): Current Real Business Cycle Theories and Aggregate Labor Market Fluctuations. *American Economic Review*, vol. 82, no. 3, pp. 430–450.

Cooley, T. F. and Hansen, G. D. (1989): The Inflation Tax in a Real Business Cycle Model. *American Economic Review*, vol. 79, no. 4, pp. 733–748.

Galí, J. (1999): Technology, Employment, and the Business Cycle: Do Technology Shocks Explain Aggregate Fluctuations? *The American Economic Review*, vol. 89, no. 1, pp. 249–271.

Galí, J., López-Salido, D. and Vallés, J. (2003): Technology Shocks and Monetary Policy: Assessing the Fed's Performance. *Journal of Monetary Economics*, vol. 50, no. 4, pp. 721–743.

Hansen, G. D. (1985): Indivisible Labor and the Business Cycle. *Journal of Monetary Economics*, vol. 16, no. 3, pp. 309–328.

Hansen, G. and Wright, R. (1992): The Labor Market in Real Business Cycle. *Federal Reserve Bank of Minneapolis Quarterly Review*, vol. 16, no. 2, 2–12.

Kydland, F. and Prescott, E. C. (1982): Time to Build and Aggregate Fluctuations. *Econometrica*, vol. 50, no. 6, pp. 1345–1369.

Kydland, F. and Prescott, E. C. (1990): Business Cycles: Real Facts and a Monetary Myth. *Federal Reserve Bank of Minneapolis Quarterly Review*, vol. 14, no. 2, pp. 3–18.

Lucas, R. E. Jr. (1977): Understanding Business Cycles. *Carnegie-Rochester Conference Series on Public Policy*, vol. 5, pp. 7–29.

Prescott, E. C. (1986): Theory Ahead of Business Cycle Measurement. *Federal Reserve Bank of Minneapolis Quarterly Review*, vol. 10, no. 4, pp. 9–22.

Sargent, T. J. (1979): *Macroeconomic Theory*. New York: Academic Press.

Solow, R. M. (1956): A Contribution to the Theory of Economic Growth. *Quarterly Journal of Economics*, vol. 70, no. 1, pp. 65–94.

Solow, R. M. (1957): Technical Change and the Aggregate Production Function. *Review of Economics and Statistics*, vol. 39, no. 3, pp. 312–320.

Summers, L. H. (1986): Some Skeptical Observations on Real Business Cycle Theory. *Federal Reserve Bank of Minneapolis Quarterly Review*, vol. 10, no. 4, pp. 23–27.

7 The cultural and psychological dimensions of economic development

Arturo Hermann

1 Introduction

In this period of economic and social distress, a thorough re-appraisal of the main aspects and problems of our economic and social development has been emerging in virtually all the most developed countries.

We will address some elements of such issues by analysing the potential of a pluralist and interdisciplinary perspective in economics for explaining significant aspects of the concepts – in particular, market, capitalism, socialism and democracy, public and private action – that have shaped this evolution.

As a matter of fact, these (apparently simple) concepts convey complex meanings which are interpreted differently according to the theories, interests and values of the subjects involved. Furthermore, these interpretations often acquire an implicit character, since, to each person, they are ingrained in deep-seated habits of thought and life in which the unconscious component is likely to play a relevant role.

For instance, there is a strong conflict between the advocates and the detractors of the market. But what is the meaning of the market? Is it, as held by classical and neoclassical economists, a kind of 'exogenous' mechanism strictly associated with capitalism? Or else, is it an institution created and maintained by public intervention and which, for this reason, can be present also in a socialist economy?

In our work, we will employ this pluralistic and interdisciplinary perspective for analysing some controversial elements of: (i) the analysis of the institutional and evolutionary nature of the market, with particular attention to the complex meaning of 'market imperfections'; (ii) the role of cultural factors in shaping the evolution of economic systems; (iii) the importance of an interdisciplinary approach for reaching out to the manifold aspects of these concepts; (iv) the role of the psychoanalytic perspective in elucidating many aspects of person–society dynamics; (v) how this more integrated approach can help identify suitable policies for our most urgent economic and social problems.

As with every complex issue, this analysis cannot address all the aspects at stake. In particular, within economics, the major focus is on a number of heterodox contributions, in particular within the field of the 'old institutional economics'; and, within psychoanalysis, we chiefly address the contributions of Freud and of 'object and interpersonal relations' theories. The reason for this choice is that, both for economics and psychoanalysis, these contributions have most often been overlooked in public debate. Hence, the objective of the work is not to lay down a complete outline of the heterodox theories and psychoanalytic contributions but only to focus attention on a number of relevant issues, also with a view to steering a pluralistic debate.

In fact, we believe that, especially for the analysis of complex phenomena, no discipline (or field or school within a discipline) is self-sufficient and perfect. The insulation process typical of many scientific approaches can really impair a far-reaching understanding of the economic and social phenomena.

In this light and with regard to our theme, a closer collaboration of Marxian theories with other theories of socialism, with institutional and Keynesian economics, and with psychology and psychoanalysis, can help to bring out their great potential for the interpretation of socio-economic evolution.

As observed by the famous sociologist Karl Mannheim (Mannheim and Wolff, 1993), a landscape can be seen only from a determined perspective and without perspective there is no landscape. Hence, observing a landscape (or phenomenon) from different angles (or disciplines) can help to acquire a much clearer insight into the features of the various perspectives.

In this light, the third, and perhaps ultimate goal of our analysis is, by employing and continually upgrading a comprehensive theoretical framework, to help improve the process of policy action, with particular attention to the problems and challenges posed by economic crisis.

2 The market in an interdisciplinary perspective

2.1 The institutional foundation of the market

As is known, the analysis of the market constitutes perhaps one of the most controversial aspects in the study of the various forms of economic organization.

For instance, the long-standing debate on 'market socialism' has triggered diametrically opposed positions[1] as concerns the role played by the market in economic and social development: on the one hand, advocates of this system posit that the market existed before capitalism and, as a consequence, can also be present in a socialist society. On the other hand, opponents maintain that the market constitutes an economic device for the exploitation of workers and, as such, can exist in its most fully fledged form only in a capitalistic economy. Even among non-socialist economists ideas widely differ with respect to the role of the market in many structural, and related, issues – for instance, scientific and technological progress, economic development, unemployment, environmental protection.

As a matter of fact, the analysis of the market lies at the juncture of many important aspects of economic and social structure and of the corresponding policy action: in particular, public action and private initiative, forms of competition, and the related concepts of capitalism, socialism, sustainable development, participation and democracy.

The main problem in this debate is that the concepts involved are extremely complex and intertwined and can be interpreted differently according to the experiences and values of the different subjects.

In fact, as we are trying to show, the market does not constitute an 'exogenous mechanism' in relation to the goals and values of the subjects involved. But, rather, it is an institution that, in J. R. Commons' terminology (1995 [1924], 1990 [1934]), with its relationships of 'conflict', 'dependence', and 'order' – to which corresponds an articulated legal framework of rights and duties – evolves along with other institutions, thus contributing to identify the distinctive features of economic, social and cultural evolution in any given context.

In this respect, if we consider the alleged more free market-oriented productive sectors, we can see that, even in these instances, consumers' demand rarely constitutes the sole criterion for the existence and development of these sectors.

Indeed, in the related policy action there often comes into play other goals which tend to be latched onto numerous policies and institutions: for example, scientific and technological development, increase in employment, industrial restructuring, social and environmental impact. Moreover, these policies tend to carry multifarious influences on consumers' demand.

This complexity tends also to be reflected in the increasing articulation of the ownership structures of companies, which tend to mirror the presence of the various – 'public' and 'private' – interest groups involved.

It is also worth noting that changes occurring in the market system directly impinge upon the forms of competition. In this sense, we can observe that competition does not constitute a static concept but evolves along with the transformations of economic and social organization.

2.2 The market as a manifold entity

Now, we try to employ these concepts for the analysis of some controversial aspects of the market. In this regard, it can be useful to look more closely into its definition. The market, in its simplest and broadest meaning, can be defined as the possibility for persons to exchange their goods and services, either directly or through the medium of any socially accepted definition of 'money.'

As can be seen, this definition includes a countless range of economic situations: for instance, isolated, barter-based, exchanges in primitive economies, or more articulated exchanges in well-developed markets – which can be more or less capitalistic or socialistic. In the related debate, and also in psychological perception, the market appears as a manifold entity, which embodies various and often contradictory features. In this sense, the market can appear, on the positive side, as:

1 An instrument for attaining more liberty and better economic coordination, in that it allows the unfolding of personal initiative and creativity through a system of decentralized actions.
2 A means for comparing and revealing information about the characteristics of goods and services.

On the negative side, the market can appear as:

3 A device, under the appearance of equal opportunities in the labour market, for exploitation of workers.
4 A way for devising, within the reality of pronounced market imperfections, unfair deals in the marketplace, through reduction in the quality of products and shrewd manipulation of information realized also by means of well-organized advertisement strategies.
5 As a consequence of these negative characteristics, the market may constitute an ineffective system for resource allocation. Also for this reason, the market is likely to entail alienation, frustration and distorted social value process for all the participants, also through its effects on the increase of economic inequalities, the uncertainty and disorder of the economic system, and environmental decay.

What is the relevance of all these aspects? In our view, they are all potentially truly significant for social life and interact among one another in a dialectic and conflicting way. The prevalence of one or the other depends on the social, economic and psychological relations underpinning market structures and the related typologies of transactions occurring therein. If these relations engender an increasingly unequal distribution of power and income – in short, if they rest on a kind of more or less sublimated 'predatory attitude' rooted in the structure of the social, cultural and institutional framework – then it follows that the market can reinforce the negative effects outlined before. But, supposing that the predatory aspects are not so predominant, the positive effects of market can, to varying degrees, outweigh the negative effects.

In our view, the real problems do not lie in the market – e.g., in the exchange activity *per se* – but in the complexity and often conflicting character of our motivations which are reflected in, and at the same time blurred by, the complexity and ambiguity of the market in any given context.

In fact, there occurs a complex reciprocal interaction between the 'individual' and 'holistic' aspects of the market, where, in the former, individual action influences market structure and, in the latter, market structure has a bearing on individual behaviour.

For instance, a professional can sell his or her services in the market chiefly out of creative and altruistic motivations – for instance, out of Veblen's (1990a [1914]) workmanship and parental bent propensities – but even chiefly out of predatory and aggressive propensities aimed at increasing without limits the quest for money and power. And, in turn, market structure impinges more or less heavily on the shaping of these propensities and the related 'freedom' of individual action within the market.

Thus, different propensities, both among different individuals and within the orientations and motivations of each individual, are likely to be always present in the market and therefore constitute one of the most intricate aspects of the socio-economic dynamics.

By adopting this approach, the market cannot realistically be appraised as an abstract mechanism amenable automatically – provided only that it be perfect enough – to individual and social utility maximization.

In fact, the market constitutes an institution that has been created and maintained by public policies and therefore is heavily embedded in the economic, social and cultural domain. This happens not only when market transactions clearly acquire the nature of a social and cultural phenomenon, as in the cases, widely investigated in social sciences, of the numerous economic relations framed within a well-established family and social network of customs, trust, kinship, friendship and citizenship.

As a matter of fact, even the (seemingly) most atomistic and impersonal transaction occurring between individuals unknown to each other is rooted within a dense framework of collective action, with all its rights, duties, values and cultural orientations.

In this sense, the 'market' implies, on the part of the actors involved, a process of social valuing which, however, can be seriously impaired in situations where the negative aspects of market prevail.

Furthermore, it is important to remember that market relations certainly constitute one important way for expressing predatory attitude but by no means the only one. In this sense, predatory behaviour can be present also in non-market relations and, in this regard, human history is full of these instances. Thus, the fundamental problem becomes to understand the psychological reasons and problems underlying predatory relations in their connections with the economic, social and cultural structure.

Likewise, the market does not constitute the sole instance for expressing personal initiative. In fact, on the one side, market can be compatible with a socialist society; and, on the other side, personal initiative can unfold very well in public administration providing that the related organization is flexible enough to allow a real involvement of the workers in its activities. As emerges from Commons' analysis and, within a different context, from the literature on quasi-markets, forms of transactions and competition can exist in any kind of public institution.

This perspective has profound implications on the analysis of market imperfections. This applies both to the 'microeconomic imperfections' – in particular, externalities, informational asymmetries, monopoly power, path-dependency and lock-in – and to the macroeconomic imperfections, in particular the difficulty of aggregate demand to reach the level of full employment (however defined).

We will address in the next paragraphs some of these aspects, also considered in their supranational dimension.

2.3 Microeconomic imperfections

An instance of the usefulness for the structural issues of considering the microeconomic – e.g., the institutional-based – foundations of macroeconomic dynamics can be found in the analysis of the so-called market 'rigidities'. These rigidities, highly present in many markets, have been deeply investigated especially within institutional and regulatory economics, and in the Keynesian developments of macroeconomics.

These rigidities are often depicted only as a negative factor as they are supposed to impair, by deviating the economic system away from the 'first best' world of perfect flexibility, the growth potential of the economy. Hence, in the discussion of the economic aspects of a market, synthesized in the general equation:

$$D(p) = S(p)$$

where D is the effective demand, S the effective supply and p the price, we can observe that the analysis of all the possible rigidities is much more complex than it appears at first sight.

In fact, these 'rigidities', as relating to complex institutional relations and expectations, should not be considered only negatively as 'market imperfections', since they also perform the fundamental function of stabilizing all the 'market' and 'non-market' institutional-based frameworks upon which the economic, social and cultural fabric rests.

In this sense, one of the fundamental roles of these rigidities is to reduce transaction costs which, in this light, should not be interpreted simply as a 'market imperfection' but as a highly institutional-rooted phenomenon.

For instance, in examining, for a given market, the slow reaction of demand and supply behaviour to changes in 'the other side' of the market (supply and demand, respectively), institutional- and Keynesian-oriented theories would point out the importance, for the demand side, of the role of imperfect and asymmetric information; and, for the supply side – in particular in the theory of 'small menu costs'[2] – of the role of transaction costs and the related difficulty of promptly modifying the firm's medium- and long-term strategy.

The difficulty or unwillingness of a firm to promptly adjust its prices whenever it would seem profit-maximizing takes, in a sense, an objective character – as when it is expensive to continually update information and/or there are administrative costs in managing too frequent changes in prices. At the same time, however, one important source of such difficulty lies in the circumstance that all the transactions in which a firm is engaged carry with them also significant social, cultural and psychological aspects. Therefore, changing a price also implies modifying these social relations and, for this reason, too frequent changes could, at real or symbolic level, jeopardize the stability and reliability of such relations.

The same reasoning can be applied to the demand side, and to all 'managerial and rationing transactions', in particular labour relations and the process of formulation of policies.

In all these instances, the search for more stable and 'institutionalized' patterns of action can also express the profound need, stressed in particular by psychoanalysis, of establishing sound interpersonal relations.

In that connection, the failures of the market in 'signalling' the negative effects of economic action on environmental and social objectives do not simply reflect some 'negative externalities' and 'imperfections' of an otherwise 'perfect mechanism'. Rather, according to our definition of the market, these failures witness and convey a more profound difficulty of economy, society, institutions and policies to really embrace these objectives within their action.

2.4 Macroeconomic imperfections

As noted before, a central trait of capitalistic institutions lies in a chronic tendency of aggregate demand to lag behind the aggregate supply of full employment (however defined).

There are a number of reasons for this tendency: in particular, both the growing productivity of labour and the satiation for certain categories of goods combine to render the objective of full employment more difficult to achieve.

In the former case, this happens because the increase in productivity signifies that, for a given level of production, fewer jobs are required; and that, in order to keep up with the same level of employment, more products should be produced and sold in the market.

In the latter case, this happens because, since the needs of consumers are becoming increasingly tied to the immaterial and intellectual side of consumption, their fulfilment tends to depend less and less on the 'material and quantitative' aspects of consumption. In fact, we do not buy books by kilos and cultural activities by mere numbers. Also, if we buy a high-tech product, we are likely to be more interested in learning how to use it, than to change it with every new model.

All this suggests that a kind of 'forced' over-consumption is the only and very imperfect way, in our present economies, for attaining some kind of full employment level.

How many high-tech items,cars, clothes, etc., should we buy to sustain the aggregate demand? For a host of economic, social and environmental reasons, this system is untenable in the long run.

These aspects constitute a significant explanation of the tendency[3] of the socio-economic system (see also later) to move from work activities resting on 'the economic motive' to activities – social, cultural, scientific, artistic – based on the true expression of the real needs and inclinations of persons.

Of course, firms can introduce new products onto the market, but this would not solve that structural issue. In fact, even if new jobs are created in these fields, in the medium and long run the increase in productivity extends also, and perhaps even more, to the new products. This could contribute to explain that every innovative wave tends to create fewer and fewer jobs. For instance, it is easily observable that, whereas the durable goods typical of the 1960s and 1970s involved hundreds of thousands of workers, the innovative cycle of today's high-tech products would employ no more than a few thousand workers.

As is known, there has been, since the inception of the industrial revolution, a rather stable increase of public spending, both in absolute and relative terms, also on account of the role of public spending in increasing the aggregate demand, and, hence, the profit of firms. In this regard, as also made evident in other works (Hermann, 2012, 2015) the present economic crises do not depend on the Keynesian policies of the past and/or in an alleged inefficient and lobbistic nature of public intervention even if, of course, it is true that public spending is not always effective and/or can be driven, to a greater or lesser extent, by the dynamics of various interest groups but in the necessity to manage the growing contradictions of the system.

Another related contradiction which has paved the way for the eruption of the present-day economic and financial crisis can be found in the relation between (a) most credit policies, which aim to uplift, also through well-organized advertisement strategies, persons' spending capacity well beyond their real earnings; and (b) business strategies which, in order to gain 'competitiveness', tend to reduce employees' incomes and work conditions to a minimum.

The relevance of these aspects is, however, only imperfectly acknowledged in our societies. Both for this reason and because of the influence of neo-liberalist attitudes, public spending is in general appraised in a negative way, as a kind of obstacle that 'crowds out' resources from the private sector.

2.5 The supranational dimension of market imperfections

In that connection, it is worth noting that the more harmful effects of market relations tend to be more pronounced in the international arena. In fact, as investigated in particular by the literature on economic development and on the 'unequal exchange', it is through the internationalization of production involving the developing and emerging countries that the worst forms of exploitation are likely to take place. There are several reasons for this. First, as highlighted in particular by Veblen's contributions, the formation of modern nation-states has its economic and cultural ancestors in ceremonial institutions chiefly rooted in emulative and predatory habits of thought and life.

In this respect, the capitalistic institutions of today, including the juridical form of nation-state, continue to express these predatory attitudes, even though in Veblen's analysis such situation could be overcome by the rationalizing role of technology. But, this being the case, then it follows that competition associated with market process comes about not only between individual and firms but also, and perhaps even more, between nations and larger supranational agglomerations. As a matter of fact, in the latter cases economic competition is likely to be more intense. Not only because a cultural and political rivalry is most often injected in such competition, but also for the reason that such competition – unlike national situations where in most cases economic competition is regulated and 'concerted' in many respects through legislative and contractual provisions – tends to be almost completely unregulated in the 'globalized' world.

True, there are important initiatives for promoting fair trade but they have not yet taken a strong foothold in developing and emerging economies. Now we briefly consider a number of relevant aspects of these phenomena.

2.6 Internationalization, research and innovation

Numerous authors[4] have emphasized that the patterns of internationalization – through exports, foreign direct investment and other forms of strategic collaboration (such as joint ventures) – play a key role in economic development: such processes, in fact, allow both the expansion of economic activities through contacts with new markets as well as the acquisition of important skills and know-how through interaction with other realities. These studies also highlight how necessary it is, especially in the case of developing nations, that foreign investments be included in a comprehensive strategy of political economy aimed at maximizing the positive impact of these investments on the growth of 'human and social capital'. Such outcome could take place through the activation of a virtuous cycle among (i) the transfer of scientific, technological and managerial capabilities; (ii) the creation of new businesses and development projects; (iii) collaboration with universities and research institutes.

These aspects have given rise to an increased importance, on the one hand, of national and international systems of innovation and of the connected structure of institutions and policies for research and technology transfer. And, on the other, of scientific and technological patterns and routines and of the related processes of path-dependency as impinging on the individual enterprise, the local systems of businesses, and the industry as a whole in its various definitions.

2.7 The difficulty of technology transfer

A key factor in the difficulties faced by underdeveloped economic systems in achieving an adequate level of innovation lies in the double nature, open and tacit, of technology (see, among others, Dosi *et al.*, 2000; Eisenhardt and Martin, 2000): on the one hand, technology has an explicit and visible side, for instance, in the form of patents and codified instructions; at the same time, however, technology possesses a 'tacit' element represented by the skills and knowledge needed to make the technologies work. Such capabilities are typically specific and path-dependent, and involve technical and organizational routines both at the firm level and at larger systems of production. In this sense, such capabilities lie not so much in the instruments of production as in the knowledge of single individuals, and tend, for this reason, to acquire an implicit and tacit nature. This happens, first, because the worker's know-how, which is the fruit of years of experience, can only be passed on very slowly and imperfectly, and second because in most cases such know-how is formed and developed within a given productive structure. For these reasons, it is difficult for inner capabilities to be 'externalized' and herein they represent the source of competitive advantage in businesses and economic systems.

These aspects of technology provide an important account for the persistent divergence in development among economic areas, and have been addressed in particular by the theories of the 'dynamic capabilities approach'. These contributions, developed in particular in the last two decades, underscore the unitary character of the firm within its environment and the role of learning at all levels of organizational structure.

This approach, by underscoring the 'holistic' and evolutionary nature of the firm, and the role of routines as a means to store and organize learning within organizations, presents a striking parallel with important concepts of institutional economics: in particular, but not only, with the role of habits of thought and life in institutional and technologic change, the role that active (and mostly tacit) knowledge residing in persons can play in determining the real 'stock of capital', and the adoption of an interdisciplinary perspective to the study of social phenomena.

In this regard, numerous studies,[5] in part linked to the previous insights, have analysed the importance of the policy and institutional context for economic and social development. Among others, the following closely intertwined actions in the public sector have been considered: (i) management of macroeconomic variables; (ii) creation of rules for conflict resolution; (iii) creation and diffusion of research and innovation; (iv) development of disadvantaged areas; (v) social and cultural policies.

2.8 Conclusion

As we have tried to outline, markets can be appraised as institutions, created and maintained by public policies, which are deeply 'embedded' in the economic, social and cultural domain. In this light, an abstract dualism between the 'State' and the 'Market', or between 'Economic Planning' and 'Capitalism', tends to miss the key feature of the economic organization: the fact that the market is not an exogenous 'mechanism' but an economic and social institution framed within, in Commons' terminology, an evolving set of 'rights', 'duties', 'liberties' and 'exposures'. And to which corresponds the multifarious realms of individuals, groups, institutions and policies which, through the various kinds of transactions reviewed before, air their different objectives, needs and values.

In the analysis of such issues, heterodox theories can contribute to achieve a better insight into the features of any given market context, through the study of the following interrelated aspects:

1 The structure of collective action, in particular the relations of conflict, dependence and order, and the corresponding systems of rights, duties, liberties and exposures among individuals, groups and social classes, and their means of expression in institutional, social and cultural forms.
2 The role of social valuing processes associated with these developments from a historical, social, economic and psychological perspective; how explicit these assessments are; and how they can be better formulated and compared.
3 The role of cultural factors in economic development.

The previous discussion, in highlighting the role of institutional and social context in the evolution of capitalistic institutions, explicitly invites a closer analysis of the role of cultural forms in shaping such evolution. Among the numerous

Cultural and psychological dimensions 149

valuable contributions, we focus attention on two that are significantly linked to the institutional economics: Dewey's *Freedom and Culture* (1989 [1939]) and K. Polanyi's *The Great Transformation* (1944).

3 The role of cultural factors in economic development

3.1 Some insights from Dewey's Freedom and Culture

This book, which is rather overlooked among Dewey's contributions, addresses[6] in a dense and concise way a number of central questions of cultural development.

3.1.1 Interactions between human nature and culture

In this context, the central problem for social sciences becomes, on the one hand, (i) recognizing and analysing the complexity of human orientations; and, on the other hand, (ii) studying how these inclinations interact with cultural factors. Indeed, in his words:

> The problem of freedom and of democratic institutions is tied up with the question of what kind of culture exists; with the necessity of free culture for free political institutions [. . .]. The question of human psychology, of the make-up of human nature in its original state, is involved [. . .]. For every social and political philosophy currently professed will be found upon examination to involve a certain view about the constitution of human nature: in itself and in its relation to physical nature.
> (Dewey, 1989 [1939], p. 18)

But what are these relations and how do they evolve? In particular, what are the factors that shape the interaction between human nature and culture?

Accepting as given the existence of different inclinations and a certain 'adaptability' of human nature – that is, its ability to develop certain features in response to social forces – Dewey focuses on analysing the role of cultural factors, intended in an extensive meaning, in fostering such development.

We can note that the characteristics of the cultural context deeply influence not only our living conditions but, more importantly, our 'patterns of thought and action'. Consequently, many concepts that might appear natural and to be taken for granted are actually the product of our cultural evolution. In this regard, Dewey emphasizes the risk that certain inclinations, more highly developed in certain cultural contexts, be considered (perhaps unconsciously) as the prevailing aspects of human nature.

3.1.2 Increasing complexity of cultural forms

These considerations, however, do not imply that human nature, due to its 'adaptability', plays a secondary role in comparison to cultural factors. In this light, Dewey pinpoints the increasing complexity of human nature and its relations to the development of cultural forms. In this sense, human nature and culture are not separate entities but, rather, interrelated aspects of human existence: in which, human nature houses individual inclinations, potential but dormant, while culture constitutes the economic, social and institutional setting where these inclinations find their concrete expression.

Indeed, cultural forms include numerous elements which, though highly intertwined, have an increasing tendency 'to specialize' and follow their 'own logic': for instance, the spheres of politics, economy, science and technology, arts and culture. A study of these interactions requires an analysis of the role of the various components of the culture in relation to economic and social development and, consequently, in relation to certain inclinations of the individual. In this regard, Dewey observes that

> the problem of freedom of cooperative individualities is then a problem to be viewed in the context of culture. The state of culture is a state of interaction of many factors, the chief of which are law and politics, industry and commerce, science and technology, the arts of expression and communication, and of morals, or the values men prize and the ways in which they evaluate them; and finally, though indirectly, the system of general ideas used by men to justify and to criticize the fundamental conditions under which they live, their social philosophy [. . .]. The fundamental postulate of the discussion is that isolation of any one factor, no matter how strong its workings at a given time, is fatal to understanding and to intelligent action. Isolations have abounded, both on the side of taking some one thing in human nature to be a supreme 'motive' and in taking some one form of social activity to be supreme.
> (1989 [1939], pp. 24 and 25)

One noteworthy consequence of the increasing complexity of cultural forms is that the concepts of freedom, democracy and participation acquire a similarly complex meaning since they are amenable to, and depend on, numerous spheres of collective action.

In this ambit, Dewey points out that economic transformations cannot be appraised as the sole 'locomotive' of social and cultural change. In fact, while it is true that the distinction between economic aspects and social aspects of human action becomes increasingly pronounced, it is also true that the interrelations between the various spheres become increasingly complex and significant. Hence, we can note that if, on the one hand, economic aspects, in particular the evaluation of monetary costs and benefits of different alternatives, permeates other areas of social relations, on the other hand, the opposite phenomenon is no less true: namely, that social and cultural aspects influence and seek adequate expression in the economic sphere. In this regard, historical analysis sheds a vivid light on the multifariousness of these processes: for example, the various experiences of capitalism and socialism, while sharing important common traits and, in turn, influencing pre-existing cultural structures, have also assumed their own specificity.

This growing complexity of the relevant spheres of collective life can be interpreted as the natural result of the increasing articulation of human needs and, hence, of the system's cultural growth; but, at the same time, that complexity leads to the creation of new problems, expectations, conflicts and challenges. In this evolutionary process, in which the establishment of appropriate goals and policies proves increasingly difficult, a thorough comprehension and social evaluation of the problems becomes paramount in order to avert the temptation to adopt authoritarian 'solutions'. In this sense

> the serious threat to our democracy is not the existence of foreign totalitarian states. It is the existence within our own personal attitudes and within our own institutions of conditions similar to those which have given a victory to external authority, discipline, uniformity and dependence upon the Leader in foreign countries. The battlefield is accordingly here – within ourselves and our institutions [. . .]. It [this battle] can be won only by extending the application of democratic methods, methods of consultation, persuasion, negotiation, communication, cooperative intelligence, in the task of making our own politics, industry, education, our culture generally, a servant and an evolving manifestation of democratic ideas.
> (Dewey, 1989 [1939], pp. 44 and 133)

According to these concepts, democracy relates not only to politics in a limited sense of the term but reaches out to the other significant spheres of interpersonal relations: in particular, family, work, and other social relations, in the broadest sense of the term. This extension of the concept of democracy consequently implies a corresponding extension of its ethical and participatory content to all realms of collective life, an important result being (in particular, Dewey, 1888) the end of the distinction – coming from a previous cultural tradition – between spiritual or 'final' activities and 'instrumental' activities related to the production process. Indeed,

> we admit, nay, at times we claim, that ethical rules are to be *applied* to the industrial sphere, but we think of it as an external application. That the economic and industrial life is *in itself* ethical, that it is to be made contributory to the realization of personality through the formation of a higher and more complete unity among men, this is what we do not recognize; but such is the meaning of the statement that democracy must become industrial.
> (Dewey, 1888, republished in Menand, 1997, p. 204)

3.1.3 How to build democracy and participation?

Once the complexity of cultural factors has been acknowledged, there remains the task of identifying the influence exerted by the various components (economy, politics, society, science and technology, and the arts) on the system. In particular, how do these factors influence one another and with what consequences in terms of realization of the goals of democracy, participation and socio-economic development?

3.1.4 Science, culture and participation

Further along in *Freedom and Culture*, Dewey explores the development of science and technology in their linkages to culture and socio-economic progress.

As a matter of fact, scientific progress tends to be applied towards increasing the technical efficiency of the systems of production, whereas its applications to social problems – that is, to the study of the organization of economic, social, and work-life – remain far more uncertain and fragmentary. And yet, a systematic use of available knowledge should be all the more important for understanding the problems to be faced in a situation marked by an increasing articulation of the system.

This is especially true of the ordinary citizen whose opinions tend to be formed more through the influence of patterns of thinking rooted in his or her cultural heritage – and which can also be considerably influenced by the mass media – rather than by a conscious use of scientific method and knowledge. A scientific approach based on pluralism which, as resting also on the concepts and methodology of the social sciences, is focused on the issue of value judgements. In fact, the influence of science and technology on collective life does not unfold in an 'objective and neutral' way but, rather, through its 'assimilation' in the complexity of the cultural system. In this sense, a situation such as the one described is particularly negative for a social development based on pluralism and participation. Indeed, 'a culture which permits science to destroy traditional values but which distrusts its power to create new ones is a culture which is destroying itself. War is a symptom as well as a cause of the inner division' (Dewey, 1989 [1939], p. 118).

In this regard, Dewey pinpoints – with considerable insight into the subsequent developments of the theories of 'human and social capital' and 'relational goods' – the crucial role played by public policies in promoting, also through the provision of public goods and services, the development of collective projects and initiatives in every articulation of the social structure. Indeed, these associative experiences constitute the core of democracy and participation and safeguard against the dangers of an excessive concentration of power in public and/or private institutions.

In this perspective, it is interesting to note that an insufficient process of participation – by tending to engender an inadequate expression of the structure of 'reasonable value', that is of the motivations and conflicts forming the basis of economic and social life, and, hence, of policy action – can be an important factor in explaining the difficulty of economic policies to meet the needs of collective life and the corresponding phenomena of 'anomie', social alienation and insufficient socio-economic development.

3.2 The links with Karl Polanyi's contribution

In this context, an especially noteworthy contribution has also been made by Karl Polanyi in his work entitled *The Great Transformation* (1944).

The *leitmotif* of this study is the recognition of the importance of cultural factors in determining forms of economic and social organization: Polanyi emphasizes in particular: (i) the great cultural variety and wealth present in ancient civilizations; (ii) how in more recent ages, the capitalistic economy has not only influenced, but has also been influenced by pre-existing cultural structures and has thus acquired different characteristics in the various countries taken into consideration.

A significant implication of this theory is that an economic system cannot exist in the absence of a social and cultural substratum. The individual needs are social and cultural, as well as economic, and these aspects should be considered for an adequate evaluation of the processes of change. For example, the negative effects on populations of the industrial revolution or of colonialism lie not so much in an economic loss, total or partial – in some cases these events might have generated economic gain for some sectors – as in the dismantling of pre-existing social and cultural relationships, resulting in a 'cultural vacuum' and increasing social and psychological malaise.

In this sense, the desired change arising from his analysis is one that moves towards a system based on workers' real participation in economic and social life: a system in which priority is no longer given to impersonal relationships that characterize the present market economy but to direct and cooperative relationships more conducive to the harmonious integration of the economic and social spheres.

In this perspective, it should be noted that while a marked differentiation between economic, social and cultural aspects of human activity has occurred over time, it is also true that the links between these spheres have become increasingly complex and significant. If, on the one hand, economic aspects (namely, the evaluation of the costs and monetary benefits of the various alternatives) permeate the rest of social relations, on the other hand the opposite also holds true, in the sense that social and cultural aspects condition and find their expression in the economic realm.

For instance, it is certainly true that, as effectively expounded by Karl Polanyi (1944), the establishment of capitalism has absorbed under its alienating framework the previous social relations, but the opposite is no less true, in the sense that the previous social relations, with all their aspects of despotism and prevarication, may have found an 'amplified' expression within capitalistic institutions.

4 The role of psychological factors in economic development

As emerges from the previous account, the economic or 'materialistic' aspects cannot be considered as the sole drivers of social evolution.

In fact, as this evolution has not arisen apart from the intended action of the actors involved, there arises the issue of understanding the cultural and psychological foundations of capitalistic society in their relations with its material basis.

In the previous part, we have focused attention on the cultural side of economic development. The interesting aspect of this analysis is that – also on account of the far-reaching definition of culture – it explicitly invites an interdisciplinary approach.

Within this ambit, we deem it appropriate to consider psychoanalytic contributions because, as noted in the introduction, they have been largely overlooked.

4.1 Psychoanalytic interpretations of social life and the role of aggressive behaviour

One central field of psychoanalytic contributions to the study of social life relates to the analysis of aggressive behaviour.

As addressed more extensively in other works (Hermann, 2010, 2015), the psychoanalytic theory of aggressiveness has not followed an easy pathway. As is known, Freud, especially in his later work, tended to regard instincts as opposing forces which, out of their conflicts, are supposed to drive human behaviour in a rather ineluctable way. This conception, especially as set forth in his theory of death instinct,[7] led him to a pessimistic view of human development, in the sense that such a view tends to imply that little can be done to reduce human aggressiveness.

In this regard, his formulation of the theory of death instinct – which, it is important to remember, Freud set out with the main aim of providing an explanation of human aggressiveness but was nonetheless never completely convinced about its real validity – triggered many controversies among psychoanalysts and is now largely dismissed chiefly as a result of an improved psychoanalytic understanding of the role played by neurotic conflicts in the formation of aggressive behaviour (see, e.g., Fine, 1979).

Within this ambit, several authors have underlined the articulated role of aggressiveness in institutional and cultural contexts: (i) on the one hand, it concurs to shape in many ways these contexts through the mutual actions of its members; (ii) on the other hand, cultural values are likely to foster the development of aggressiveness especially in the early stages of individual life – for instance, indirectly through their influence on the child's caretakers and directly through their role of 'cultural models' to be imitated and internalized by the child.

In this context, psychoanalytic studies underscore that in many cases social relations are based, at various levels, on a fight for power having its focus in – at real and/or symbolic level – 'possessing institutions'. But, since an institution constitutes an organized whole of collective action controlling, liberating, and expanding individual action, this implies that 'possessing' an institution relates to an unconscious fantasy of omnipotent control over all the relations occurring therein. This means that, for instance, ownership in its predatory and acquisitive meaning embodies – as shown in particular by Marx and Veblen – not a person-to-goods but a person-to-person relation. According to this interpretation, the reason why, under these predatory and neurotic habits, institutions are considered like 'things' to be owned does not rest in the circumstance that institutions are conceived of like things in any meaning of the word, but in the fact that 'the owner' of the institutions, in trying 'to control and dominate' the social relations taking place therein, disregards the needs and opportunities that might potentially arise from the people involved in these (frustrating and neurotic) social relations.

For the same reason, the various forms of economic action – consumption, saving, investment – embody profound psychological meanings which interact in a complex way with the social and institutional structure. For this reason, economic action cannot realistically be reduced to an abstract 'maximizing behaviour'.

For example, considering an instance of individual consumption, psychoanalysis can help identify the profound reasons, largely unconscious, that can underlie this act. If persons buy a product chiefly out of imitation, emulation, and conformism to the prevailing social canons – a pattern well described by Veblen's theory (1899) of 'conspicuous consumption' – it can hardly be the case that they are maximizing their behaviour.

In this regard Freud, in discussing Marx's theory, stresses the necessity of considering not only the influence of the economic organization of society on individual psychology, but also the role of psychological factors in shaping the 'materialistic aspects' of society. As he notes:

> The communists believe that they have found the path to deliverance from our evils. According to them, man is wholly good and is well-disposed to his neighbour; but the institution of private property has corrupted his nature. The ownership of private wealth gives the individual power, and with it the temptation to ill-treat his neighbour; while the man who is excluded from possession is bound to rebel in hostility against his oppressor. If private property were abolished, all wealth held in common, and everyone allowed to share in the enjoyment of it, ill-will and hostility would disappear among men. Since everyone's need would be satisfied, no one would have any reason to regard another as his enemy; all would willingly undertake the work that was necessary. I have no concern with any economic criticisms of the communist system; I cannot inquire into whether the abolition of private property is expedient or advantageous [Here, there is a footnote in which Freud stresses his solidarity, also in relation to his own experience, with the situations of economic deprivation.] But I am able to recognize that the psychological premises on which the system is based are an untenable illusion. In abolishing private property we deprive the human love of aggression of one of its instruments, certainly a strong one, though certainly not the strongest; but we have in no way altered the differences in power and influence which are misused by aggressiveness, nor have we altered anything in its nature. Aggressiveness was not created by property. It reigned almost without limit in primitive times, when property was still very scanty.
>
> (Freud, 1930, pp. 70–71)

Despite these cautious remarks, when discussing the difficulty of lessening human aggressiveness, he observes that,

> at this point the ethics based on religion introduces its promises of a better after-life. But so long as virtue is not rewarded here on earth, ethics will, I fancy, preach in vain. I too think it quite certain that a real change in the relations of human beings to possessions would be of more help in this direction than any ethical commands; but the recognition of this fact among socialists has been obscured and made useless for practical purposes by a fresh idealistic misconception of human nature.
>
> (1930, p. 109)

And then, he clearly points to a closer collaboration between Marxism and psychoanalysis:

> The strength of Marxism clearly lies not in its view of history or the prophecies of the future that are based on it, but in its sagacious indication of the decisive influence which the economic circumstances of men have upon their intellectual, ethical and artistic attitudes. A number of connections and implications were thus uncovered, which had previously been almost totally overlooked. But it cannot be assumed that economic motives are the only ones that determine the behaviour of human beings in society. The undoubted fact that different individuals, races and nations behave differently under the same economic conditions is alone enough to show that economic motives are not the sole dominating factor. It is altogether incomprehensible how psychological factors can be overlooked where what is in question are the reactions of living human beings; for not only were these reactions concerned in establishing the economic conditions, but even under the domination of those conditions men can only bring their original impulses into play, their self-preservative instinct, their aggressiveness, their need to be loved, their drive towards obtaining pleasure and avoiding unpleasure. In an earlier enquiry I also pointed out the important claims made by the super-ego, which represents tradition and the ideals of the past and will for a time resist the incentives of a new economic situation.
>
> (Freud, 1933, pp. 220–221)

These aspects are closely related to the dynamics of group behaviour. As noted by Freud (in particular, 1921) and by subsequent psychoanalysts, group cohesion tends to be based on the following processes: (i) emotional links among the members of the group; (ii) projection of individual aggressiveness into people and/or institutions lying outside the group; (iii) identification with the group leader – who symbolizes the parental instance (typically, the father) – in order to repress the conflicts related to the *Oedipus* complex.

These processes – which operate partly at an unconscious level and may be driven by neurotic conflicts – can help explain the scission that often occurs between 'the good and right', lying inside the group, and 'the bad and mistaken', lying outside.

These contributions highlight the role of groups and institutions for expressing the needs and conflicts of the person. For instance, for the person, the group may represent an idealized *ego*; and, in that connection, its 'morals' and 'code of conduct' symbolize parental figures that, through a process of 'internalization', play the role of *superego*.

Thus, it is worth note that the *superego* stems also from a normal human tendency to establish sound interpersonal relations and, accordingly, to behave with affection and solicitude towards each other and continually improve the positive aspects of personality. However, whereas in non-neurotic situations the 'code of conduct' emerging from such tendencies asserts itself as a genuine behaviour, in neurotic situations leading to the formation of *superego* things can be quite different. Here, the tendency of improving personality tends to be, under an appearance of goodness and morality, subordinated to the expression of neurotic contents at cross-purposes with such tendency.

In particular, quite often the severity of *superego* leads – through the so-called paranoid and narcissistic transformation of personality, extensively studied in psychoanalysis – single individuals, groups or societies to do nasty and persecutory actions towards other individuals, groups or societies into which their aggressiveness has been projected, and so to sabotage the possibility of establishing sound interpersonal relations. These psychological processes can help explain – and history is full of such instances – the neurotic roots of racism, xenophobia and other phenomena of exclusion and marginalization. These phenomena tend to be reinforced by economic and social crises.

The foregoing discussion implies that any process of social change requires a thorough process of social valuing in order to bring to the fore the profound needs, orientations and conflicts of the persons, groups and classes involved.

On that account, historical analysis shows that feudalism and capitalism, for instance, have acquired different forms in the various countries and that, in the evolutionary shaping of these forms, a crucial role was played by political and social action, with all the set of distinctive psychological and cultural features.

4.2 Psychoanalysis and social change

As we have seen, Freud and subsequent psychoanalysts[8] have provided relevant insights into the conflicts of individual and collective life and the possibility of social change. However, notwithstanding these contributions, among social scientists Freud is rarely regarded as a social reformer. Rather, social scientists – owing, perhaps, to a rather pessimistic vein arising from his theory of death instinct – tend to regard his theory as essentially 'conservative', as it would seem to imply that little can be done to abate human aggressiveness and the social relations resting upon it.

Certainly, there is such a vein in Freud's theory. But, at the same time, his theory is more far-reaching than this interpretation would suggest, as it contains aspects that clearly point to the possibility of social change. For instance, in discussing the October Revolution, he is not against such transformation but underlines the importance for social reformers, in order to build a truly better society, to acquire a deeper understanding of human nature.

In this regard, individual self-understanding is not without consequences for social self-understanding, since psychoanalysis is (Freud, in particular 1921) at the same time an individual and a collective psychology. Therefore, the application of psychoanalysis to the comprehension of social phenomena, although not entailing a direct ethical impact as such, can have important consequences in this respect. Freud thinks that psychoanalysis, in collaboration with other social sciences, can find interesting applications in a host of social issues. As he points out, in a lively discussion with an imaginary interlocutor:

[Psychoanalysis] as a 'depth-psychology', a theory of the mental unconscious, it can become indispensable to all the sciences which are concerned with the evolution of human civilization and its major institutions such as art, religion and the social order. It has already, in my opinion, afforded these sciences considerable help in solving their problems. But these are only small contributions compared with what might be achieved if historians of civilization, psychologists of religion, philologists, and so on would agree themselves to handle the new instrument of research which is at their service. The use of analysis for the treatment of neuroses is only one of its applications; the future will perhaps show that it is not the most important one [. . .]. Then let me advise you that psycho-analysis has yet another sphere of application [. . .]. Its application, I mean, to the bringing-up of children. If a child begins to show signs of an undesirable development, if it grows moody, refractory, and inattentive, the paediatrician and even the school doctor can do nothing for it, even if the child produces clear neurotic symptoms, such as nervousness, loss of appetite, vomiting, or insomnia [. . .]. Our recognition of the importance of these unconspicuous neuroses of children as laying down the disposition for serious illnesses in later life points to these child analyses as an excellent method of prophylaxis [. . .].Moreover, to return to our question of the analytic treatment of adult neurotics, even there we have not yet exhausted every line of approach. Our civilization imposes an almost intolerable pressure on us and it calls for a corrective. Is it too fantastic to expect that psycho-analysis in spite of its difficulties may be destined to the task of preparing mankind for such a corrective? Perhaps once more an American may hit on the idea of spending a little money to get the 'social workers' of his country trained analytically and to turn them into a band of helpers for combating the neuroses of civilization.

(Freud, 1926, pp. 83–86)

5 Conclusions: how can an interdisciplinary approach contribute to policy action?

Let us now address how an interdisciplinary approach can help acquire a more complete understanding on a number of questions which are relevant also for policy action: (i) Is, for instance, the quest for money a direct and sole target, or does it cover other motivations of the person? For example, the (partly unconscious) need for affection and consideration, which the person tries to pursue through a perceived socially accepted behaviour? (ii) In other words, is the quest for money a primary or secondary goal to the person? (iii) And what are the psychological, social and cultural factors (including the role of mass media) leading the person to a given consumption, work, investment and saving pattern? (iv) In particular, what is the role of any given context in orienting, fostering or frustrating the various propensities, values, conflicts and needs of the person?

On that account, it can be very interesting to analyse how people perceive and interpret their economic and social realities and the reasons that can hinder the attainment of a more equitable and sustainable society.

We can see these aspects by investigating how people tend to perceive and interpret the increase in public spending of the past decades. In this situation, a vicious circle tends to arise: as a result of the structural tendency towards increase in public spending, the opinion has gained ground, even across various sectors of the progressive domain, that the only remedy to the present crisis consists in a progressive reduction of public spending. The basic and widespread perception is that public spending is in any case 'too high' and so must be abated at any cost.

In these situations, in which the only faith in economic progress rests on a kind of a wild and unregulated competition, the market tends to be psychologically perceived as an inflexible and punitive *superego*. In that vision, the only possible thing we should do is to comply with the 'needs of the market', without any further enquiry on the adequacy of the system to respond to the profound needs of economy and society.

In this regard, an interdisciplinary approach can help gain a deeper insight into the factors underlying the emergence of the recent economic and financial crisis, and into the multiple links between the various spheres of policy action. We can mention, in particular:

1   the economic and psychological significance of economic and social crisis;
2   how a pluralistic interpretation of pivotal concepts such as market, socialism and social justice can improve our understanding of these phenomena;
3   the most suitable macroeconomic policies and their interaction with structural policies.

The significance of this approach for policy action can be shown by a simple example. If we wish to further personal initiative at economic and social level, a narrow conception of the *Homo oeconomicus* will suggest policy measures centred only on pecuniary incentives. Conversely, a proper acknowledgement of the significance for the person of establishing sound interpersonal relations will help devise more effective and far-reaching policies, as they would be more tailored to the real needs and orientations of the person.

Thus can be created the basis for the definition of a policy strategy more centred to the real features and problems of any considered context.

Notes

1   For more details on this debate see, among others, Cole (2003), Ollman (1998), Salsano (1982). We have also treated a number of these aspects in Hermann (2014).
2   This theory belongs to the field of the 'new Keynesian economics' and was first set out by G. Mankiw (1985) in order to underscore that firms, even in the presence of low costs of adjustment – as in the case of a restaurant's menu – often do not quickly adapt their prices in response to a change in demand. The same phenomenon has been observed in labour markets, where both firms and workers prefer to negotiate long-term contracts.

It can also be interesting to note that many of these issues have already been addressed by Commons in his enquiry into the emergence of unions and labour contracts in the US (in particular in the essays contained in *Labor and Administration*, 1964), where he

stresses the importance of ensuring reliable contractual relations in order to abate the uncertainty and the transactions costs associated with it. In this sense, the issues related to market imperfections can receive new insights by considering the concepts of the 'old' institutional economics.
3 These aspects have been developed in particular by J. M. Keynes (1963 [1931]) and J. K. Galbraith (1998 [1958]).
4 For important contributions on the theories of internationalization and their relations with the national systems of innovation, refer, among others, to Buckley and Casson (2009); Casson (1987, 1991); Dicken (2010); Dunning and Tsai-Mei (2007); Dunning and Lundan (2008); Hall and Rosenberg (2010); Ietto-Gillies (2012); Nelson (1993); Nelson and Winter (1982); Rugman (2012).
5 Among the many contributions that have addressed these issues, refer to Commons (1995 [1924], 1990 [1934]); Hamilton (1940); Hodgson *et al.* (1994); Rutherford (2011); Tugwell (1924); Veblen (1899, 1990a, 1990b, 2012).
6 This paragraph is partly based on Hermann (2011).
7 For a good acquaintance with Freud's theory, also regarded in its social implications, refer in particular to Freud (1912–1913, 1915, 1920, 1921, 1924, 1926, 1930, 1933, 1937, 1940).
8 For significant contributions that have underlined the importance of object and interpersonal relations, also in their connection with the possibilities of social change, refer to Klein (1964, 1975); Horney (1939); Bion (1970); Kernberg (1998, 2004); Sullivan *et al.* (1953); Winnicott (1988).

References

Bion, W. R. (1970): *Attention and Interpretation: A Scientific Approach to Insights in Psychoanalysis and Groups*. London: Tavistock Publications.
Buckley, P. J. and Casson, M. (2009): *The Multinational Enterprise Revisited: The Essential Buckley and Casson*. London: Palgrave Macmillan.
Casson, M. (1987): *The Firm and the Market*. Oxford: Blackwell.
Casson, M. (ed.) (1991): *Global Research Strategy and International Competitiveness*. Oxford: Blackwell.
Cole, G. D. H. (ed.) (2003): *A History of Socialist Thought*. London: Palgrave Macmillan.
Commons, J. R. (1964 [1913]): *Labor and Administration*. New York: Kelley.
Commons, J. R. (1990 [1934]): *Institutional Economics: Its Place in Political Economy*. New Brunswick: Transaction Publishers.
Commons, J. R. (1995 [1924]): *Legal Foundations of Capitalism*. New Brunswick: Transaction Publishers.
Dewey, J. (1989 [1939]): *Freedom and Culture*. New York: Prometheus Books.
Dicken, P. (2010): *Global Shift: Mapping the Changing Contours of the World Economy*. London: Sage Publications.
Dosi, G., Nelson, R. R. and Winter, S. G. (eds.) (2000): *The Nature and Dynamics of Organizational Capabilities*. Oxford: Oxford University Press.
Dunning, J. H. and Tsai-Mei, L. (eds.) (2007): *Multinational Enterprises and Emerging Challenges of the 21st Century*. London: Elgar.
Dunning, J. H. and Lundan, S. M. (2008): *Multinational Enterprises and the Global Economy*. Cheltenham: Elgar.
Eisenhardt, K. and Martin, J. (2000): Dynamic Capabilities: What Are They? *Strategic Management Journal*, vol. 21, pp. 1105–1121.

Fine, R. (1979): *A History of Psychoanalysis*. New York: Columbia University Press.
Freud, S. (1912–1913): *Totem und Tabu*. Lipsia, Vienna and Zurich: Internationaler Psychoanalytischer Verlag. English version, *Totem and Taboo*. Standard Edition. New York: Norton, 1990.
Freud, S. (1915): Das Unbewusste. *Internationale Zeitschrift für ärztliche Psycoanalise*. English version, *The Unconscious*. London: Penguin, 2005.
Freud, S. (1920): *Jenseits des Lustprinzips*. Lipsia, Vienna and Zurich: Internationaler pychoanalytischer Verlag. English version, *Beyond the Pleasure Principle*. Standard Edition. New York: Norton, 1990.
Freud, S. (1921): *Massenpsychologie und Ich-Analyse*. Lipsia, Vienna and Zurich: Internationaler Psychoanalytischer Verlag. English version, *Group Psychology and the Analysis of the Ego*. Standard Edition. New York: Norton, 1959.
Freud, S. (1924): Vorlesungen zur Einführung in die Psychoanalise. *Gesammelte Schriften*, vol. 7. English version, *Introductory Lectures on Psycho-Analysis*. Standard edition. New York: Norton, 1990.
Freud, S. (1926): *Die Frage der Laienanalyse. Unterredungen mit einen Unparteiischen*. Lipsia, Vienna and Zurich: Internationaler Psychoanalytischer Verlag. English version, *The Question of Lay Analysis*. Standard edition. New York: Norton, 1990.
Freud, S. (1930): *Das Unbehagen in der Kultur*, Lipsia, Vienna and Zurich: Internationaler Psychoanalytischer Verlag. English version, *Civilization and Its Discontents*. Standard edition. New York: Norton, 1990.
Freud, S. (1933): *Neue Folge der Vorlesungen zur Einführung in die Psychoanalise*. Lipsia, Vienna and Zurich: Internationaler Psychoanalytischer Verlag. English version, *New Introductory Lectures on Psycho-Analysis*. Standard edition. New York: Norton, 1990.
Freud, S. (1937): Die endliche und die unendliche Analyse. *Internationale Zeitschrift fur Psychoanalyse*, vol. 23. English version, Analysis Terminable and Interminable. International Psychoanalytical Association; 1st edition (1987).
Freud, S. (1940): Abryss der Psychoanalyse. Internationale Zeitschrift fur Psychoanalyse. *Imago*, vol. 25. English version, *An Outline of Psychoanalysis*. New York: Norton, 1990).
Galbraith, J. K. (1998 [1958]): *The Affluent Society*. New York: Mariner Books.
Hall, B. H. and Rosenberg, N. (eds.) (2010): *Handbook of the Economics of Innovation*. Amsterdam: Elsevier.
Hamilton, W. H. (1940): *The Pattern of Competition*. New York: Columbia University Press.
Hermann, A. (2010): Institutionalism and Psychoanalysis: A Basis for Interdisciplinary Cooperation. *International Journal of Pluralism and Economics Education*, vol. 1, no. 4, pp. 372–387.
Hermann, A. (2011): John Dewey's Theory of Democracy and Its Links with the Heterodox Approach to Economics. *Eidos*, no. 14 (http://rcientificas.uninorte.edu.co/index.php/eidos/article/view/2140/1377).
Hermann, A. (2012): Policy Responses to Economic and Financial Crises: Insights from Heterodox Economics and Psychoanalysis. *International Journal of Pluralism and Economics Education*, vol. 3, no. 1, pp. 8–22.
Hermann, A. (2014): Market, Socialism and Democracy in an Interdisciplinary Perspective. *International Journal of Pluralism and Economics Education*, vol. 5, no. 4, pp. 327–353.
Hermann, A. (2015): *The Systemic Nature of the Economic Crisis: The Perspectives of Heterodox Economics and Psychoanalysis*. Abingdon: Routledge.

Hodgson, G. M., Samuels, W. J. and Tool, M. R. (eds.) (1994): *The Elgar Companion to Institutional and Evolutionary Economics*. Aldershot: Elgar.
Horney, K. (1939): *New Ways in Psychoanalysis*. New York: Norton.
Ietto-Gillies, G. (2012): *Transnational Corporations and International Production: Trends, Theories, Effects*. Cheltenham: Edward Elgar.
Kernberg, O. (1998): *Ideology, Conflict and Leadership in Groups and Organizations*. New Haven, CT: Yale University Press.
Kernberg, O. (2004): *Contemporary Controversies in Psychoanalytic Theory, Technique, and Their Applications*. New Haven, CT: Yale University Press.
Keynes, J. M. (1963 [1931]): *Essays in Persuasion*. London and New York: Norton.
Klein, M. (1964): *Contributions to Psychoanalysis 1921–1945*. New York: McGraw-Hill.
Klein, M. (1975): *Envy and Gratitude and Other Works 1946–1963*. New York: Delacorte Press.
Mankiw, G. (1985): *Small Menu Costs and Large Business Cycles: A Macroeconomic Model of Monopoly*. The Quarterly Journal of Economics, vol. 100, no. 2, pp. 529–538.
Mannheim, K. and Wolff, K. H. (1993): *From Karl Mannheim*, 2nd (expanded) ed. New Brunswick, NJ: Transaction Publishers.
Menand, L. (ed.) (1997): *Pragmatism: A Reader*. New York: Vintage Books.
Nelson, R. (ed.) (1993): *National Innovation Systems*. Oxford: Oxford University Press.
Nelson, R. and Winter, S. G. (1982): *An Evolutionary Theory of Economic Change*. Cambridge, MA: Harvard University Press.
Ollman, B. (ed.) (1998): *Market Socialism*. Abingdon: Routledge.
Polanyi, K. (1944): *The Great Transformation*. New York: Rinehart.
Rugman, A. (2012): *The End of Globalization: What It Means for Business*, new. ed. Cornerstone Digital.
Rutherford, M. (2011): *The Institutional Movement in American Economics, 1918–1947: Science and Social Control*. Cambridge: Cambridge University Press.
Salsano, A. (ed.) (1982): *Antologia del Pensiero Socialista*. Bari: Laterza.
Sullivan, H. S., Perry, H. S. and Gawel, M. L. (eds.) (1953): *The Interpersonal Theory of Psychiatry*. New York: Norton.
Tugwell, R. G. (ed.) (1924): *The Trend of Economics*. New York: Knopf.
Veblen, T. (1899): *The Theory of Leisure Class*. New York: Penguin.
Veblen, T. (1990a [1914]): *The Instinct of Workmanship and the State of the Industrial Arts*. New Brunswick, NJ: Transaction Publishers.
Veblen, T. (1990b [1919]): *The Place of Science in Modern Civilization*. New Brunswick, NJ: Transaction Publishers.
Veblen, T. (2012 [1904]): *The Theory of Business Enterprise*. London: Forgotten Books.
Winnicott, D. W. (1988): *Human Nature*. London: The Winnicott Trust by Arrangement with Mark Paterson.

Part III
History in the Italian tradition of economic thought

8 Economics and history in Italy in the twentieth century

Piero Roggi

1 Introduction

The theme of this chapter is the multifarious relationship between fact and theories in the thought of Italian economists: a subject so vast that it can be depicted only with rapid brush strokes and brief glimmers.

The view Maffeo Pantaleoni held about history is widely known (Pantaleoni, 1907; Bruni, 1999). He thought in different terms than we do today. History was simply a line on the Cartesian plane, an unpretentious interpolative curve to soften dents and peaks of reality. No scientist has ever had, I think, a poorer and faultier idea of history.

If in this chapter I should follow the geometrical vision of Pantaleoni, a meagre chapter indeed would it become! Others, instead, already and readily embraced his method, in history of science as in history of economic thought. Luigi Einaudi (1936), for example, observed that during the *Methodenstreit* of the nineteenth century many intellectuals strayed from it, causing a waste of intellectual powers that could have found a better use. Kuhn (1962) also approved Pantaleoni's criteria by describing the dynamics of science as a broken interpolated line made of normal science, anomaly and scientific revolution.

The content of this chapter, alas, will not follow the curve of Pantaleoni. His coordinates on the Cartesian plane pertain to a region unattainable by any median curve, while the question of the *Methodenstreit* cannot be treated in its singularity.

I want to clarify, immediately, my frank position: after one hundred and seventy years, that very special catastrophic event has not been yet adequately analysed. We could adopt, as an analogy, the explanation an elderly Sismondi gave, in 1819, of the contrast in technological methods on the market for production factors (labour against machines). An analogy not devoid of perils, first and foremost in comparing the market for production factors of goods with the market for intellectual services, offering 'interpretations' of reality. The analogy is haphazard and could result in bizarre outcomes, far from historical reality.

In declaring my uneasiness with this theme, I am not merely making a rhetorical excuse. As an historian of economic thought, in fact, I am myself part of the history I want to relate and so I am biased. The question, perhaps, could have been better studied by a sociologist of academic life. Another problem pertains to the works I will cite: just a few of all that have been written on the issue. My line of interpolation could thus assume the form of a proscription curve. On this, I will only underline that precisely the ones I will not quote are closer to my own point of view.

Given these clarifications, I can begin my reasoning. I will centre my reflections on the destructive force of the *Methodenstreit* and its long-term consequences. I will begin with those isolated scholars who, in the inter-war period, felt uneasy as a consequence of the historical proximity to it.[1] I will then discuss those who, in the 1970s and 80s, wanted to distance themselves from it, erasing even its memory. I will observe, in the end, how that long-passed dispute influences scholars even today.

2 The *Methodenstreit* in Italy until the 1930s

Everything originated from the crisis of the classical school, regarding, at the same time, economic policy, economic methodology and academia (Roggi, 1978, pp. 17–19; Zagari, 1989, pp. 25–42; Koot, 1988, pp. 10–38). Economic policy because English liberalism, with its mystic faith in comparative costs, was immediately suspected of being the expression of England's national interests. Economic methodology because the cognitive results of classical political economy appeared a way too generic, in their abstractness, to understand and explain the development process of particular countries. Academia because it was easily grasped that a decisive innovation in research methods could increase chairs and financing.

In conclusion, all these factors came together in a movement prone to reforming economic science, a science that from Adam Smith onward had experienced many cumulative changes, pruning of branches, but no real alterations in the roots. The reform of the middle of the nineteenth century, instead, wished to be radical, changing the methodology itself of the economic science (Shackle, 1972). The further evolution of knowledge, from being physiologic and cooperative, became revolutionary and comparative.

Censures and excommunications followed suit and the orthodox side immediately worked on a 'post-Reformation'. As with dinosaurs in front of the meteorite, an entire generation of economists felt the threat of extinction.

From the high walls of Vienna, Carl Menger (1883) began the fight against the invading barbarians. Forges vibrated with industrious effort, weapons were sharpened and a defensive shield carefully prepared. The shield had a very complicated name: 'a priori methodological exclusivism'. Whichever form it took it had to possess two precise characteristics: only an economist should hold it and it should project enough force to discourage amateurs and charlatans.

In this way, the conservatives of the economics school could act on the market for intellectual services, offering an interpretation protected by a patent, impeding the competition of non-adherents. This defensive strategy soon crossed the Alps and caused in Italy the birth of two counterpoised associations of economists: the *dogmatists* of Francesco Ferrara in the Adam Smith Society, and the *mesologists* in the Society for the Development of Science (Poettinger, 2013; Faucci, 2000; Maccabelli, 2000).

The constitutive act of this last society – undersigned by Antonio Scialoja, Luigi Cossa, Luigi Luzzatti and Fedele Lampertico – stated:

> The economic science, having overcome all the obstacles that in feudal states opposed freedom, today is called upon to investigate whichever economic function should be responsibility of the State, so that freedom might become fruitful and prolific and not subject of the optimists' fatalism.[2]

The cleft had so been created: Lampertico, Luzzatti, Cossa, Scialoja on one side; Ferrara, Pareto, Pantaleoni and Einaudi on the other.

The events of the German methodological reform and of the purists' post-reformation are well known. The severe contraposition of methods and economic schools would later become a deep psychological encumbrance for authors such as Benedetto Croce and Alberto Bertolino.

Benedetto Croce believed that after 1848 historiography could never be the same as before. Ancient historiography had been the history of liberation, of transcendence and enfranchisement from the environment; the history made with a view to the sky to reach serenity, the history of art, of philosophy and of religion. Modern history, instead, after Marx and Engels, is earthly historiography, with struggle and 'crashing of the teeth', historiography of the clashes of classes in the brutal social environment: 'It appears that man traces the history of his own passions in search for serenity [. . .]. But before 1848, two young Germans cautioned that the drama of human race consisted exclusively in the ownership of the means of production' (Croce, 1960 [1950], p. 116).

With the passing of time, the attention of historians shifted from the sky toward earth: a difficult process. In the case of Alberto Bertolino, for example, the discomfort following the battle of methods caused unceasing torment. Should the historian of economic thought escape into Pantaleoni's dogmatism, an identifying refuge that, excluding amateurs and charlatans, parades the flag of a history written only by economists, or should he avoid it, following the natural inclinations of his mind?

Bertolino interiorizes the external quandary, transforming it into an intellectual dilemma, internal conflict between the natural freedom of spirit and the institutional organization of culture.

The first option injures the intellectual's freedom. Every a priori methodological exclusivism, underlines Bertolino, would be unreasonable and detrimental, because it causes insufferable limitations to the individual aptitudes of researchers. On the other side, there would be a 'social division, perhaps even political and academic' of the intellectual work that cannot be ignored. Such division imposes the necessity to choose sides: 'The indetermination of the observation field is the cause of unfruitful and superficial studies' (Bertolino, 1939 [1926], p. 127). It also imposes a choice to escape the threat of being confused with low-end mesologists. We are not mesologists, stresses Bertolino: 'Against this method, we are in the good company of Maffeo Pantaleoni' (Bertolino 1979 [1927], p. 16). Again: 'We have nothing to do with the Schmollerian historicism' (p. 55).

In the end, Bertolino concludes that the history of economic thought has to be written by economists and guided by a science devoid of value judgements. Value judgements cannot scientifically pertain to an economics clearly separated from morals. In the contradiction between the *natural* and the *academic* division of intellectual labour, the reality principle vanquishes the natural right of the mind: the author capitulates.

The discomfort of individual scientists speaks for them alone, but that of opposed schools speaks to all. The fronts had in time their standard-bearers, as in the case of Luigi Einaudi and Ugo Spirito. Spirito immediately recognized the methodological manoeuvre of economistic purism attempted by Einaudi to delegitimize generic historians.

Excommunications, though, can fall back on the one who delivered them. 'We witness a curious display of pure scientists who, exceeding in purism, drown in the same dilettantism they despise, endorsing the most illicit and monstrous abuses' (Spirito, 1930, p. 322). Their ignorance of the role of the state is disarming, in the eyes of Spirito, and their pretence of methodological independence illusory. So to say, anathemas can be returned to the sender.

Luigi Einaudi reacted to the provocation of Spirito: 'Squabbles and excommunications amuse the audience when those who want to overthrow and exclude others do not have the capacity themselves to write any history at all' (Einaudi, 1936, p. 82). In his view, conflicts over methodology refer to struggles of academic power rather than to the noble research of truth.

It is fascinating to study the methodological war as a conflict among leaders, but hearing the voices of the troops makes it a choral experience. In the 1930s, the historicist front comprised Mondaini, Verlinden, Fanfani and Dal Pane.

Mondaini (1947) recognized in the historical understanding a unique and irreplaceable form of knowledge, while hastily doing away with all pseudo-functions that in the past were credited to it. History was neither a form of pedagogy nor a *magistra vitae*, because contexts remain incomparable; history was also different from morals because it was averse to value judgements; history could not even be the trivial expression of insatiable curiosity. Mondaini considered the true value of history, instead, to be its epistemological function. Its method is unique, because it uncovers the past as 'difference' and thus allows the hidden sedimentation of tradition inside every man to be recognized. This task is exactly what no theory without history could ever accomplish. This is the reason why the dignity of this cultural sector could never be questioned by any theoretical dogmatism.

While Mondaini underlined the specificity of history, Verlinden (1960 [1948]) introduced the concept of 'stage system'. He never doubted the epistemological superiority of economic history in respect to theory. The 'infinite ubiquity' of theory (a single general law with universal and extemporal validity), in his view, generates a dull and inaccurate knowledge. The opposite pertains in respect to the 'stage system', the art of German economists to fracture historical time as with a chocolate bar.

Friedrich List would fracture time with the knife of the prevalent production (hunting, farming, trade and industry); Hildebrand with the criteria of the characteristic mean of exchange (barter, money and credit); Bücher and Schmoller broke historical time with the knife of the distance between production and consumption, small in a domestic economy, greater in an urban economy and greatest in the national economy.

Whatever the fracture criteria, Verlinden credits the method of the 'stage system' for having efficiently contained the infinite ubiquity of economists: 'This brief excursus of mine proved the utility of the stage system in economic history' (Verlinden, 1960 [1948], p. 60).

The Italian followers of German historicism are legion and it would be pleonastic to retrace all their expressions, although it might still be useful to follow one particular declination of it, the Catholic one, in view of the lasting influence it had on Italian historiography.

The 'stage system' was indeed adopted by two economic historians of Catholic inclinations: Mauri (1924) and Fanfani (2011), who held, respectively, the chairs of History of Economic Thought and Economic History in the Catholic University of Milan. Exercising the art of time fracturing, they adopted the knife of the prevailing economic morals in the periods considered (Porta, 2001; Parisi Acquaviva, 2001).

During the Middle Ages, according to these authors, the moral of the '*limited* acquisition of wealth' prevailed, particularly thanks to the Church. Only later the bourgeois French revolution diffused the moral of '*unlimited* acquisition'. In post-capitalist time, then, *tempered* acquisition emerged: *unlimited* in production and *limited* in distribution. According to this interpretation, while at the beginning the will of the civil and religious powers (hence the denomination: *voluntarism*) alleviated the hedonistic instinct, subsequently (in the time of *naturalism*) natural instincts became free, giving birth to a capitalism that exacted a high tribute from labour. When, later, a demand for social justice became general, morals changed toward a dialectic form: free natural instinct in the production and state imperative in the distribution (*neo-voluntarism* or *tempered voluntarism*).

Splitting the continuity of history into economic steps defined by different moral attitudes has two major advantages: to render the evolution of economic history efficaciously and to point out the prospective target of humanity: a society with a contractive economy where social conflict can be easily overcome.

The historicism of all these interpretations is immediately recognizable by the use of the 'stage system'. That of Dal Pane, instead, is hidden and more personal. In effect, Dal Pane even if defining himself as a historicist, does not frontally attack dogmatism. He instead affirms that to enlighten historical research a theoretical assumption that ensures hermeneutical value is necessary:

> Muratori misses the theoretical instruments of an economist who interprets the flowing of events on the base of theoretical principles [. . .]. Pagnini, instead, supplies principles guiding the intelligence of facts [. . .]; but it is Labriola the one who uses the new and richer interpretative canon [. . .] merging the economy with the rest of life.
>
> (Dal Pane, 1960 [1952], pp. 185–193)

170 *Piero Roggi*

Dal Pane champions the idea that there is a historiographical evolution guided by the enrichment of the researcher's theoretical assumption. The historical reconstruction requires guiding criteria, but, in the view of Dal Pane, these criteria possess different grades of complexity. The criteria of pure economics are insufficient, while those of the enlarged Marxian dynamics are more satisfying. In other words, taproots are less apt to studying history than rhizomatous roots and the best economic historiography is the one known as *economic and social history*.

3 The *Methodenstreit* in Italy from the 1970s to the new millennium

Fractures, in bones as in historiography can be compound or not. Historicists, such as those quoted earlier, worsened the fracture of economics from history, but others tried to resolve it. I will metaphorically call this last group the 'orthopaedists'. Every one of them used his own method, but curiously, each developed it during the 1970s.

Already in 1929, Roberto Michels observed that the *Methodenstreit* assumed an identifying character. Scholars had to take a stance and adhere to one of the two opposing sides. His contribution intended to overcome this dualism. In his view, both methods held their own validity. Some questions called for the one, some for the other. 'Facts have often preceded theory and gave origin to it. Sometimes, though, the process had reversed. The task of the historian is to understand which connection chronologically preceded the other' (Michels, 1929, p. 106). Certainly, 'there is a causal relationship between theory and facts. The analysis of this relationship constitutes the main task of the historian of economic thought' (ibid.).

Given this point of view, the main problem is no longer the rivalry between intellectuals, but the alternative use of working instruments. The identity struggle between schools of thought becomes, in the hands of Michels, the pragmatic choice and personal responsibility of every historian. As the artisan chooses the best instrument to work iron or wood, so the historian will adapt his method to his object of study.

Where Michels' solution to the *Methodenstreit* is pragmatic, Aurelio Macchioro proposed a rather cultural and political one.

In Perugia, in 1971, Giuseppe Calzoni hosted the first congress of Italian historians of economic thought. Participants pertained to the most diverse schools of thought and methodological traditions. The Marxian Aurelio Macchioro gave the keynote speech. At the very beginning, he immediately stated his methodological preference. History of economic thought should unveil the ideologies of classes bent on appropriating the surplus of the working class: history of economic thought should be 'civil history'. All convenors now expected from Macchioro a severe critique of the diffused method 'from theory to theory' (in Macchioro's terms the dogmatic, teleological and superstructural method). Macchioro, instead, surprised all by stating that he still preferred the dogmatic method to the 'KK' one (he called it 'KK', an invented term, to avoid offending anyone by adopting a debasing term). Hermaphrodite, erudite and confusing, the 'KK' is the method of historians devoid of any theoretical background, guided by mere curiosity and incapable of distinguishing among different theories. Macchioro summarized: 'We prefer dogmatism to the confusion of KK [...] we must assume that KK is the erroneous corruption of the other two methods' (Macchioro, 1974, pp. 12–18). What Macchioro proposed was an alliance of Marxists and dogmatists against a new adversary: the 'KK'.

It seems that reconciling the fracture of the *Methodenstreit* is possible, but the solution must be one of cultural politics. Not all orthopaedists work with the same instruments. Those of Antonio Fusco (1969 and 1974), differ from those of Michels or Macchioro. Fusco prefers an instrument that is neither pragmatic nor political but purely historical: historiography.

In his view, the advocated methodological purism and the following *conventio ad excludendum* were not natural categories of political economy but appeared in a very precise historical moment. They are neither natural nor absolute but, rather, historical and relativistic. Medieval economic thought centred on theology and the thought of the eighteenth century centred on the philosophy of social welfare. Only with the advent of positivism, mimicking physics, the methodologic dependency became independency through the acceptance of 'the a prioristic methodologic exclusivism'. Only then did specialization overcome general knowledge. Fusco underlines that the methodologic dependency and independency of economics are historical contingencies, alternatives that cyclically recur. Nothing can guarantee that in the future the process of methodologic specialization will prove irreversible. Fusco's orthopaedic solution has a strong historicist connotation.

More complex than the compositions proposed by Michels, Macchioro and Fusco, is the one offered by Piero Barucci between 1971 and 1998. First, because it has its own internal evolution, and second, because it represents a first tentative solution of the 'unsettled question' evoked by Alberto Bertolino in 1937.

Barucci (1998) expressed a very strong judgement on the *Methodenstreit:* an unyielding fight to win over academic positions and resources, begun by German historicists and continued by purists to lock their vantage point and exclude external 'invaders'.

How does he, then, recompose the fracture? Which orthopaedics does he apply? He first tries out a psychological solution, but then prefers a dialectic one. Barucci – in the period of his review of Macchioro (Barucci, 1971) and his essay on the economic dogma of Einaudi (Barucci, 1974) – softens his negative judgement on the *Methodenstreit.* Macchioro's method can be as acceptable as Einaudi's.

Barucci then proceeds to construe a theory of the production, circulation and consumption of economic theory of which mesologism and dogmatism are just two dialectic phases. Mesology represents the first movement of the circulation, theorization the second. 'Facts are one of the most common elements in the laboratory of an economist; so that a continuous circulation movement ensues between theory and factual environment' (Barucci, 1983, p. 515). In consequence, the historian of economics 'studying economists of the past can only be an economist' (Barucci, 1998, p. 156).

The circulation also has a third movement, back to mesology, but to an upturned mesology. 'Economists', writes Barucci, 'cannot live without intervening in economic policy matters' (1983, p. 505). Economists thus become journalists, producers of economic culture and even politicians. Economists, stepping down from the isolated tower of theorization, want to transform from *Sacerdos ad excludendum* into *Sacerdos ad imprimendum.*

The circuit 'production/circulation/distribution' of economic theory is thus complete, but not for all times. The circuit continuously repeats itself, continuously changing historical contingencies. Summing up: mesology to start with, dogmatism, upturned mesology in the end, and so on ad infinitum. The contradiction denounced by Alberto Bertolino has herewith found a dialectical and cyclical solution.

Historicists and purists spoke of a methodological irreparable contradiction, orthopaedists of a compoundable one. Who won the battle for the unity or uniformity of economics? Nobody, apparently, considering that the question remained unsettled even after the 1970s.

Let us take the case of Vera Zamagni (1992). In her view, the knowledge of the past is no easy feat: it requires a cumulative and comprehensive capability. There are, essentially, two available methods: the exclusive one with separation effects (the island in the metaphor of the author) and the federative method with aggregation effects. Which one maximizes the total interpretative power? The exclusive method tends toward the exclusion of all alternative researches judged as amateurish and inadequate. The federative method, on the contrary, looks for a convergence of alternative research techniques. The first will diminish the total interpretative power of the discipline; the second will augment it. As with human aggregation, in general the rule holds: the greater the grouping the more powerful it is; so it is with scholars.

Zamagni speaks for a complete refusal of specialism and isolationism, while at the same time recognizing the existence of an original fracture that cannot easily be mended.

How, then, is an economic historian distinguishable from a historian of economic thought? Just by looking her/him in the eye, answers Marco Cattini (1992). The economist's eye is selective, the historian's one completive. If the theoretical assumption of the economist selects just a few variables for his limited sight, the eye of the historian maintains his peripheral view, including all variables left in the shadows by the economist. In sum: 'Economists use the exception clause, while historians do not' (Cattini, 1992, pp. 26–27).

In conclusion, the methodological fracture became, in the essay of Cattini, a different eye conformation between the two types of scholars, as in different ethnical groups.

Again, the cases of Vera Zamagni and Marco Cattini show different attitudes concerning the originating *Methodenstreit*. Zamagni would like to bridge the gap and close the dispute, while Cattini transforms the cultural diversity into a physiological one.

This dividing line recurs also in the debate hosted at the end of the twentieth century by the *Rivista di Storia Economica*.

Schumpeter denied that theorization could follow facts. Historically, facts evolve from a confused multiplicity to a purified quintessence. The economist who decided to start from the multiple uncertainty of the past instead of considering the simplified purity of the present would incur many a risk. So concludes De Vecchi (2001): 'Schumpeter votes against the use of history as a reliable point of reference for economists' (p. 367). It would, thus, be correct to put Schumpeter among dogmatists.

Marcello De Cecco (2001) tries to evaluate the place to be assigned to Keynes in reference to the *Methodenstreit*. It would be difficult to put him among dogmatists, because still many a manual insists that Keynes' underemployment equilibrium theory followed the great crisis of 1929. How could his theory be detached from the failed correspondence between the animal spirits of investors and the aspirations of consumers without income? How could De Cecco save Keynes from the accusation of mesologism? He did so by insisting that Keynes used facts not as an inspiration source, but only to confirm his a priori intuition and explain his thought to the larger public. So purified, also Keynes could enter the paradise of pure theoreticians with no relationship to history and facts.

One last economist analysed on the *Rivista di Storia Economica* in his relation to historical reality is Marx. Giorgio Gilibert (2002) has no doubts on Marx's mesologism. The main proof is obviously his systematics of historical stages: Asiatic, antique, feudal, capitalist and socialist. Marx's breaking up time into historical steps, connected to each other, brought him far away from generalising dogmatism. Gilbert thus judges Marx as a dialectical mesologist.

All of these recent analyses implicitly refer to the fracture of the *Methodenstreit* in the nineteenth century, but never directly address the problem. Pierangelo Toninelli (1999), instead has openly tackled the nineteenth-century events in search for the cause. Toninelli underlines the differences in style between Anglo-Saxon academics and Europeans. He looks for an explanation by using the tools of a sociologist of science. In his view the methodological manoeuvres of the end of the nineteenth century represented nothing other than a war for academic positions and resources. To appropriate funds and chairs, academics of both opposing fronts condemned the others as charlatans and amateurs, banning them from the academic discourse. The main weapon of this war was the construction of methodological fences that resulted in veritable scientific monopolies. Anyone who did not abide by the set of methodological rules would be immediately excommunicated and excluded from all academic positions. Academics, judged Toninelli, acted in the same way as little children in front of a limited number of sweets.

4 Conclusions

This long *excursus* can be summarised synthetically in four points.

1   The methodological systematization of the end of the nineteenth century was no routine evolution of thought in the sense of Pantaleoni or Einaudi.
2   The *Methodenstreit* is more like a catastrophic event that endangered the existence of an entire set of scholars.

3 Its devastating effects did not go unnoticed and claimed the attention of many historians who tried to mend the cleft between historicists and dogmatists.
4 However, the fracture still remains and is occasionally revived when resources and chairs in academia become scarce, as at present.

My thesis is that historians should learn from the past a more open attitude toward methodological eclecticism and not repeat the errors of the *Methodenstreit*.

The war on methods has been a hypocrite and paradoxical pretext. Hypocrite, because it attributed to science unscientific characters. Paradoxical, because dogmatists adopted a liberalist attitude in their doctrine while remaining strenuously monopolistic in their methodological stance. A pretext, because it concealed its real intent behind a methodological façade.

Notes

1 For a review of the debate about the *Methodenstreit* which arose in Italy in the last decades of the eighteenth century, see Poettinger (2014).
2 The document is also to be found in Lampertico (1996, p. 406).

References

Barucci, P. (1971): Considerazioni di metodo a proposito di una recente 'storia' del pensiero economico. *Rivista internazionale di scienze sociali*, vol. 42, no. 2–3, pp. 239–254.
Barucci, P. (1974): Luigi Einaudi e la storia del dogma economico. *Note economiche*, no. 4, pp. 39–67.
Barucci, P. (1983): Teoria economica e politica economica nella evoluzione storica del pensiero economico. *Rivista di politica economica*, no. 3, pp. 499–519.
Barucci, P. (1998): Economia e storia: una relazione difficile. *Nuova economia e storia*, vol. 4, no. 2, pp. 147–161.
Bertolino, A. (1939 [1926]): Riflessioni sulla nozione di dottrina economica. In: F. Battaglia and A. Bertolino (eds.), *Problemi metodologici nella storia delle dottrine politiche ed economiche*. Rome: Società editrice del Foro Italico (orig. ed. in *Studi Senesi*, vol. 40, 1926, pp. 243–260).
Bertolino, A. (1979 [1927]): Sulla storiografia del pensiero economico. In: *Scritti e lezioni di storia del pensiero economico*. Milan: Giuffrè, pp. 4–24 (orig. ed. in *Studi senesi*, vol. 41, no. 3, 1927, pp. 232–260).
Bruni, L. (1999): The Historical School Taken Seriously: The Debate on the Economic Principle According to De Viti, Pantaleoni and Paret. *Revue européenne des sciences sociales*, vol. 37, no. 116, pp. 149–172.
Cattini, M. (1992): Questione di sguardo. *Rivista di storia economica*, vol. 9, no. 1–2, pp. 26–27.
Croce, B. (1960 [1950]): Un ammonimento circa la storiografia economica. In: M. R. Caroselli (ed.), *Natura e metodo della storia economica*. Milan: Giuffrè, pp. 49–50 (orig. ed. in *Quaderni della Critica*, no. 17–18, 1950, p. 116).
Dal Pane, L. (1960 [1952]): Storia economica e storia sociale. In: M. R. Caroselli (ed.), *Natura e metodo della storia economica*. Milan: Giuffrè, pp. 181–215 (orig. ed. in *Giornale degli economisti*, vol. 11, no. 3–4, 1952, pp. 131–165).

De Cecco, M. (2001): John Maynard Keynes. *Rivista di storia economica*, no. 3, pp. 373–382.
De Vecchi, N. (2001): Schumpeter economista: il posto della storia e il posto della logica. *Rivista di storia economica*, no. 3, pp. 361–370.
Einaudi, L. (1936): Postilla [to G. Luzzatto, Per un programma di lavoro]. *Rivista di storia economica*, vol. 1, no. 3, pp. 199–204.
Fanfani, A. (2011): *Storia delle dottrine economiche: un'antologia*, ed. by O. Ottonelli. Florence: Le Monnier.
Faucci, R. (2000): La Società Adamo Smith. In: M. M. Augello and M. E. L. Guidi (eds.), *Associazionismo economico e diffusione dell'economia politica nell'Italia dell'Ottocento. Dalle società economico-agrarie alle associazioni di economisti*. Milan: Angeli, pp. 279–298.
Fusco, A. (1969): Economia e storia: qualche riflessione. *Rassegna economica*, no. 2, pp. 443–468.
Fusco, A. (1974): Lo storico dell'economica e gli economisti italiani del Settecento: qualche riflessione di metodo. *Rivista di politica economica*, no. 6, pp. 724–762.
Gilibert, G. (2002): Storia economica e teoria: Marx. *Rivista di storia economica*, no. 1, pp. 71–81.
Koot, G. M. (1988): *English Historical Economics, 1870–1926. The Rise of Economic History and Neomercantilism*. Cambridge: Cambridge University Press.
Kuhn, T. S. (1962): *The Structure of Scientific Revolutions*. Chicago: University of Chicago Press.
Lampertico, F. (1996): *Carteggi e diari: 1842–1906*, vol. 1. Venice: Marsilio.
Maccabelli, T. (2000): La Società d'incoraggiamento di Padova e l'Associazione per il progresso degli studi economici (1846–1878). In: M. M. Augello and M. E. L. Guidi (eds.), *Associazionismo economico e diffusione dell'economia politica nell'Italia dell'Ottocento. Dalle società economico-agrarie alle associazioni di economisti*. Milan: Angeli, pp. 299–328.
Macchioro, A. (1974): La storia del pensiero economico fra storia e scienza (relazione presentata a Perugia al primo convegno di studiosi di pensiero economico, marzo 1971). *Nuova rivista storica*, vol. 58, no. 1–2, pp. 1–28.
Mauri, A. (1924): La storia delle dottrine economiche nell'economia sociale. *Rivista internazionale di scienze sociali e discipline ausiliarie*, vol. 98, no. 374, pp. 122–141 and no. 375, pp. 215–230.
Menger, C. (1883): *Untersuchungen über die Methode der Sozialwissenschaften und der politischen Ökonomie insbesondere*. Leipzig: Duncker und Humblot (latest English reprint: *Investigations into the Method of the Social Sciences with Special Reference to Economics*, ed. by L. Schneider. Auburn: The Ludwig von Mises Institute, 2009).
Michels, R. (1929): Disamina di alcuni criteri direttivi per la storia delle dottrine economiche. *Giornale degli economisti*, vol. 69, no. 3, pp. 105–121.
Mondaini, G. (1947): La storiografia nella esperienza semisecolare di un docente. *Nuova rivista storica*, no. 3–6, pp. 217–257.
Pantaleoni, M. (1907): Una visione cinematografica del progresso della scienza economica. *Giornale degli economisti*, vol. 35, pp. 964–992.
Parisi Acquaviva, D. (2001): L'idea che genera il fatto e il fatto che si riverbera sull'idea: storia del pensiero economico nella didattica nell'Università Cattolica negli anni Venti e Trenta. *Bollettino dell'archivio per la storia del movimento sociale cattolico in Italia*, vol. 36, no. 2, pp. 240–251.

Poettinger, M. (2013): La diffusione della scienza economica come strumento di propaganda liberale: 'L'Economista' (1874–1881). *Il pensiero economico italiano*, vol. 21, no. 1, pp. 151–176.

Poettinger, M. (2014): Besieging the French Liberal Fortress: The Diffusion of Italian and German Economic Thought in the Last Quarter of the 19th Century. *Rivista di storia economica*, vol. 30, pp. 37–58.

Porta, P. L. (2001): La storia delle dottrine economiche negli studi di Angelo Mauri e Amintore Fanfani. *Bollettino dell'archivio per la storia del movimento sociale cattolico in Italia*, vol. 36, no. 2, pp. 59–84.

Roggi, P. (1978): *L'economia politica classica, 1776–1848*. Florence: Le Monnier.

Shackle, G. L. S. (1972): Marginalism: The Harvest. *History of Political Economy*, vol. 4, no. 2, pp. 587–602.

Sismondi, J. C. L. S. (1819): *Nouveaux principes d'économie politique, ou de la richesse dans ses rapports avec la populations*. Paris: Delaunay.

Spirito, U. (1930): La storia dell'economia e il concetto di Stato. *Nuovi studi di diritto, economia e politica*, vol. 3, no. 5, pp. 321–324.

Toninelli, P. (1999): Fra stile analitico e stile continentale: la Storia economica alla ricerca di uno statuto metodologico. *Rivista di storia economica*, no. 1, pp. 53–86.

Verlinden, C. (1960 [1948]): Cicli e periodi nella storia economica. In: M. R. Caroselli (ed.), *Natura e metodo della storia economica*. Milan: Giuffrè, pp. 51–60 (orig. ed. Introduction à l'histoire économique générale. Coimbra: Universidade de Coimbra, 1948).

Zagari, E. (1989): La crisi dell'economia classica: Sismondi e Mill. In: C. Perrotta (ed.), *Momenti di svolta nel pensiero economico*. Lecce: Congedo, pp. 25–42.

Zamagni, V. (1992): Storia economica: isola o crocevia? *Rivista di storia economica*, no. 1–2, pp. 9–12.

9 Labour as culture
The Lombardo-Veneto School

Gianfranco Tusset

1 Introduction

While the use of neoclassical economics in the analysis of economic facts and the study of the development of a country or a region enables exploration of the role of labour and capital, it does not clarify everything that concerns the role of both institutions and time. Moreover, the neoclassical view completely ignores the role of culture, even when cultural features find expression in informal economic behaviours. This occurs even though ideas, ideologies, and myths matter, and understanding of how they evolve is crucial for grasping social and economic changes (North, 1996, p. 347).

This chapter deals with culture over time in regard to a specific economic change process. It does not treat culture *tout court*, but rather the 'culture of labour': that is, the well-defined approach to labour relationships characterizing an economic area. The aim is to show how the 'culture of labour' that took root in a particular region, the Italian north-east, played a role in the economic growth which connoted that area from the 1980s onwards. In particular, the entrepreneurial culture that typifies that area cannot be separated from the 'culture of labour' widespread in it, according to the view that labour was one of the pillars of that successful experience, but also one of the least recognized (Anastasia and Corò, 1996, p. 209).

The method applied here is that of *path dependence*, meaning that current facts are investigated by assuming that they may be influenced by past events. Postulating the principle that a system follows one path instead of another according to its past history (Day, 1994), the path dependence approach allows us to consider the 'history' of a socio-economic system, that is, its evolutionary trajectory showing both its linearity and irregularity. This interpretative approach seems suitable for grasping the role played by 'culture of labour' in economic development, also when such a culture is of an entrepreneurial nature. At the same time, since culture expresses the set of relationships connecting past and present, it implicitly evokes a path dependence perspective.[1]

The notion of 'culture of labour' makes direct reference to the values of both workers and entrepreneurs as expressed in their preferences and choices: we can say that culture is a sort of meta-preference. Consequently, the evolution of this meta-preference should be reconstructed in order to understand what kind of labour relations have originated from such culture.

The definition of such culture can be simplified by examining the theoretical principles characterizing the 'Lombardo-Veneto' school of economic thought, which during the second half of the nineteenth century included economists and statisticians mainly from that region. This is not to claim that the 'culture of labour' recognizable in the Italian north-east originated with the Lombardo-Veneto School, but the contents of that body of thought, beginning with its pragmatism, can be of help in reconstructing the economic features that were constants in that culture. In order to represent the theoretical liveliness and originality of economists and politicians such as Fedele Lampertico, Angelo Messedaglia, Luigi Luzzatti, but also the less well-known Emilio Morpurgo, all representatives of that school, the idea of the 'Veneto laboratory' has been introduced (Camurri, 1992a, p. 4), in accordance with its use with reference to the economic experience of the late twentieth century.

The conduct of a mainly historical analysis which starts from Italian unification and ends in the second half of the twentieth century is justified by the fact that values and ideologies anchored to a specific cultural context evolve very slowly, even more so if the intention is to consider the preferences and beliefs that in some sense pertain to the material sphere (Lal, 1998), as is the case of the culture of labour. However, examination of a process involving cultural sedimentation can only be historical-evolutionary in nature.

The culture of labour as defined by the Lombardo-Veneto School reflects the features of the entrepreneurial and economic relationships of the region considered here. It gave origin, in the last century, to a specific relation between workers and entrepreneurs that can be synthesized as 'paternalism', first 'philanthropic' and then entrepreneurial and social: a specific version of the labour/capital conflict, one might say (Favaro and Solari, 2015). Precisely because it was part of the existing 'culture of labour', paternalism survived industrialization and the spread of social policies to become an authentic organizational strategy of social consensus in given industrial areas during the 1930s. It is not rash to argue that the 'culture of labour' and the deep-rooted experience of paternalism were important causes of the growth of small enterprises from the post-Second World War years onwards. The Italian north-east was effectively characterized by a network of medium and small enterprises whose growing dynamism reached a peak during the 1980s.

The period examined here, which begins in the 1870s and 1880s and ends in the 1980s, can be explained by the two 'laboratories' that arose in the same area but with a time span of around one hundred years between them. The first 'laboratory' was theoretical in nature; the second can be identified with the extraordinary economic growth. We can anticipate a first outcome of the analysis. It will be confirmed that the Schumpeterian schemes grounded on entrepreneurial creativity and novelties are not sufficient to explain the vertical mobility that could be observed in Veneto. Obviously, this does not reduce the weight and importance of any kind of innovation, but it rather stresses the importance of imitation concerning entrepreneurial roles. Vertical mobility was fuelled by a culture of labour which gradually transformed itself into an entrepreneurial culture.

The first section of the chapter describes the original features of the 'culture of labour' as it emerged in the first 'laboratory' in the decades around Italian unification. The second section focuses on the corporate and social paternalism that accompanied the application of the Lombardo-Veneto School's precepts. The third section dwells on the spread of small enterprises during the 1950s and 1960s, here presented as a form of imitation within an entrepreneurial culture. A sort of 'attraction to self-employment' took shape, giving rise to a reorganization of the production system and shaping the so-called 'laboratory' of the end of the century, here considered in section four. Finally, the chapter will seek to show that the 'culture of labour' is a variable endogenous to the economic system, not an exogenous one.

2 The culture of labour in the late nineteenth-century Veneto 'laboratory'

The Lombardo-Veneto School grouped together economists who often assumed political and governmental appointments, thus playing a role in the definition of Italian economic policy between the two centuries. Governing and engaging in economics were conceived as mutually reinforcing actions, and this explains the strongly pragmatic approach taken by this school. Theory did not prescind from real economic relationships, even if this might entail a lack of analytical rigour. Consequently, the economic theory appeared closer to an economic culture.

Two points should be stressed. First, economics was not conceived as the *science of wealth*, but rather as the *science of man*. Second, labour was treated as a social or public value that determines the *social relations* prevailing within a community or area. Labour meant *social economy*.

Let us consider the first point in detail. Like the contemporaneous German *Kathedersozialisten* (socialists of the chair), who by breaking with *laissez-faire* laid the bases for the successive development of the German welfare state (Scaldaferri, 1992), so the Lombardo-Veneto economists stated a work ethic that subsequently influenced industrial development. The originality of those economists resided not only in their moderate political and economic tones and in the establishment of Catholic solidarism, but also in the conception of worker/entrepreneur relationships that would characterize organization of the firm for a long time.

The Lombardo-Veneto scholars are often likened to the historical German-speaking economists (Cognetti de Martiis, 1886) for having inherited the socialism of the chair doctrine. On reading Fedele Lampertico's *Economia dei popoli e degli Stati* (1874–1876), which according to the author is a textbook of the Lombardo-Veneto School (De Rosa, 1996), one gains the impression that the features typical of German historicism are certainly many – Schäffle's organism; von Hermann's economic relationships; the link between law and economics – but that the school to which Lampertico belonged cannot be considered a legacy of

German historicism. On the contrary, its recurrent pragmatism seems to evoke elements drawn from the British tradition.

However, Lampertico's theory was fully organicistic when he stated that social harmony is not a natural outcome of individuals' relationships, but rather is an objective that must be pursued. In this organicist representation of society, labour is not only a productive and distributive fulcrum but also an authentic social 'glue'.

Although Lampertico recognized the minimum means as a natural law of economic behaviour, he combined that principle with another natural law, that of 'universal solidarity', according to which any individual is constantly 'in relation with the labour of the whole of humankind' (Lampertico, 1874, p. 14). This view of production relationships makes the following statement more understandable: 'It is not goods, products, or wealth that are at the centre of economics, but man, who is the point of departure and arrival' (Lampertico, 1874, pp. 136–137). This perspective justifies the shift of the core of economics from the production of wealth to the labour of man, from the individual to the society.

Although they might appear ingenuous, these notes drawn from the *Economia dei popoli* are crucial for grasping the core of the economic theory propounded by the Lombardo-Veneto School. Lampertico, on the basis of the thought of Angelo Messedaglia and the 'Italian school', considered not an abstract or medium individual, but 'man as he is according to the variety of social and economic conditions'. Lampertico did not challenge the principle of freedom as the guide for any individual action, but he added that economic science should consider individual interests in all 'their expressions', that is to say, 'family, community, state, humankind'; and this 'because the fulcrum of the entire national economy is the person' in accordance with 'his or her moral, religious, national, political conditions, that is, all the relationships that influence the economy' (Lampertico, 1874, pp. 138–139). Thus a social dimension of the economy gradually took shape: to use Lampertico's expression, the 'social economy' (Cardini, 1993).

To support the idea of an economics focused on man and, consequently, on labour, Lampertico cited the Italian school of the mid-sixteenth century – Genovesi, Beccaria, Ortes, Palmieri – who put 'human industriousness' at the centre of political economy. This idea of economic science was different from that prevailing in the English-speaking countries, where 'political economy mainly treated wealth *per se*', wrote Lampertico. On the other hand, 'Italian thought considered man not as a wealth factor alone, but as the subject of wealth'. What mattered was the conclusion. Lampertico and the other Lombardo-Veneto scholars were persuaded that labour was the fulcrum of economic science. Labour, on which the existence of goods depends, should not be considered in a strictly instrumental perspective as a production factor, because, like any other economic behaviour, it 'obeyed not only economic laws but all the laws governing human intelligence, heart and strength' (Lampertico, 1874, p. 121 and 1876a, pp. 6–7). Economic behaviours should not be explained on rational bases alone, such as minimum means; nor should labour be conceived only as a production factor.

Compared with Böhm-Bawerk's work published ten years later, Lampertico's view was still an ingenuous conception of the economic process, pragmatic more than scientific, but equally meaningful because it treated labour as a 'value' *per se* before being a productive factor – a view far from being a strictly materialist one. By treating labour as a social relationship, as well as a production factor, Lampertico could state that the destinies of both worker and entrepreneur are interwoven, to the point that each of them should earn a fixed 'income', accumulating the remainder in a common reserve as a contribution to the original capital (Lampertico, 1876b, p. 317). Consequently, labour was a sort of social wealth before it was an individual source of income, in accordance with the civilizing function that the Lombardo-Veneto School assigned to production activity.

The idea of labour as the regulator of social and interpersonal relationships gained ground. It partially obscured the classical conception of labour as a mere production factor and, hence, as a source of conflict. To be stressed is that labour was not viewed in moral terms alone: Lampertico, and especially Morpurgo, did not detach labour from wealth. The Lombardo-Veneto School took together the moral and strictly economic perspectives on labour, without one of them becoming the unique dimension of labour. It can be said that the encounter between materialism and the moral view led to the consideration of labour as a 'strategy' of production, but also of the community and the society, as a source of civilization.

At that time, the principle that workers consider the firm's output as an 'accepted behavioural rule' became a sort of 'organizational ethic.' It was the origin of the social value of labour which still today is a crucial resource involving both worker and entrepreneur as local economic subjects.

This kind of 'added social value' attributed to labour can be understood also by considering the importance that Lampertico gave to the relational characteristics accompanying production activities, a concept that evoked the German idea of *Lebensverhältnisse*, life relationships, which von Hermann introduced in a political economy text of 1832. Following von Hermann, Lampertico made reference to some features such as loyalty in exchanges, goodwill, and benevolence, which connote economic relationships. Thus, labour must yield material and 'immaterial' goods, the latter being necessary to guarantee social order and 'civil progress'.

3 Social economy and institution

The economic and social system should be grounded on individuals whose relations involve loyalty, goodwill and mutual support. In short, there should be cooperation instead of conflict, as stated by Luigi Luzzati in 1892:

> To spread friendly societies, cooperation, social security institutions [. . .] to promote arbitrations in rural and town areas, negotiations between capital and labour, to favour the participation of workers in profit distribution, to anchor any progress to individual security, which must be strengthened with specific laws.
>
> (Luzzatti, 1935, p. 352)

The outcome is a society based on cooperation among the parts composing it.

This is neither classicism nor socialism of the chair, nor reformism, but social economy – the other pillar, with the focus on labour, of the theoretical perspective of the school analysed here. The entire social economy is built on the assumption that 'the economic law presupposes man', the latter considered not only as an individual but also in terms of the aggregates that he creates: 'Family, municipality, state, and church'. Evoked here is an idea of reformism – a word that Lampertico was reluctant to use – stressing the differences from Manchester School liberalism, on the one hand, and German socialism on the other. Social economy is grounded on friendly societies, on mutual support among individuals, and also on legislative intervention by the state (Lampertico, 1874, p. 321).

The Lombardo-Veneto School combined the British notion of *self-help* (Romani, 1985), of which mutual support was a form, with that of institutional self-government, both based on hierarchy, on the one hand, and interpersonal loyalty on the other. Emilio Morpurgo's studies (Morpurgo, 1861, 1871) demonstrated that in the proto-industrial phase mutual support schemes were fully consistent with a model of labour relations management oriented towards maintaining the apolitical character of friendly and self-help societies (Monteleone, 1871), while at the same time excluding alternative forms of unions.

Mutualism among workers and between workers and owners involves a high degree of interdependence of preferences. To put the 'man at work' at the centre of a view, which seemingly banished accumulation, required basing production relations on the 'labour family', 'benevolence', and 'interest of the group', with a lack of clarity in regard to roles and tasks. This opacity is typical of organizations in which labour is a 'public capital' that yields well-being for all. The distributional criteria did not appear rigorously defined on productive bases, but instead were decided according to relational features – as occurs in any paternalistic scheme.

The model of the mutual aid society, strongly advocated by Morpurgo (1871), was totally functional to such a view of production relationships, which avoided increasing isolation of social classes and its consequent potential conflict. A mutual aid society acts as a 'house of arbitration' where potential conflicts are mitigated if not resolved. The arbitration serves to strengthen the worker's loyalty towards the industrial or rural owner and the guarantees provided by the latter on the social condition of the worker and his family. This exchange explains why Veneto society was marked by the shift from blind benevolence to *individual responsibility* and *mutual aid*. Morpurgo (1871) recognized that labour relationships must contain bilateral features signifying a detachment from the philanthropy and patronage of the first part of the century. He also denied what Cattaneo termed *legal charity* (1956 [1836–1837], 1983 [1843]): that is, public aid, but which maintains the aided subjects in poverty. In Morpurgo's texts, it is possible to discern the relational or bilateral dimension that marked the transformation of *patronage* into *paternalism*.

The same relational characteristic was apparent at that time in the banking credit, first rural and then industrial. Giuseppe Toniolo (1871) – drawing on Luzzatti – stressed the importance of personal securities besides real ones: that is, the borrower's moral reliability as well as his financial position. In this way, he drew attention to credit, subsequently considered to be crucial for the development of rural areas, and to the need to strengthen popular and rural banks inspired by the 'spirit of family' characterizing both production relationships and social ones.

Functional to the strengthening of 'proximity' credit relationships would be the spread of territorial garrisons, as shown by the German experience. With this direct reference to interrelationships, it was clear that both Luzzatti and Toniolo sought to associate credit with the personal characteristics of the individual concerned, consistent with the then dominant ethics of work.

The function assigned to the state is no less interesting. According to Lampertico's view, shared by almost all the Lombardo-Veneto economists, the state should paternalistically contribute to the improvement of economic relationships by means of legislation (Lampertico, 1874). Among others, Luzzatti (1874) stressed two points. First, the need for entrepreneurs to be aware of the importance of wider social guarantees for all, workers included, and the need for the legislator to intervene when the interest of entrepreneurs involved morally unacceptable practice, such as child labour. Second, education must be guaranteed by the state, even though this might undermine the producers' immediate advantage because it was the only instrument with which to transform the 'unlearned plebs suffering in the spirit and body' into 'safe and industrious inhabitants'. Luzzatti appealed to the Italian middle class, which should promote 'with love and wisdom the intellectual and moral progress of the masses'. And he indicated the combination between private and public paternalism as the road to follow: protection of soul and body; laws on education and factory work.

The idea of cooperation between social bodies was strong, and legislation was not conceived as a means to regulate social conflict but as an instrument of pedagogy. The law yields positive outcomes only if it is applied in an environment that already accepts the cooperative principle. For example, Luzzatti used the expression 'reserve army' to denote the supplementary function of the state (Luzzatti, 1874, p. 246). This view was shared by Morpurgo, who argued for a 'weak and self-restricted' (Camurri, 1992b) state confined to the role of intermediary between the parts of a social body.

Thus, supplementary educational tasks were recognized to be duties of the state because not all owners/entrepreneurs had the far-sightedness and morality necessary to understand that the cooperative environment between workers and owners – that is, the exchange between social security including education and labour loyalty – is not only the core of social and economic prosperity but is also an indubitable source of advantages for the owners themselves. Theorized, as a consequence, was a first idea of subsidiarity between the state and owners/entrepreneurs in the supply of social services.

This conception may have been influenced by the legacy of the previous Austrian administration, so attentive to bureaucracy, education, and security for poorer individuals. This occurred in the presence of essentially free working relationships. Before Austria, philanthropy was not unfamiliar to the 'great repertory of Venetian landowners' (Franzina, 1992, p. 380).

Toniolo, on emphasizing the centrality of man and the civilizing function of the firm, focused on the negative consequences of a production increase detached from a 'more than proportional progress of morality in both people and public institutions' (Toniolo, 1921 [1908], p. 83). This entailed adequate 'education' for entrepreneurs, who only in this way could better safeguard their interests.

The state's intervention in workers' security was entirely excluded by Alessandro Rossi (1871), an entrepreneur/economist, who on the contrary supported a fully private security system. According to Rossi, the morality of both workers and entrepreneurs was sufficient to guarantee the self-organization necessary to mitigate any possible source of conflict. He supported the cause of the supremacy of labour because only 'the improvement of labour' could reduce the divide between those who supplied labour and those who demanded it. According to Rossi, the entrepreneur sought to improve national and local well-being, not to increase his profit alone. This personal view of industrialization grounded on defence of the national community was anchored to the moral principle affirming the implicit 'goodness of workers' and the 'non-ruthlessness' of Italian capitalism – a view characterized by strong religious sentiment. Thus, by affirming 'mutual respect', the 'prime root of true political freedom', Christianity must constitute the moral value of political economy.

In this climate marked by social cooperation there occurred what Franzina (1990) called the 'soft transition', that is, the passage from a proto-industrial to an industrial economy. The idea that 'cooperation' must shape private economic relationships was rooted in both owners and workers and, according to Rossi, it was the basis for the future development of Veneto's industry. Rossi agreed that the above-mentioned exchange between social security and labour loyalty was the most advanced attempt to control the workforce and to restrain the workers' costs of management and surveillance.

It seems clear that a 'culture of labour' of this kind could not express clear and well-defined relationships within the firm and the local community. Relations were of the informal type, dominated by the personal features of the parties. In short, within a legal framework that did not undermine the substantial freedom of exchange, what prevailed was complete self-organization. The lack of a sharp division between social classes, at least in regard to identity if not the economic sphere, and the idea that the community must regulate itself, contributed to explaining what already at the end of the nineteenth century was depicted as 'entrepreneurial liveliness' (Roverato, 1986, p. 119). In effect, the appearance of industrial units, many of small size, in certain respects anticipated the spread of small enterprises that occurred in the post-Second World War years.

4 From 'patronage' to enterprise paternalism

While patronage ('a voluntary bond grounded on interest and affection' typical of rural society; Debouzy, 1988, p. 6), defines social relationships moulded on the servant/owner couple – that is, on the personal power exercised by the owner over the servant and his family, as analysed by Baglioni (1974) with regard to rural pre-industrial society – the paternalist exchange of the late nineteenth century prefigured a contractual more than hierarchical relationship.

In effect, pragmatic economists such as Lampertico, Morpurgo, Luzzatti, and an entrepreneur like Rossi, theorized the transition from rural patronage to industrial paternalism: a hierarchical establishment characterized by servile relations was gradually replaced by an *agreement* between owners/entrepreneurs and workers.

Using the transaction costs approach, Alston and Ferrie (1999), in their study on the paternalism characterizing work relationships in the Southern cotton plantations of the United States between the nineteenth and twentieth centuries, explain that the *loyalty* that workers promised to owners allowed the latter to reduce the costs associated with both production conflicts and the surveillance of workers. For their part, the workers enjoyed some social improvements. This agreement was similar to the one discussed and supported by the Lombardo-Veneto School.

The paternalist exchange reproduces, in a production context, ties typical of the family, and which, by their nature, are considered superior to legislative regulation. Thus paternalist practice was strengthened not only by the advantages deriving from the reduction of costs for both parties, but also by the symbolic equalization of production relationships to familial ones. Finally, analogously to the family, what seems advantageous for the firm *must* appear advantageous for each of its components, workers included.

The paternalist response to the advance of industrialization was therefore the expression of a tendency to revise habits, customs and beliefs into informal rules concerning the organization of the firm and the settlement of social disputes. These work relationships were finally extended to the community in which workers and their families lived, according to a conception of paternalism as a strategy structuring social and territorial identities on the basis of meanings and symbols drawn from work relationships.

Recent studies have emphasized (Roverato, 1986) that entrepreneurs, by attempting to coordinate relief and philanthropic initiatives, from 1920s onwards sought new legitimization for entrepreneurs themselves. Besides the worker/ entrepreneur relationships taking place within the firm, the paternalist doctrine identified in the building of the 'social town' the ideal response to the need to reaffirm the factory as a 'social subject' (Roverato, 1986, pp. 322 ff.). Therefore, the late nineteenth-century culture or ethics of work concurred in shaping the territory on the basis of a necessary contiguity between the workplace and the life place: a trend that took further root in the subsequent decades with the development of the small firm.

The rise to power in the 1920s of an authoritarian regime certainly favoured the institutionalization of the paternalist order. On the one hand, the social mediation guaranteed by paternalism was functional to the social surveillance wanted by the then fascist regime. On the other hand, firms worked in a strongly bureaucratic and inefficient administrative system, to the point that they preferred to replace the state by taking direct action to establish public structures and services. The firm, by proposing itself as the producer of 'common goods', acquired the status of a 'work authority' (Roverato, 1986, p. 327).

In cases where the entrepreneur organized work within the firm according to the paternalism strategy pushing social relationships towards the 'family model', workers' productivity was higher than that in other firms following different organization strategies. However, although in a different production environment, differences with respect to the previous patronage did not appear substantial. In fact, the final outcome was the same: higher productivity assured by the lack of social conflicts, besides greater general well-being.

The paternalist agreement within the firm was so binding that compliance with it did not require a third party's intervention. It was marked by a 'mutual trust' similar to that characterizing implicit contracts and very distant from paternalism conceived as a unilateral act.

During the 1930s, paternalism spread in Veneto's more industrialized areas, although with local differences. According to that strategy, being an owner meant more to manage relations and technical competencies than wealth (Roverato, 1986, p. 341), as the Lombardo-Veneto School had stated some years previously. It was clear that paternalism involved more complexity than the exchange engendered by mutual interest in reducing transaction costs.

If paternalism represented – as affirmed by Noiriel (1988) – an intermediate stage between patronage and firm management, in Veneto it maintained its features also beyond the spread of management. Throughout the twentieth century, apparent in the small enterprises of the Italian north-east were the three conditions implied by a paternalist firm organization: (1) physical presence of the owner in the production place; (2) familiar language and practice between owners and workers; (3) workers' adherence to such a type of organization (Debouzy, 1988, pp. 8–9).

It should be emphasized that the above three conditions involve the transmission of organizational and technical knowledge from the entrepreneur to the worker, to the point that the paternalist enterprise becomes an incubator of future generations of entrepreneurs. Consequently, workers developed a propensity towards entrepreneurial activities. In short, 'loyalty and obedience' may constitute a strategy for emancipation and social redemption.

This interpretation explains the growth of entrepreneurial actors in Veneto from the post-Second World War years onwards. To cite the studies on 'tradition' by Boyd and Richerson (1985, 1993), if the prevailing 'culture of labour' is inclined towards compromise and paternalism, rather than conflict and competition, the average belief will be far from the belief considered optimal in regard to a division of labour guaranteeing productive efficiency. The fact that the entrepreneur, in contrast to the model of a strict distinction of tasks, favours a cooperative atmosphere well represents the paternalist aim.

In a way, the practice of paternalism prepared the ground for imitation processes expressing the already-existing tradition or 'culture of labour'. The thesis argued here is that the behaviour of the paternalist entrepreneur, the sharing of knowledge, and workers' involvement contributed to lessening the workers' risk aversion, favouring their 'jump' to entrepreneurship.

Summing up, paternalism was a strategy useful for reducing what Luzzatti (1935) called the 'fatal rift' between capital and labour. In other words, it was a means to induce empathy between the two parties, as suggested by Luigi Einaudi (1961, p. 336) when he ascribed social conflict to the fact that 'one party refused to understand the mental position of the other'. Moreover, paternalism was also a way to create and transmit knowledge, triggering an 'imitation rush' of the entrepreneurial role.

5 Entrepreneurial culture and tradition

The contiguity between capital and labour can be viewed as one of the causes of the entrepreneurial liveliness of the small and medium-sized north-east Italian enterprise after the post-war years, when also because of the lack of dependent employment many workers tried the 'risky step' of entrepreneurial activity, even if on a small scale (Roverato, 1995, p. 122). The strengthening of this trend led to a growth in the number of firms, as testified by the fact that a large part (90 per cent) of the small enterprises operating in Veneto during the 1980s had been created during the 1950s.

The paternalistic cooperating atmosphere assigned to so-called 'industriousness' a meaning that goes beyond a supposed but nebulous anthropological feature of a given community. That concept, which can be replaced by 'work intensity', is of interest because the idea of industriousness synthesizes familiarity with the entrepreneurial activity, the latter considered a resource or even a production factor at the disposal of the worker.

This industriousness, by shaping individual beliefs, can influence the decision to take the 'jump' of setting up an own-account business. It can reduce the perception of enterprise risk. Briefly, as a consequence of such a work-based culture, the idea that work intensity may off-set other shortages, of a technical or financial origin, was socially shared and increased the enterprise risk. Finally, the acceptance of industriousness as a social value reduces the level of blame if such initiatives should fail. It was that culture of 'work for work' by means of which Corrado Gini (1952, p. 15) connotes the work ethic of the United States' 'captains of industry' that differentiates it from the 'bourgeois' character of the European work ethic.

A constructive legislative initiative favoured the entrepreneurial initiative. From the post-Second World War years onwards, numerous legislative acts established a context propitious to strengthening the entrepreneurial skills. Laws were enacted on credit to small and medium-sized enterprises (1947), the development of mountain communities (1950), again on the financing of small and medium-sized enterprises (1952), credit facilitations (1959) and measures to support depressed areas in central and north Italy (1966). Other legislative interventions can be added. Those consequent on ratification of the first European Community agreements (1961) included the protection of enterprises during the transition towards the European market by establishing a fund for industrial renewal and the purchase of machine tools (1965) (Bianchi, 1990, p. 189).

Finally, decentralization and fragmentation of production favoured the multiplication of small–medium-sized enterprises (10–99 employees, particularly those with up to 50 employees), whose importance increased from the 1960s onwards with regard to both the micro-enterprise and the big company, determining a 'dimensional specialization' of the north-east (Anastasia and Corò, 1996, p. 106).

Familiar with a 'reduction' of social and class differences, having grown up in a paternalistic environment that favoured individual initiative, and encouraged by a legislative context affording access to finance for entrepreneurial activity, blue- and white-collar workers were induced to make the 'jump' to an entrepreneurial role. Consequently, the existing culture of labour was integrated by a completely new *entrepreneurial culture* visible because of the growing number of small businesses. This vertical social mobility induces one to speak of *imitation*, in this case concerning not technological aspects but economic roles.

Incubated in the experience of paternalism, imitation entered the 'culture of labour' of north-east Italy, contributing to the development of small enterprises. What are imitated are first roles, then productive processes. Imitation and innovation could coexist in the same individuals and processes.

The resulting entrepreneurial dynamism cannot be assumed as a given because it is endogenous to the economic system generating it. In effect, imitation results from relationships that have grown within the production system; it is not brought in from outside. This is how to conceive the transformation from 'culture as labour' as 'entrepreneurial culture'. More than a choice resulting from a calculus on efficiency, imitation of the entrepreneurial role is a fruit of tradition.

According to Boyd and Richerson (1993, p. 131) tradition often acts in a useful way because it reduces the costs of acquiring information and the possibility of committing errors. Imitation and tradition have also been presented as strategies alternative to optimization (Conlisk, 1980, 1988). However, on considering the sphere where expectations and beliefs are shaped – thus before choices are made on technological aspects – imitation cannot be compared with optimization. Imitation is a product of cultural evolution and is thus path dependent, which is different from the outcome of a choice among alternative solutions.

In sum, while during the late nineteenth century the preference order of work was shaped by 'life relationships' such as loyalty; with enterprise paternalism such relations were transformed into 'cooperation', the latter representing a fertile ground because aversion to risk made room for the imitation processes. The early exchange based on loyalty gave way to an imitative trend that set the entrepreneur/worker relationship on new bases.

6 The culture of labour in the second Veneto 'laboratory'

Finally, one might wonder whether and how the 'culture of labour' contributed to the dynamism characterizing the north-east's economy from the 1980s onwards. Economic indexes have shown performance higher than the national averages. Although this result may be of a cyclical nature, such a 'discontinuity' (or bifurcation) can be treated as resulting from the encounter of previously separate 'events'. Among the latter, certainly to be mentioned are 'technological decomposition'; the internationalization of markets; increasing productivity; and other qualitative features such as the distribution of knowledge. But to these widely recognized factors can be added the 'culture of labour' and, consequently, the 'entrepreneurial culture', as defined above.

Admitting that discontinuity or bifurcation is determined by the encounter of 'events' like those just mentioned (Masulli, 1991) means renouncing an explanation based on a causal logic affirming that every event always has a cause. However, history cannot be left to chance. One can speak of a local causality bounded to specific events: path dependence entails considering the trajectory not of the entire system, but of each of its components. This means that the rapid growth of the north-east is the outcome not so much of a generic 'story' of the system as of the story of each event that, on encountering others, yields bifurcations: that is, single steps, 'singularity' instead of cyclical conditions.

Resorting to the image of an 'encounter' among different 'events' – for example, market internationalization and culture as work – in order to explain an extraordinary fact like an economic jump, requires that such events be separately analysed because they are structurally different in both contents and evolutionary dynamics. The evolution of labour as culture is certainly different from the spread of a technological innovation or the creation of a new market. However, only by analysing the slow evolution of the culture is it possible to comprehend how such an event contributed to an economic discontinuity.

Thus an evolutionary analysis is needed to understand any cultural aspect. A study limited to simultaneous variables does not allow one to distinguish cultural beliefs from material ones (Lal, 1998), the latter conditioning consumption choices. This explains why it has been argued here that the late nineteenth-century culture of labour was not so different from the culture of one hundred years later. On the contrary, the second economic laboratory was the result of the first cultural one.

According to this view, cultural features can no longer be treated as exogenous aspects of a discontinuity or change. They constitute endogenous variables that change with the economic system itself.

7 Concluding remarks

The foregoing analysis has shown that work can become a criterion regulating social relationships. Concretely, here this has meant the strengthening of paternalism as a strategy leading to self-regulation of owner/worker relationships particularly in small and medium-sized enterprises. According to the economic context's change, the culture of labour has enriched what can be called entrepreneurial culture, as a self-organizing strategy by means of which the system produces entrepreneurs as guarantors of its preservation. Finally, such cultures, on encountering other factors, determine a discontinuity or economic jump.

This sequence of changes shapes the system's evolution, where each of them is a stage in this trajectory: patronage, mutualism, paternalism, small enterprise. Each choice does not represent an innovation alone – a rather amorphous concept – but a continuous reorganization of the system. Paternalism should be treated as reorganization of relationships at local level leading to the emergence of new identities.

What has been proposed here does not correspond to a deterministic interpretation of economic facts. On the contrary, it can be said that each stage or bifurcation in which the system reorganizes itself is explained not only by the 'events' determining it, but by the 'stories' of such events and by their encounter. A historical-dynamic approach (Lordon, 1996), which synthesizes path dependence with the theory of bifurcation, allows us to tell such 'stories'.

Note

1 Simmie and Martin wrote: 'Standard path dependence theory has relatively little to say about where paths of regional economic development come from, how they arise. Indeed, the typical assumption is that such paths originate in random [. . .] But there is both good empirical evidence and strong conceptual founds for arguing that new paths are often shaped by old paths' (Simmie and Martin, 2010, p. 32).

References

Alston, L. J. and Ferrie, J. P. (1999). *Southern Paternalism and the American Welfare State: Economics, Politics, and Institutions in the South, 1865–1965*. Cambridge, New York and Melbourne: Cambridge University Press.

Anastasia, B. and Corò, G. (1997): *Evoluzione di un'economia regionale. Il Nordest dopo il successo*. Portogruaro: Ediciclo.

Baglioni, G. (1974): *L'ideologia della borghesia industriale nell'Italia liberale*. Turin: Einaudi.

Bianchi, P. (1990): Le politiche industriali per le piccole e medie imprese e il riorientamento delle politiche comunitari. In: M. Baldassarri (ed.), *La politica industriale in Italia dal '45 ad oggi*. Rome: SIPI, pp. 171–201.

Boyd, R. and Richerson, P. J. (1985): *Culture and the Evolutionary Process*. Chicago, IL: The University of Chicago Press.

Boyd, R. and Richerson, P. J. (1993): Rationality, Imitation, and Tradition. In: R. H. Day and P. Chen (eds.), *Nonlinear Dynamics and Evolutionary Economics*. Oxford: Oxford University Press, pp. 131–149.

Camurri, R. (ed.) (1992a): La scienza moderata. Fedele Lampertico e l'Italia moderata. Milan: Angeli.

Camurri, R. (1992b): Tradizione e innovazione nel pensiero di Emilio Morpurgo. In: R. Camurri (ed.), *La scienza moderata. Fedele Lampertico e l'Italia moderata*. Milan: Angeli, pp. 339–376.

Cardini, A. (1993): *Le corporazioni continuano . . . Cultura economica e intervento pubblico nell'Italia unita*. Milan: Angeli.

Cattaneo, C. (1956 [1836–37]): Della carità legale. In: C. Cattaneo, *Scritti economici*, ed. by A. Bertolino. Florence: Le Monnier.

Cattaneo, C. (1983 [1843]): Dell'economia nazionale di Federico List. In: C. Cattaneo, *Memorie di economia pubblica dal 1833 al 1860*. Milan: Banca del Monte di Milano, pp. 455–512.

Cognetti de Martiis, F. (1886): L'economia come scienza autonoma. *Giornale degli economist*, vol. 1, no. 2, pp. 166–203.

Conlisk, J. (1980): Costly optimizers versus cheap imitators. *Journal of Economic Behavior and Organization*, vol. 1, no. 3, pp. 275–293.

Conlisk, J. (1988): Optimization Cost. *Journal of Economic Behavior and Organization*, vol. 9, no. 3, pp. 213–228.

Day, R. H. (1994): *Complex Economic Dynamics*. Cambridge, MA: The MIT Press.
Debouzy, M. (1988): Permanence du paternalism. *Le Mouvement Social*, no. 144, pp. 3–16.
De Rosa, G. (1996): Prefazione. In: E. Franzina (ed.), *Fedele Lampertico. Carteggi e diari 1842–1906*, vol. 1. Venice: Marsilio, pp. xv–xxix.
Einaudi, L. (1961): Il governo democratico del lavoro e la gioia di lavorare. In: *Cronache economiche e politiche di un trentennio (1893–1925)*, vol. 5. Turin: Einaudi.
Favaro, A. and Solari, S. (2015): Giuseppe Toniolo e la scuola etico-giuridica dell'economia di Padova. *Mimeo*.
Franzina, E. (1990): *La transizione dolce. Storie del Veneto tra '800 e '900*. Verona: Cierre.
Franzina, E. (1992): Le strutture elementari della clientele. In: R. Camurri (ed.), *La scienza moderata. Fedele Lampertico e l'Italia moderata*. Milan: Angeli, pp. 377–430.
Gini, C. (1952): *Patologia economica*, 5th ed. Turin: Utet.
Hermann, F. B. W. (1832): *Staatswirthschaftliche Untersuchungen*, München: Werber.
Lal, D. (1998): *Unintended Consequences. The Impact of Factor Endowments, Culture, and Politics on Long-Run Economic Performance*. Cambridge, MA: The MIT Press.
Lampertico, F. (1874): *Economia dei popoli e degli stati. Introduzione*. Milan: Treves.
Lampertico, F. (1876a): *Economia dei popoli e degli stati. Il lavoro*, 2nd ed. Milan: Treves.
Lampertico, F. (1876b): *Economia dei popoli e degli stati. La proprietà*. Milan: Treves.
Lordon, F. (1996): Formaliser la dynamique économique historique. *Economie Appliquée*, vol. 49, pp. 55–84.
Luzzatti, L. (1874): Libertà economica ed ingerenza governativa. *Rivista Veneta*, vol. 3, pp. 242–249.
Luzzatti, L. (1935): *Memorie tratte dal carteggio e da altri documenti*. Bologna: Zanichelli.
Masulli, I. (1991): *La storia e le forme*. Rome: Editori Riuniti.
Monteleone, G. (1871): *Economia e politica nel padovano dopo l'Unità (1866–1900)*. Venice: Deputazione.
Morpurgo, E. (1861): *La popolazione agricola padovana nei suoi rapporti colla moralità e cogli sviluppi intellettuali*. Padua: Randi.
Morpurgo, E. (1871): Intorno alla distribuzione economica del lavoro. *Rivista Periodica dell'Accademia patavina di Scienze Lettere Arti*, vol. 20, pp. 81–112.
Noiriel, G. (1988): Du Patronage au Paternalisme. *Le Mouvement Social*, no. 144, pp. 17–35.
North, D. C. (1996): Epilogue: Economic Performance through Time. In: L. J. Alston, T. Eggertsson and D. C. North (eds.), *Empirical Studies in Institutional Change*. Cambridge: Cambridge University Press, pp. 342–355.
Romani, R. (1985): L'anglofilia degli economisti lombardo-veneti. *Venetica*, no. 4, pp. 5–27.
Rossi, A. (1871): *Di una nuova economia politica*. Padua: Prosperini.
Roverato, G. (1986): *Una casa industriale. I Marzotto*. Milan: Angeli.
Roverato, G. (1995): *Scritti di storia economica*. Padua: Università degli Studi.
Scaldaferri, R. (1992): I modelli stranieri nel socialismo della cattedra italiano. In: R. Camurri (ed.), *La scienza moderata. Fedele Lampertico e l'Italia moderata*. Milan: Angeli, pp. 235–254.
Simmie, J. and Martin, R. (2010): The Economic Resilience of Regions: Towards an Evolutionary Approach. *Cambridge Journal of Regions, Economy and Society*, vol. 3, no. 1, pp. 27–43.
Toniolo, G. (1871): Sull'importanza delle Banche Agricole. *Rivista Periodica dell'Accademia patavina di Scienze Lettere Arti*, vol. 20, pp. 81–113.
Toniolo, G. (1921 [1908]): *Trattato di economia sociale. La produzione*, 2nd ed. Florence: Libreria Editrice Fiorentina.

10 Sergio Paronetto

An economist in deed, from Alberto Beneduce to Alcide de Gasperi, 1934–1945

Stefano Baietti and Giovanni Farese[1]

1 An economist without sources?

Sergio Paronetto (1911–1945), economist and industrial manager, was long eclipsed, hidden within a historiographical umbral shadow (Paronetto Valier, 1991; Baietti and Farese, 2010, 2012). In fact, also authoritative works in prestigious publications would sometimes get his name wrong, as 'Peronetto', 'Baronetto', or 'Peronetti', even replicating these errors in the name index. Were these mere typographical errors?

For a scholar interested in Sergio Paronetto – in particular, for an economic historian – two questions are unavoidable. First, can you write the history of a leading actor in the economy without sources, or rather, without the traditional sources? Sources of information on Paronetto are scanty and dispersed in a number of archives. Second, can we call someone who never wrote a treatise on economics an 'economist'? For Sergio Paronetto never did write such a treatise.

These are not mere idle questions but questions that have been posed by eminent scholars (Barucci, 2012). Our own answer is affirmative, to both. True, the primary sources on Paronetto are scanty and dispersed, and secondary sources in which he is mentioned rarely deal with his work in depth. So we have had to rely on tertiary sources, the testimony of contemporaries. And we devised a series of stratagems. One problem was attributing to Paronetto writings published by IRI which were either unsigned or attributed to others (for instance, Alberto Asquini and Donato Menichella) (Banca d'Italia, 1986). We have taken the writings of others, some of them after Paronetto's death, as a means of examining his thought and work (works by Guido Carli, Pasquale Saraceno and Ezio Vanoni) (Carli, 1993; Saraceno, 1951; Vanoni, 1955). Where there were historiographic holes, Paronetto's life and thought proved helpful in filling them.

On the second question, whether we can consider someone who never wrote a specific treatise an economist, the answer is only apparently simpler. Sergio Paronetto was the author of a good number of essays, articles and reviews, often unsigned, that demonstrated that he kept regularly up to date with developments in economic theory (Paronetto, 1930, 1931, 1933, 1936, 1937, 1940, 1941, 1943). However, no treatise of his is to be found. But isn't this the case with other, better known protagonists of Italian economic history? Where are the treatises of Alberto Beneduce (Bonelli, 1974), Guido Carli or Donato Menichella – all men, significantly, who were in Sergio Paronetto's circle. Our conclusion, naturally, is that one can qualify as an economist not only by one's words but by one's deeds. This applies to people who have *only* acted, only performed concrete actions: those who have changed the history of economic thought, the economic system, the management of the economy, the institutions of national economic life (Mortara, 1984). And this is an important point, if we are dealing with facts and theories in economic history.

2 From Morbegno to IRI: a strenuous life

Sergio Paronetto, like Pasquale Saraceno and Ezio Vanoni, was born in Morbegno, in the province of Sondrio in Northern Italy, near the Swiss border (Cavazza Rossi, 1993; Bonuglia, 2006; Quadrio Curzio, 2007; Arena, 2011). These three native sons exerted such an intense reciprocal influence on one another that in the exchange it is hard to tell who gave and who received what. Paronetto, born in 1911, was not of exactly the same generation as the other two (both born in 1903). His was the generation of Paolo Baffi and Giuseppe Di Nardi (both born in the same year as Paronetto) and Guido Carli (born in 1914). Their mentors were Alberto De' Stefani (for Paronetto), Giorgio Mortara (Baffi), Giovanni Demaria (Di Nardi) and Marco Fanno (Carli). They all converged on Rome, to the Bank of Italy and to the Institute for Industrial Reconstruction (IRI), centres of intensive study and action (Gigliobianco, 2006; Castronovo, 2013).

Paronetto graduated from the newly established Faculty of Political Science in Rome with a thesis in economic history. His advisors were the former minister of Treasury and Finance Alberto De' Stefani, and historian Gioacchino Volpe (Paronetto Valier, 1991). As a student, he worked with Camillo Manfroni, who taught history and science of the colonies. He was a member of the Italian Catholic University Students Federation (FUCI) (Moro, 1979), directed by Monsignor Giovanni Battista Montini and by Igino Righetti, and in 1932, together with these same men, he founded the Movement of Catholic University Graduates in Cagliari. In January 1934 he joined IRI, with the intermediation of Pasquale Saraceno, who had come to the Institute six months earlier through Donato Menichella. In 1937, in his turn, at the request of Monsignor Montini, Paronetto brought in Guido Carli (Carli, 1993). Paronetto headed the technical secretariat of IRI's director-general, Donato Menichella, under the chairmanship first of Alberto Beneduce and then of Francesco Giordani (Avagliano, 1979). In the second half of the 1930s, Paronetto deepened his interest and developed his thought along the lines and the results of Franklin Delano Roosevelt's economic policy (Paronetto, 1933).

'I study, Saraceno sees, Menichella acts', wrote Paronetto in his posthumously published diary, which carried a preface by Montini (Paronetto, 1948). He helped in the drafting of the Banking Law in 1936 (a contribution defined as 'invaluable' by Menichella, who together with Alberto Beneduce and Alfredo De Gregorio was the law's primary framer) (Calabresi, 1996); played a role in establishing the Finmare holding company (1936) and the Finsider steel corporation (1937), with their bond issues; and worked on the conversion of IRI into a permanent institution

(1937). He also worked on the design of a new sectoral holding company, Fincant (renamed Fincantieri after the war, when it was eventually established), and the sectoral economic plans from 1938 on (Baietti and Farese, 2010, 2012).

Under Donato Menichella's protective wing, Paronetto was an appreciated, acute and affable interlocutor of the leading managers who headed IRI's subsidiary corporations: Oscar Sinigaglia, Agostino Rocca, Giuseppe Cenzato, Raffaele Mattioli, Guglielmo Reiss Romoli, Paride Formentini, Giovanni Malvezzi (Mortara, 1984). He was regularly responsible for drafting the first version, for Menichella, of the annual report accompanying IRI's financial statement and accounts.

He collaborated with the review *Studium*, soon becoming a tireless editor and acute commissioner of articles (Paronetto Valier, 1991). This position highlighted one of the characteristics of his working method: the encyclopedic approach, i.e. the resort to every possible branch of knowledge, in the observation of the latest developments, in order to infer a fundamental ('integral') meaning of modernity. He then applied this approach to his own favourite subjects: economics (practised in the economic laboratory that was IRI) and the study of society (pursued together with Montini and Righetti) (Paronetto, 1930). The encyclopedic or multidisciplinary method, however, would have been valueless unless accompanied by intense interchange with others, to harvest and share knowledge and ideas. This was Sergio Paronetto's *pedagogy*. Along with his reflection concerning Joseph Alois Schumpeter's *homines novi* (Paronetto, 1941), Paronetto produced a series of writings – and commissioned others – on entrepreneurs, including banking entrepreneurs, and on their social responsibility (Paronetto, 1940). In practice, he introduced management science and culture to Italy (Paronetto, 1943; Saraceno, 1943, 1944).

In the 1940s he brought together, at his Roman home, a group of men (Pietro Campilli, Giuseppe Spataro, Ezio Vanoni, Pasquale Saraceno, Giulio Andreotti, Guido Gonella) who would play leading roles after the war, all followers of Alcide De Gasperi, who attached great importance to these private lessons in economics (Andreotti, 1986). 'Keep on counseling me, with your consciousness illuminated by reality', wrote De Gasperi, who evidently found in Paronetto's views the solution for many of the difficult issues of the day (De Gasperi, 1974). All were engaged in seeking to imagine what would come 'after'.

Paronetto was the pivot of these encounters. On economic and financial matters, no one else had De Gasperi's ear to the same extent, as Andreotti has testified (Andreotti, 1986). Above all what was convincing, beyond the unsurpassed depth of his understanding of economic science, was Paronetto's rigorous adherence to the concrete, the practical, namely real things and action. He devoted an insightful piece of writing in 1943 precisely to the 'need for concreteness in economics' (Paronetto, 1943). His approach convinced De Gasperi that here he had found the right formula for facing, in practice, the mammoth task of postwar reconstruction. From Paronetto he learned who should be assigned to represent Italy's interests in international gatherings and in managing the American funds that Paronetto had been predicting (since 1942) would be forthcoming (Paronetto Valier, 1991).

Paronetto had a hand in 'Christian Democracy's ideas for reconstruction', issued in 1942, and above all in the 1943 'Camaldoli Code', for which he bore the main responsibility in the eyes of Montini and De Gasperi (Damilano, 1967). He was the Code's actual author – first among peers – with Saraceno, Vanoni and jurist and philosopher Giuseppe Capograssi. Montini and De Gasperi would have delegated this responsibility to no one but him (the proofs of the first edition of the Camaldoli Code lay on Paronetto's death bed, along with those of the new Statutes of IRI). Other future leaders present in Camaldoli (Tuscany) were Guido Gonella, Giulio Andreotti, Giorgio La Pira, Amintore Fanfani, Paolo Emilio Taviani and Aldo Moro (De Rosa, 1966; Roggi, 1979; Giovagnoli, 1982; Taviani, 1988). Nor must we forget the major Italian economic figures who always professed their 'Camaldolian' civil faith, such as Pietro Campilli and the internationally renowned statistician Marcello Boldrini, future president of Agip and ENI. The Code of Camaldoli was meant to be the updating of the Social Code of Malines-Mechelen (1927–1933), and therefore a document expressed by an ecclesial, not civil, circle; and yet it eventually became the main source for the articles of the Italian Constitution dealing with economics (Baietti and Farese, 2012).

Through the intermediation of Guido Gonella, Paronetto served as ghost writer for the economic and social portions of Pope Pius XII's radio talks (Paronetto Valier, 1991). Through radio talks of 1941 and 1942, Pope Pius XII made a radical innovation of the social doctrine of the Church, overcoming and giving up Christian corporatism envisaged fifty years before by Pope Leo XIII. This was widely due to the influence of Sergio Paronetto.

After Italy's surrender to the Allies on 8 September 1943, Donato Menichella (formally resigning as director-general but still running things behind the scenes) made Paronetto deputy director-general, a job he accepted only on condition of a pay cut (Paronetto Valier, 1991). At the Institute's separate office in Rome, he worked with Milan-based IRI commissioner Alberto Asquini, a disinterested Fascist, a jurist and a fine mind, with experience at IRI under Beneduce. He was determined to keep Paronetto on in the newly 'fascistised' IRI, retaining him for the management of the group's corporations – against the desires expressed in some quarters to essentially break up IRI and pursue the appointment of separate 'political commissars' for every firm – and to preserve the efficiency of the firms in circumstances that were difficult in the extreme. At the same time, he was essential to carrying out the secret plan of Donato Menichella and Giovanni Malvezzi to shield Italy's industrial assets from both partisan liberation fighters and the Germans, who simultaneously sought (though in different ways) to appropriate it, till the dismantling of the most modern and productive steelworks in Europe, located in Genoa Cornigliano, and to transfer it to Germany (Baietti and Farese, 2012). Menichella and Paronetto were united by the passionate thought of 'afterwards', of reconstruction.

Within IRI, Paronetto protected his colleague Luigi Chialvo, who under Paronetto's coordination kept the partisans' secret funds. In his own house, risking his own life and that of his family, he hid several fugitives from the Nazis and their collaborators of the Fascist Italian Social Republic authorities. In 1944, after the liberation of Rome, he served as coordinator of the technical secretariat of Giovanni Gronchi, Minister for Industry in the democratic government of Ivanoe Bonomi. Here he collaborated with the Minister for Reconstruction, Meuccio Ruini, and with the young head of his secretariat, Federico Caffè, introduced by the same Paronetto (Baietti and Farese, 2012).

Sergio Paronetto died in 1945, just 34 years old and already universally considered – by Guido Carli, Ezio Vanoni, Enrico Cuccia, Federico Caffè and De Gasperi himself – a master (Vanoni, 1955). He had not yet been acquitted of the paradoxical charge of collaborating with the Nazis, along with Menichella and Saraceno (they were accused of having transferred the paper shares of IRI companies to the Nazi-occupied north of Italy at the orders of the Italian Social Republic authorities, collaborating with IRI commissioner Asquini). He would not be cleared until 1946, posthumously.

3 Savings from Giolitti and Nitti to De Gasperi (via Paronetto)

There is a unifying element in the thought and action of Sergio Paronetto: saving, seen as the fruit of one's labour, as social insurance and as the foundation for investment. In a sentence, he considered saving to be a concrete tool for growth and social justice, for the establishing of economic democracy in a country dominated by a handful of large capitalists and a handful of large firms. This stress on saving was not merely theoretical, drawn from his reading of the classics of economic thought. It was rooted in acts, documents, organisations, institutions, facts. In Pope Leo XIII's encyclical *Rerum Novarum* (1891), of which Paronetto was a leading scholar and commentator (Paronetto, 1931), saving is accorded a place of honour as a prime instance of the proper sphere of State intervention in the economy. The Pope wrote:

> If a workman's wages be sufficient to enable him comfortably to support himself, his wife, and his children, he will find it easy, if he be a sensible man, to practice thrift, and he will not fail, by cutting down expenses, to put by some little savings and thus secure a modest source of income. The law, therefore, should favour ownership, and policy should be to induce as many as possible of the people to become owners. Many excellent results will follow from this; and, first of all, property will certainly become more equitably divided.
>
> (Leo XIII, 1891)

In fact, the second decade of the century, when Paronetto was born, had seen a historically unprecedented development: the growth in the volume of popular saving in Italy. It was this saving that Alberto Beneduce multiplied with the foundation, under his direction, first of the National Insurance Institute (INA) in 1912, then the National War Veterans Organisation (ONC) in 1917, whose financial unit was decisive, and finally the Credit Consortium for Public Works (Crediop) in 1919 (Cianci, 1977; Cassese, 1983).

The essential role of saving was affirmed in the 1936 Banking Law, of which, as we have seen, Paronetto was one of the principal drafters (Calabresi, 1996). The law enshrined the fundamental principle of the protection of saving (Cassese, 1974; Guarino and Toniolo, 1993). Nor is that all. Two of the era's main financial innovations, namely State-guaranteed bonds and IRI's convertible bonds, embodied a major new idea, that of enabling small savers to become shareholders (Cianci, 1977). These were practical steps towards real economic democracy.

But there was something else. What could protect and shield savings, especially popular savings, against conjuncture and business cycle, against risk and uncertainty? Besides the insurance mechanisms, there was a new tool named *plan*. Paronetto is a major theoretician of economic plans for national systems to pursue social justice and *bonum commune*, the common wealth (Paronetto, 1937). The plan is not the fruit of a bureaucratic job, as in the Soviet experience. The operators who favour capital accumulation are both public and private. In this respect Paronetto's legacy would then be assumed by Ezio Vanoni and Pasquale Saraceno. The relevant knowledge acquired in this field will be used by Allied authorities before the European Recovery Program (ERP), the Marshall Plan.

Saving was central to the Code of Camaldoli of 1943 as well. Article 58 reads:

> For workers, the accumulation of the fruits of labour cannot mean the enhancement of his tools, so instead it takes the form of a savings of money, which the worker cannot but entrust to the ability and honesty of third parties about whom he has no direct way of forming a thorough judgment. Government intervention is indispensable: 1) to protect the savings of the community by ensuring the proper management of banks, insurance companies and other financial institutions, whose task is to channel savings towards productive uses (thus performing the function that in simpler economies is performed by savers themselves); and 2) to regulate the process of distribution of the community's wealth with a view to providing workers – in part using their own contributions – with a series of supplementary benefits, beyond wages, that are adequate to the nation's level of civic and economic development.
> (ICAS, 1945; Baietti and Farese, 2012)

The subsequent tunnelling of the Code's formulas and ideas into the Constitution by the Camaldolian Catholic components of the Constituent Assembly, La Pira and Vanoni above all, is well known (Roggi, 1980). Article 47 of the Constitution, certainly a rarity among modern constitutional laws, directly concerns savings, its forms and uses:

> The republic encourages and protects savings in all its forms, regulates, coordinates and controls the provision of credit. It favours access to savings for the purchase of homes, for worker-owned farms, and for direct or indirect investment in shares of the country's large productive enterprises.

The constitutional provision for channelling savings into investment in home ownership, land property and industrial shares (with the particularity of workers' investment in the capital of the enterprise in which they work) came solely through the influence of Beneduce and Paronetto. Without their contribution, none of the members of the Assembly would have written this synthesis of the philosophy behind INA, the Veterans Fund, Crediop, the Credit Institute for Public Utilities (Asso and De Cecco, 1994), IMI (Farese, 2009) and IRI into the Constitution (Baietti and Farese, 2012). If it was only for this focus on savings, even then, Paronetto would deserve a central place in the history of Italian economic thought and policies in the first half of the twentieth century. His work was decisive to the incorporation of the Beneduce system into the postwar Italy of De Gasperi and Vanoni (Saraceno, 1977; Vanoni, 1977; Magliulo, 1991; Forte, 2009; Ivone, 2009).

4 Enterprises, organisations, the Academy: deeds and words

Those years were remarkable for the primacy of deeds (enterprise) over words (the Academy), albeit inscribed within a dialectic between the two. But the fact remains: within IRI and its orbit, we find the 'magnificent seven': Beneduce, Menichella, Giordani, Saraceno, Paronetto, De Gregorio and Vanoni (Avagliano, 1979).

At the Bank of Italy under governor Vincenzo Azzolini, Beneduce and Mortara set up in 1936–1938 a Research Office where capable young economists like Paolo Baffi (a future governor) and Giuseppe Di Nardi emerged (Caracciolo, 1992; Gigliobianco, 2006). At Banca Commerciale Italiana, under the direction of Raffaele Mattioli, we find Antonello Gerbi, Enrico Cuccia, Ugo La Malfa, Giovanni Malagodi, Cesare Merzagora and Raimondo Craveri. At Istat there was Alessandro Molinari (Misiani, 2010). This was the age of research offices, in the private sector as well as the public. Such large private enterprises as Edison, Montecatini, and Pirelli (many of which were in the Banca Commerciale's sphere of influence) created their own research departments, calling eminent scholars and economists to head them, such as Ferdinando Di Fenizio, Libero Lenti and Ferruccio Parri (Baietti and Farese, 2012). Comparable developments were taking place in the United States and the most advanced countries of Europe.

All these organisations, these men, were singularly advanced, modern, by comparison with the economics discussed in the Academy. They were more advanced in their reading – the American Institutionalist school, Keynes and his followers, German ordoliberalism, the Stockholm school; in their method – namely, the effort to reach a synthesis between business economics, traditional political economy, economic policy and modern macroeconomic theory; and in their tools – from industrial censuses to national accounting and national plans and models (Baietti and Farese, 2012).

Little or none of these was to be found in the academic environment. At the universities of Milan and Pisa, and elsewhere, the discussion was focused on the debate on whether corporatism constituted a new economic science or only a new economic policy (Fausto, 2007; Barucci *et al.*, 2015). But the people who attended international meetings (such as those with Per Jacobsson, chief economist at the newly formed Bank for International Settlements in Basel, of which Alberto

Beneduce was co-founder and Vice-Chairman) were exposed to quite a different sort of intellectual interchange.

5 The current relevance of Sergio Paronetto's work

The foregoing should corroborate the thesis put forward at the outset: namely, that Sergio Paronetto was an economist, and that one can do research on an economist even without the standard set of sources. Once the methodological strategy has been defined, one can flank to some extent sources with *actions*, and writings with *deeds*. Economic history can come to the aid of the history of economic thought, and vice versa (Di Taranto, 2012).

Paronetto was a practical economist in a large State-owned enterprise. His gauge was facts, acts, the concrete. There were powerful echoes of American institutionalism, in the background, and of American pragmatism too. He was in line with the most recent Swedish and Dutch experiences in economics (Per Jacobsson, Gunnar Myrdal, Jan Tinbergen) at the end of the 1930s (Baietti and Farese, 2012).

For an assessment of Sergio Paronetto as an economist, it is enough to consider how he was treated by Alcide De Gasperi, Donato Menichella, Giovanni Battista Montini, Pasquale Saraceno, Ezio Vanoni, Guido Carli, Federico Caffè, Mario Ferrari Aggradi and Enrico Cuccia, fine minds to whom he served as 'maestro' and who honoured him, though some of them had been, in turn, master to him (Vanoni, 1955; De Gasperi, 1974; Carli, 1993; Baietti and Farese, 2012).

And his thought and action are now peculiarly relevant to the current situation. The world is no longer split between East and West, nor solely between North and South, but between structural deficit countries and structural surplus countries. The issue of savings has regained a central place in Europe and in Italy. In *Finance and the Good Society*, Nobel laureate Robert Shiller maintains that we need a new dispersion of capital to serve a new sort of democracy in economy and finance. Shiller writes of citizen-owners and worker-shareholders, proposing a housing plan and an enterprise plan (Shiller, 2012). These are recipes to be found in Sergio Paronetto's deeds as well as in his writings – and, significantly, in the action of those Italian postwar ministers who were inspired by his vision and his example.

Note

1 Paragraph two is attributable to Stefano Baietti; paragraphs three and four are attributable to Giovanni Farese; paragraphs one and five to both.

References

Andreotti, G. (1986): *De Gasperi visto da vicino*. Milan: Rizzoli.
Arena, G. (2011): *Pasquale Saraceno commis d'état. Dagli anni giovanili alla Ricostruzione (1903–1948)*. Milan: Angeli.
Asso, P. F. and De Cecco, M. (1994): *Storia del Crediop. Tra credito speciale e finanza pubblica (1920–1960)*. Rome, Bari: Laterza.
Avagliano, L. (1979): La gestione finanziaria e la nascita del Brain Trust dell'IRI. *Rassegna economica*, no. 9–10, pp. 1137 ss.

Baietti, S. and Farese, G. (2010): Sergio Paronetto and the Italian economy between the industrial reconstruction of the 1930s and the reconstruction of the country in the 1940s. *The Journal of European Economic History*, vol. 39, no. 3, pp. 411–425.

Baietti, S. and Farese, G. (eds.) (2012): *Sergio Paronetto e il formarsi della costituzione economica italiana*. Soveria Mannelli: Rubbettino.

Banca d'Italia (1986): *Donato Menichella: testimonianze e studi*.Rome, Bari: Laterza.

Barucci, P. (2012): Sergio Paronetto e le difficoltà culturali dell'economia politica in Italia dopo la metà degli anni Trenta. In: S. Baietti and G. Farese (eds.), *Sergio Paronetto e il formarsi della costituzione economica italiana*. Soveria Mannelli: Rubbettino, pp. 93–102.

Barucci, P., Misiani, S. and Mosca, M. (eds.) (2015): *La cultura economica tra le due guerre*. Milan: Angeli.

Bonelli, F. (1974): Alberto Beneduce. *Economia Pubblica*, no. 3, pp. 4–6.

Bonuglia, R. (2006): Tre valtellinesi al servizio dello Stato: Saraceno, Vanoni e Paronetto. *Élite e storia*, no. 1, pp. 44–64.

Calabresi, G. F. (1996): *L'Associazione bancaria italiana. 1919–1939*. Rome, Bari: Laterza.

Caracciolo, A. (ed.) (1992): *La Banca d'Italia tra l'autarchia e la guerra*. Rome, Bari: Laterza.

Carli, G. (1993): *Cinquant'anni di vita italiana*. Rome, Bari: Laterza.

Cassese, S. (1974): La preparazione della riforma bancaria del 1936 in Italia. *Storia contemporanea*, vol. 5, no. 1, pp. 3–46.

Cassese, S. (1983): Gli aspetti unitari degli statuti degli enti Beneduce. In: *Alberto Beneduce e i problemi dell'economia italiana del suo tempo*, Atti della giornata di studio per la celebrazione del 50° anniversario dell'istituzione dell'IRI, Caserta, 11 November 1983. Rome: Edindustria, pp. 105–110.

Castronovo, V. (ed.) (2013): *Storia dell'IRI: dalle origini al dopoguerra*. Rome, Bari: Laterza.

Cavazza Rossi, M. (1993): Sergio Paronetto e Pasquale Saraceno: un incontro (1943–1945). *Economia Pubblica*, no. 4–5, pp. 159–172.

Cianci, E. (1977): *La nascita dello Stato imprenditore in Italia*. Milan: Mursia.

Damilano, A. (1967): *Atti e documenti della Democrazia cristiana, 1943–1967*. Rome: Cinque Lune.

De Gasperi, M. R. (ed.) (1974): *De Gasperi scrive. Corrispondenza con capi di stato, cardinali, uomini politici, giornalisti, diplomatici*. Brescia: Morcelliana.

De Rosa, G. (1966): *Il partito popolare italiano. Storia del movimento cattolico in Italia*. Rome, Bari: Laterza.

Di Taranto, G. (2012): La centralità di Sergio Paronetto. In: S. Baietti and G. Farese (eds.), *Sergio Paronetto e il formarsi della costituzione economica italiana*. Soveria Mannelli: Rubbettino, pp. 61–64.

Farese, G. (2009): *Dare credito all'autarchia: L'IMI e il governo dell'economia negli anni Trenta*. Napoli: Editoriale Scientifica.

Fausto, D. (ed.) (2007): *Intervento pubblico e politica economica fascista*. Milan: Angeli.

Forte, F. (2009): *Ezio Vanoni economista pubblico*, ed. by S. Beretta and L. Bernardi. Soveria Mannelli: Rubbettino.

Gigliobianco, A. (2006): *Via Nazionale. Banca d'Italia e classe dirigente. Cento anni di storia*. Rome: Donzelli.

Giovagnoli, A. (1982): *Le premesse della ricostruzione. Tradizione e modernità nella classe dirigente cattolica del dopoguerra*. Milan: Nuovo Istituto Editoriale Italiano.

Guarino, G. and Toniolo, G. (eds.) (1993): *La Banca d'Italia e il sistema bancario 1919–1936*. Rome, Bari: Laterza.
ICAS (1945): *Per la comunità cristiana. Principi dell'ordinamento sociale. A cura di un gruppo di studiosi amici di Camaldoli*. Rome: Edizioni Studium.
Ivone, D. (ed.) (2009): *Ezio Vanoni tra economica, politica, cultura e finanza*. Naples: Editoriale Scientifica.
Leo XIII (1891): *Rerum Novarum*. Rome.
Magliulo, A. (1991): *Ezio Vanoni: la giustizia sociale nell'economia di mercato*. Rome: Studium.
Misiani, S. (2010): Luci e ombre nella storia della statistica pubblica. Il censimento del 1937–1939 e il calcolo del reddito nazionale. *Quaderni storici*, no. 2, pp. 445–476.
Moro, R. (1979): *La formazione della classe dirigente cattolica (1929–1937)*. Bologna: Il Mulino.
Mortara, A. (ed.) (1984): *I protagonisti dell'intervento pubblico in Italia*. Milan: Angeli.
Paronetto, S. (1930): Ambiente e metodo nelle scienze sociali. *Studium*, vol. 25, no. 5, pp. 279–291.
Paronetto, S. (1931): Il pensiero sociale cattolico in rapporto alla Rerum Novarum. *Studium*, no. 5–6, pp. 312–320.
Paronetto, S. (1933): Roosevelt e il demiurgo. *Azione Fucina*, no. 35, pp. 1–2.
Paronetto, S. (1936): L'imprenditore in regime corporativo. *Azione Fucina*, no. 12.
Paronetto, S. (1937): Dottrina e realtà in un recente esempio di economia diretta. *Studium*, vol. 32, no. 2, pp. 109–117.
Paronetto, S. (1940): Profilo del banchiere e dell'uomo di finanza. *Bollettino di Studium*.
Paronetto, S. (1941): Profilo del capo d'azienda. *Studium*, vol. 38, no. 6, pp. 221–226.
Paronetto, S. (1943): Il bisogno di concretezza nella dottrina economica e nello studio dell'azienda. *Studium*, no. 1.
Paronetto, S. (1996): *Ascetica dell'uomo d'azione*. Rome: Studium.
Paronetto Valier, M. L. (1991): *Sergio Paronetto: libertà di iniziativa e giustizia sociale*. Rome: Edizioni Studium.
Quadrio Curzio, A. (2007): Pasquale Saraceno. In: *Economisti ed economia. Per un'Italia europea: paradigmi tra il XVIII e il XX secolo*. Bologna: Il Mulino, Bologna.
Roggi, P. (1979): Le indicazioni di politica economica del Codice di Camaldoli. *Civitas*, vol. 30, nos. 11–12, pp. 41–55.
Roggi, P. (1980): Il mondo cattolico e i grandi temi della politica economica. In: G. Mori (ed.), *La cultura economica nel periodo della ricostruzione*. Bologna: Il Mulino, pp. 57–100.
Saraceno, P. (1943): Proprietà e direzione aziendale nella moderna organizzazione industriale. *Studium*, vol. 39, nos. 11–12, pp. 337–343.
Saraceno, P. (1944): Mete della giustizia sociale: monopoli privati e monopoli sociali nella moderna organizzazione industriale. *Studium*, vol. 40, nos. 5–7, pp. 103–111.
Saraceno, P. (1951): *Lo sviluppo economico dei paesi sovrappopolati*. Rome: Studium.
Saraceno, P. (1977): *Intervista sulla ricostruzione, 1943–1955*, ed. by L. Villari. Rome, Bari: Laterza.
Shiller, R. (2012): *Finance and the Good Society*. Princeton, NJ: Princeton University Press.
Taviani, P. E. (1988): La svolta di Camaldoli. *Civitas*, vol. 35, no. 4, pp. 3–7.
Vanoni, E. (1955): Sergio Paronetto, amico e maestro. *Il Popolo*, March 29.
Vanoni, E. (1977): *La politica economica degli anni degasperiani: scritti e discorsi politici ed economici*, ed. by P. Barucci. Florence: Le Monnier.

Index

Ádám, M. 110, 118
Akerlof, G. A. 47–8, 56
Albert, H. 102, 118
Alston, L. J. 18, 190–1
Alt, J. E. 119
Anastasia, B. 177, 188, 190
Andreotti, G. 194–5, 199
Ankersmit, F. R. 7, 12
Archibald, Z. H. 41
Arena, G. 193, 199
Arensburg, C. M. 13
Aristippus 87
Aristotle 32–3, 37–9, 76, 84, 89
Arnal, J. T. 11
Asquini, A. 192, 195–6
Asso, P. F. 198–9
Augello, M. M. 12, 175
Austin, M. 18, 42
Avagliano, L. 193, 198–9
Azzolini, V. 198

Backhaus, J. G. 4, 12
Baffi, P. 193, 198
Baglioni, G. 184, 190
Baien, M. 35, 40
Baier, H. 94–5
Baietti, S. 11, 192, 194–200
Baldassarri, M. 190
Baloglou, C. P. 33, 38
Barucci, P. 171–2, 174, 192, 198, 200–1
Battaglia, F. 174
Bauer, O. 83
Beccaria, C. 180
Beck, M. 110, 118
Beckerath, E. von 39
Bekker, Z. 119

Beneduce, A. 192–3, 195–6, 198–200
Benhabib, J. 127, 137
Beretta, S. 200
Bernanke, B. 132, 135, 137
Bernardi, L. 200
Bertolini, F. 94–5
Bertolino, A. 167–8, 171–2, 174, 190
Bianchi, P. 187, 190
Bion, W. R. 160
Bismarck, O. 81
Blaug, M. 22, 37
Bodenhorn, H. 12
Böhm-Bawerk, E. 26, 39, 76, 83–4, 180
Böhm, F. 101–2, 106–8, 117–8
Böhmert, V. 94–5
Boldizzoni, F. 12–3
Boldrini, M. 195
Bonelli, F. 192, 200
Bonomi, I. 196
Bonuglia, R. 193, 200
Bortkiewicz, L. 83
Botero, G. 30, 37
Boyd, R. 186, 188, 190
Brakelmann, G. 106, 118, 120
Brodersen, K. 38
Bruni, L. 165, 174
Buchanan, J. M. 100, 119
Bücher, K. 4, 12, 18–9, 39, 169
Buckley, P. J. 160
Burnside, C. 131, 137

Caffè, F. 196, 199
Calabresi, G. F. 193, 197, 200
Calzoni, G. 170
Campilli, P. 194–5
Camurri, R. 178, 183, 190–1

Cangiani, M. 11, 57, 64, 70
Cantillon, R. 22
Capograssi, G. 195
Caracciolo, A. 198, 200
Cardini, A. 180, 190
Carli, G. 192–3, 196, 199, 200
Carnap, R. 93, 95
Caroselli, M. R. 174, 176
Cartelier, J. 35, 37
Cartesio 78
Cartwright, N. 82, 89, 92–5
Cassese, S. 196, 197, 200
Casson, M. 160
Castronovo, V. 193, 200
Cat, J. 95
Cattaneo, C. 182, 190
Cattini, M. 172, 174
Cavazza Rossi, M. 193, 200
Cenzato, G. 194
Chen, P. 190
Chialvo, L. 195
Christiano, L. J. 127, 137
Cianci, E. 196–7, 200
Cicero, M. T. 83, 95
Clark, V. S. 12
Cognetti de Martiis, F. 179, 190
Cohen, R. S. 75, 76, 96–9
Colbert, J.-B. 18, 42, 81
Cole, G. D. H. 159–60
Commons, J. R. 141, 143, 148, 159–60
Conlisk, J. 188–190
Cooley, T. F. 127–8, 137
Copernicus, N. 24, 37
Corò, G. 177, 188, 190
Cossa, L. 167
Craveri, R. 198
Croce, B. 167, 174
Cuccia, E. 196, 198–9

D'Alembert, J.-B. 35
Dal Pane, L. 168–70, 174
Dalton, G. 70
Damilano, A. 195, 200
Davies, J. K. 41
Day, R. H. 177, 190–1
De Cecco, M. 173, 175, 198–9
De Gasperi, A. 194, 199–200
De Gasperi, M. R. 194–6, 198–200
De Gregorio, A. 193, 198

De Rosa, G. 179, 191, 195, 200
De Vecchi, N. 173, 175
De Viti De Marco, A. 174
De' Stefani, A. 193
Debouzy, M. 184, 186, 191
Demandt, A. 94–5
Demaria, G. 193
Dewey, J. 149–52, 160–1
Di Fenizio, F. 198
Di Nardi, G. 193, 198
Di Taranto, G. 199, 200
Dicken, P. 160
Diderot, D. 35, 39
Dietze, C. von 101, 106, 120
Dilthey, W. 6, 12, 76, 96
Dmitriev, V. K. 25, 37
Dopfer, K. 35, 37
Dosi, G. 147, 160
Droysen, J. G. 76, 96
Drukker, J. W. 39
Duhem, P. M. M. 76, 92, 96
Dunning, J. H. 160

Eggertsson, T. 191
Eichenbaum, M. 127, 131, 137
Einaudi, L. 165, 167–8, 171, 173–5, 187, 191
Eisenhardt, K. 147, 160
Engels, F. 27, 38, 167
Epikur 97
Ermis, F. 18, 37
Eucken, W. 100–9, 116–20

Faccarello, G. 41
Fanfani, A. 2, 6, 7, 12, 168–9, 175–6, 195
Farese, G. 11, 192, 194–200
Faucci, R. 166, 175
Fausto, D. 198, 200
Favaro, A. 178, 191
Fay, C. R. 12
Fayazmanesh, S. 70
Ferrara, F. 166–7
Ferrari Aggradi, M. 199
Ferrie, J. P. 185, 190
Feyerabend, P. 75
Fine, R. 154, 161
Finley, M. I. 19, 37
Fistetti, F. 78, 92–3, 96
Fleck, L. 95

Follmann, S.-U. 94, 96
Formentini, P. 194
Forte, F. 198, 200
France, A. 88, 96
Frank, A. G. 20, 37
Franzina, E. 183–4, 191
Freud, S. 139, 154–8, 160, 161
Freudenthal, G. 92, 96
Friedman, M. 55, 57, 127
Fukuzawa, Y. 36–7
Fulbrook, M. 109, 118
Fusco, A. 171, 175

Gabrielsen, A. 41
Galbraith, J. K. 160–1
Galí, J. 131–2, 137–8
Gawel, M. L. 176
Gazdasági, K. 119
Gedeon, P. 118
Genovesi, A. 180
Gerbi, A. 198
Gerken, L. 102–3, 105, 118
Gertler, M. 132, 135, 137
Gigliobianco, A. 193, 198, 200
Gilchrist, S. 132, 135, 137
Gilibert, G. 173, 175
Gini, C. 187, 191
Giordani, F. 193, 198
Giovagnoli, A. 195, 200
Glaeser, J. 32, 37
Goethe, J. W. von 29, 41
Goldschmidt, N. 117–8
Goldstone, J. A. 20, 38
Gonella, G. 194–5
Gramsci, A. 46, 56, 67, 70
Grantham, G. 12
Gras, N. S. B. 12
Greenspan, A. 132
Gronchi, G. 196
Grossmann-Doerth, H. 101, 107, 117
Guarino, G. 197, 201
Guidi, M. E. L. 175

Hagemann, H. 70, 83, 96,
Hahn, H. 92
Hall, B. H. 160–1
Haller, R. 75, 77, 96–8
Hamilton, W. H. 160–1
Hammerstein, N. 39

Hands, D. W. 94, 96
Hansen, G. D. 126–8, 137–8
Hayek, F. A. von 46, 48–51, 55, 56, 69, 70, 106, 119
Heaton, H. 5, 12
Heertje, A. 41
Heidegger, M. 6
Heinrich, R. 98
Hensel, K. P. 101
Hermann, A. 11, 146, 154, 159–61
Hermann, F. B. W. 179, 181, 191
Herrmann-Pillath, C. 106, 118
Herz, P. 35, 38, 41
Hierholzer, V. 41
Hildebrand, B. 4, 13, 168
Hilferding, R. 83
Hodgson, G. M. 8, 13, 160, 162
Hodrick, R. J. 129
Höfer, U. 75, 96
Hofmannsthal, H. 88, 96
Horney, K. 160, 162
Hu, J. 28, 38
Husserl, E. 103, 117

Ietto-Gillies, G. 160, 162
Ikeda, Y. 70
Iselin, I. 84, 96
Itelson, G. 76, 79, 92, 96
Ivone, D. 198, 201

Jacobsson, P. 199
Jähnichen, T. 106, 118, 120
James, W. 92
Jenks, L. H. 12
Justi, J. H. G. von 34, 40

Kahane, J. 57
Kaldor, N. 24, 38
Kaplan, J. 3, 13
Kaposi, Z. 110, 118
Karachentsev, T. 92, 96
Karácsony, A. 112, 119
Kaunitz-Rietberg, W. A. von 86
Kautsky, K. 38
Kernberg, O. 160, 162
Keynes, J. M. 31, 32, 34, 38, 39, 46–51, 56, 105, 109, 119, 122, 160, 162, 173, 175, 198
Khaldun, I. 35, 40

Kirzner, I. M. 107, 119
Klein, M. 160, 162
Klock, K. 29, 30, 33, 38
Koot, G. M. 166, 175
Kopányi, M. 116, 119
Köster, R. 94, 96
Krugman, P. 55, 57
Kuhn, T. S. 75, 165, 175
Külp, B. 119
Kurz, H. D. 41, 94, 96
Kydland, F. 122–4, 126, 128–9, 132, 138
Kyrkos, B. A. 33, 38

La Malfa, U. 198
La Pira, G. 195, 197
Labriola, A. 169
Lal, D. 178, 189, 191
Lampe, A. 101
Lampertico, F. 167, 174, 175, 178–83, 185, 190, 191
Landau, H. de 96
Lederer, E. H. 83, 96
Lenel, H. O. 105, 119
Lenti, L. 198
Leo XIII 195–6, 201
Lessius, L. 20, 38, 40
Leßmann, O. 94, 96
Levi, M. 119
Liefmann, A. J.
Liefmann, R. 109–19
Liefmann, S. 111
Linzbichler, G.
Lippmann, C. W.
List, F. 76, 89, 168, 190
Liverani, M. 2, 13
Locke, J. 26, 40
López-Salido, D. 132, 138
Lordon, F. 190, 191
Louis XV 37
Love, J. R. 39
Löwe A. 68–70
Lucas, R. E. Jr. 123–4, 138
Lundan, S. M. 160
Lunghini, G. 70
Lutz, F. 101
Luzzatti, L. 167, 178, 181–3, 185–6, 191
Luzzatto, G. 175
Lysias 33, 38

Maccabelli, T. 166, 175
Macchioro, A. 170–1, 175
Mach, E. 12, 13, 76, 88, 93, 96, 119
Machiavelli, N. 5, 8, 13, 30, 38
Madarász, A. 106, 119
Maddison, A. 20, 38
Magliulo, A. 198, 201
Magris, C. 76, 96
Maier, C. S. 68, 70
Maier, K. F. 101
Malagodi, G. 198
Malthus, T. R. 43
Malvezzi, G. 194–5
Manfroni, C. 193
Mankiw, G. 159, 162
Mann, F. K. 34, 38
Mann, G. 109, 111, 119
Mann, T. 109
Mannheim, K. 6, 65, 70
Marcks, E. 42
Marshall, A. 25, 32, 38, 197
Martin, J. A. 147, 160
Martin, R. 190–1
Marx, K. 3, 14, 21, 24, 26–8, 31–2, 38–9, 45–6, 56–7, 63, 70, 81, 83, 97, 154–5, 167, 173, 175
Masulli, I. 189, 191
Mattioli, R. 194, 198
Mátyás, A. 100, 104, 119
Mauri, A. 169, 175, 176
Mayer, J. P. 99
McCloskey, D. N. 8, 12, 13
Meadow, P. 12, 13
Menand, L. 151, 162
Menger C. 5, 13, 27, 63–4, 70, 92, 166, 175
Menger, K. 70
Menichella, D. 192–6, 198–200
Merton, R. K. 53, 56–7
Merzagora, C. 198
Messedaglia, A. 178, 180
Meyer, E. 4, 13, 18–9, 83, 92, 94–5
Meyer, F. W. 101
Michels, R. 170–1, 175
Miksch, L. 101
Mill, J. S. 32, 44–5, 51, 57, 176
Mirabeau, V. R. de 41
Mises, L. von 19, 48–9, 55–7, 83–4, 92, 94, 96, 107, 119
Misiani S. 198, 200–1

Mokyr, J. 12, 13
Molinari, A. 198
Mondaini, G. 168, 175
Monteleone, G. 182, 191
Montini, G. B. 193–5, 199
Mori, G. 201
Moro, A. 195
Moro, R. 193, 201
Morpurgo, E. 178
Mortara, A. 193, 194, 201
Mortara, G. 193, 198
Mosca M. 200
Motta, M. 110, 119
Müller-Armacks, A. 29, 38, 40, 100
Müller, K. A. von 42
Muratori, L. A. 169
Myrdal, G. 199

Nau, H. 23, 38
Nell, E. J. 35, 38
Nelson, E. 55, 57
Nelson, R. 160, 162
Nelson, R. R. 160
Nemeth, E. 96, 98
Németh, I. 109, 119
Neurath, M. 76, 97
Neurath, O. 3–5, 7, 11–3, 75–99
Neurath, P. 98
Neurath, W. 82, 93–5, 98
Niehans, J. 22, 24, 38
Nietzsche, F. 82, 88, 92–3, 98
Nishizawa, T. 70
Nixon, R. 34
Nobis, H. M. 37
Noiriel, G. 186, 191
North, D. C. 14, 177, 191
Nottelmann, N. 93, 98
Nuti, D. M. 37

Ollman, B. 159, 162
Oncken, A. 94, 98
Ortes, G. 180
Ostrom, E. 119
Ostrom, V. 100, 119
Ottonelli, O. 12, 175

Pagnini, G. A. 169
Palmieri, G. 180
Pantaleoni, M. 67–8, 70, 165, 167, 173–5

Pareto, V. 31, 42
Parisi Acquaviva, D. 169, 175
Paronetto Valier, M. L. 192–201
Paronetto, S. 11, 192–5, 201
Parri, F. 198
Pasinetti, L. L. 24, 38
Pearson, H. W. 70
Pelle, A. 11, 110, 119
Perrotta, C. 176
Perroux F. 69, 70
Perry, H. S. 162
Peschka, V. 110, 118
Petty, W. 34, 39
Pies, I. 106, 119
Pius XII 195
Plato 32, 38–9, 93, 98, 109, 119
Plumpe, W. 35, 38
Poettinger, M. 1–3, 11–3, 37, 94, 98, 166, 174, 176
Poincarè, H. 92
Polanyi-Levitt, M. K. 57
Polanyi, K. 12–3, 32, 38, 46, 51–7, 62, 65, 69, 70, 149, 152–3, 162
Pombo, O. 96, 98
Pomeranz, K. 20, 39
Poni, C. 35, 39
Popper, K. 96
Porta, P. L. 169, 176
Prescott, E. C. 122–6, 128–32, 138
Ptak, R. 105, 199

Quadrio Curzio, A. 193, 201
Quesnay, F. 41, 76
Quine, W. V. O. 79, 93–4, 98

Rabossi, E. 93, 98
Rau, K. H. 26, 39, 40
Rebelo, S. 131, 137
Reinert, S. A. 41
Reisman, D. A. 6, 13
Reiss Romoli, G. 194
Renner, A. 102–3, 105, 118
Rey, A. 92
Ricardo, D. 24, 26, 31–2, 39, 41, 43–4, 51–2, 57,
Richardson, A. 75, 98
Richerson, P. J. 186, 188, 190
Richter, S. 41
Rickert, W. 61

Rieter, H. 35, 39
Righetti, I. 193–4
Riquetti Marquis, V. 41
Robbins, L. 66–8, 70
Robinson, J. 27, 39, 116–7, 119
Rocca, A. 194
Rodriguez, A. 11
Rogerson, R. 127, 137
Roggi, P. 11–2, 166, 176, 195, 197, 201
Romani, R. 182, 191
Roosevelt, F. D. 193, 201
Röpke, W. 100
Rosenberg, N. 160–1
Rossi, A. 184–5, 191
Rossi, P. 6, 12–3
Rostow, W. W. 3, 5, 13, 21, 23, 39
Roth, G. 71
Rothbard, M. M. 107, 117, 119
Roverato, G. 184–7, 191
Roy, T. 7, 8, 13
Rugman, A. 160, 162
Ruini, M. 196
Russell, B. 92
Rüstow, A. 100
Rutherford, M. 160, 162
Rutte, H. 97
Ryden, D. B. 10, 13

Sahlins, M. 22, 39
Salin, E. 21, 28–9, 33–4, 39
Salin, P. 107, 119
Salsano, A. 159, 162
Salvadori, N. 94, 96
Samuels W. J. 58, 70, 162
Samuelson, P. A. 22, 128
Sandner, G. 92, 98
Saraceno, P. 192–201
Sargent, T. J. 123, 138
Sawers, L. 14
Say, J.-B. 43
Scaldaferri, R. 179, 191
Schapire-Neurath, A. 84, 87, 98
Scheer, C. 41
Schefold, B. 11, 17–20, 22–3, 25–6, 28–9, 32–42
Schlecht, O. 103, 119
Schliesser, E. 35, 41
Schmitz, S. W. 96
Schmoller, G. 12, 75, 83, 167, 179

Schneider, L. 175
Schröder, J. 41
Schullern zu Schrattenhofen, H. R. 94, 98
Schumpeter, J. A. 21–2, 34, 39, 41, 61, 68, 70, 82, 83, 96, 98, 173, 175, 194
Schwartz A. J. 55, 57
Scialoja, A. 167
Sebestik, J. 79, 94, 98
Sen, A. 86, 94, 96
Serra, A. 20, 22, 40–1
Shackle, G. L. S. 10, 13, 166, 176
Shaw, G. B. 56
Shiller, R. J. 47–8, 56, 199, 201
Siebert, H. 101, 119
Simmie, J. 190–1
Sinigaglia, O. 194
Sismondi, J. C. L. S. 76, 165, 176
Smith, A. 3, 24–6, 29, 32, 34, 41, 43, 76, 84, 88, 95, 102, 119, 166, 175
Solari, S. 178, 191
Solow, R. M. 122–5, 129–31, 137–8
Sombart, W. 27–9, 39, 41
Soulez, A. 93, 98
Spataro, G. 194
Spencer, H. 55
Spierling, V. 96
Spiethoff, A. 9, 14, 21, 29, 30, 41
Spirito, U. 168, 176
Sraffa, P. 24–6, 39, 41
Starbatty, J. 39
Steedman, I. 96
Steuart, J. 87
Sullivan, H. S. 160, 162
Summers, L. H. 125, 138
Sumner, W. J. 55
Symons, J. 96, 98
Szlezák, T. 38

Taviani, P. E. 195, 201
Taylor, J. 137
Thomas, D. 53, 57
Thomas, W. I. 53, 57
Thomasberger, C. 11, 51, 57
Tinbergen, J. 199
Tokody, G. 109, 119
Toninelli, P. 173, 176
Toniolo, G. 182–4, 191, 197, 201,
Tool, M. R. 70
Torres, J. M. 96, 98

Tsai-Mei, L. 160
Tuchtfeld, E. 105, 120
Tugwell, R. G. 160, 162
Turgot, A. R. J. 81
Tusset, G. 11–2

Uebel, T. E. 75, 82, 93–6, 98–9

Vaccaro, E. L. 88, 92, 99
Vallés, J. 132, 138
Vanberg, V. 100, 107, 119–20
Vanoni, E. 192–201
Vara Crespo, O. 11
Veblen, T. 6, 13, 64–5, 69, 71, 142, 146, 154–5, 160, 162
Verlinden, C. 168–9, 176
Vico, G. 27
Vidal-Naquet, P. 18, 42
Villari, L. 201
Volcker, P. 132
Volkert, J. 107, 120
Volpe, G. 193
Dietze, C. von 101, 106, 120

Wagener, H. J. 39
Wallerstein, I. 7, 14

Walras, L. 27
Weber, M. 6, 12, 19–22, 27–9, 31, 32, 36, 39–42, 58–67, 69, 71, 77–8, 81, 92, 94–5, 99, 111,
Whaples, R. 12–4
Whewell, W. 25, 42
Wicksell, K. 31, 42
Wieser, F. 64, 71, 94
Willoughby, J. 14
Wilson, T. 109
Winkler, H. A. 109, 120
Winnicott, D. W. 160, 162
Winter, S. G. 160, 162
Winterbottom, M. 95
Wisman, J. D. 3, 14
Wittgenstein, L. 88
Wittich, C. 71
Wolters, F. 18, 42
Woodford, M. 137
Wright, R. 126–7, 137–8

Xenophon 33–3, 40

Zagari, E. 166, 176
Zamagni, V. 172, 176
Zoepffel, R. 37